John Joseph Shillinglaw

Historical Records of Port Phillip

The First Annals of the Colony of Victoria

John Joseph Shillinglaw

Historical Records of Port Phillip
The First Annals of the Colony of Victoria

ISBN/EAN: 9783337327125

Printed in Europe, USA, Canada, Australia, Japan

Cover: Foto ©ninafisch / pixelio.de

More available books at **www.hansebooks.com**

OF

PORT PHILIP

THE

First Annals of the Colony of Victoria.

EDITED BY

JOHN J. SHILLINGLAW,

Fellow of the Royal Geographical Society of London; Author of "Arctic Discovery," &c.

[From Papers presented to Parliament in return to an Order of the Legislative Assembly of Victoria, on the motion of Mr. W. J. O'Hea, M.P., 14 August 1878.]

By Authority:
JOHN FERRES, GOVERNMENT PRINTER, MELBOURNE.

1879.

CONTENTS.

I.—Letter to the Honourable Graham Berry.
II.—Prefatory Note by the Editor.
III.—Journal of Exploration of Port Phillip made by Charles Grimes, Surveyor-General of New South Wales, 1802-3.
IV.—Order Book of Lieutenant-Governor Collins during the stay at Port Phillip, 1803-4.
V.—Journal of the Rev. Robt. Knopwood, Chaplain to the Settlement. From 24th April 1803 to 31st December 1804.

	PAGE
Sketch.—The Heads of Port Phillip.	
Portrait of Mr. James Hobbs	15
Fac-simile Chart of the Survey of Port Phillip by Grimes	15
Portrait of Lieutenant-Governor Collins	30
„ Rev. Robert Knopwood	64
„ Captain Woodriff, R.N., H.M.S. *Calcutta*	65

MR. SHILLINGLAW TO THE HON. THE CHIEF SECRETARY.

To the Honourable Graham Berry, Premier of Victoria.

SIR,

The documents now submitted to you may fairly be called the First Annals of this colony. They are important as being official records, and they set at rest some points which have hitherto been in dispute or doubt regarding the settlement attempted by Governor Collins at Port Phillip Heads three quarters of a century ago.

As you have thought these early historical MSS. worthy of national publication, I have compressed in the form of a Prefatory Note a few facts necessary to the illustration of their character and value, and showing how they were brought to light.

I take leave to add that when future writers of Australian history come to tell the story of that marvellous national career which in less than fifty years has transformed a coast whaling-station and a few turf huts on the banks of an unnamed river into the noble Province of Victoria, they will not fail to recognize the public spirit which has induced you to preserve these memorials of an earlier attempt at its colonization, which, happily for us all, came to nought.

I have the honour to be,

Your very obedient servant,

JOHN J. SHILLINGLAW, F.R.G.S.

Melbourne, 28th October 1878.

PREFATORY NOTE BY THE EDITOR.

To get a clear idea of the space of time in which the great English colonies have grown up in Australasia, as well as to mark the period to which the following historical records refer, an illustration, at once simple and striking, may be given in a few words.

At a little village a few miles from Hobart Town there still walks about a hale hearty man, who was born at Port Phillip Heads on the 25th November 1803. His parents had landed there with the rest of the intended colony about six weeks before.

On the following Christmas Day, under the gum trees overlooking what is now called "Sorrento," after the chaplain's sermon to the assembled civil and military officers, the settlers and the convicts,[1] Lieutenant-Governor Collins handed the little son of the sergeant of marines to the Rev. Mr. Knopwood, and stood godfather to *William James "Hobart" Thorne*, the first-born of the settlement. In another month godfather and godson, officers, emigrants, and outlaws had got on board their ships again, had hove up their anchors and sailed away for Tasmania, where Hobart Thorne and Hobart Town grew up together.

Lieutenant-Governor Collins was born in 1756. At the age of nineteen he was with his father's regiment at "Bunker's Hill," in the American Revolutionary War, and at thirty-two he went out, in 1788, as Judge-Advocate with Governor Phillip in the "FIRST FLEET," and so helped to found SYDNEY.

When we reflect that at that time there was not a white man resident on any part of the vast island-continent of Australia, or in New Zealand, Tasmania, or any of the islands washed by Australasian seas, we may form some idea of what has been done in the span of these two lives.

The journals of the early discoverers and explorers, which led to Collins being sent out by the British Government to establish a penal colony at Port Phillip, together with the records of the settlement itself,

---

[1] The First Sermon Preached in Port Phillip, on the 13th November 1803, by the Revd. Mr. Knopwood, has been printed in the Melbourne "Church of England Messenger," 14th February 1878.

have hitherto been very imperfectly known. The disappearance of some has been a bar to accurate historical narrative and the cause of many perplexities. Very recently, however, the archives of the Public Record Office of England have been successfully ransacked by the son of an early Victorian colonist, who has lately published the result of his five years' painstaking research.[1] To Mr. Labilliere belongs the credit of having gathered from the vast collection of State Papers preserved in the Colonial and Admiralty offices in London most of the missing records; and, for the first time, we read in his volumes the true story of the first discovery and subsequent exploration of this province, given in the exact words of the men who did the work.

But for some of these missing documents Mr. Labilliere sought in vain; and the Journals of GRIMES and KNOPWOOD, now published, are of that number.

These fill up gaps in his collection, and their value will be best seen when read in connection with his full and clear narrative, which at the same time has rendered it unnecessary in this place to do more than sketch-in a few outlines left by Mr. Labilliere untouched.

The fears of Governor King at the beginning of the century that France had a design to establish herself somewhere in Australia—to convert Western Port perhaps into a second Pondicherry—lent weight to the concurrent testimony of Bass, Grant, Murray, and Flinders, as to the suitability of the south coast as a place for settlement; and the expedition of Lieutenant-Colonel Collins was the prompt result determined on by the British Government. But meantime Governor King saw fit to have a more particular survey made of Port Phillip. For this purpose the colonial schooner *Cumberland*, of 29 tons (the same in which Flinders, exactly twelve months afterwards, was made prisoner in the Isle of France), was equipped in Sydney, and placed in charge of Lieutenant CHARLES ROBBINS of H.M.S. *Buffalo*. Robbins carried despatches to the French Commodore BAUDIN, then known to be on the coast, in case he should fall in with him. Besides the crew, the party consisted of CHARLES GRIMES, the Acting Surveyor-General of New South Wales; Dr. MCCALLUM, surgeon; JAMES MEEHAN, a surveyor; and JAMES FLEMMING, a man in whom the Governor had great confidence, who was to observe the nature of the country explored. Their orders were to "walk round" Port Phillip.

The journal of the expedition, herein related, was kept by Flemming, and the chart attached is a *fac-simile* of the survey made by Grimes.

---

[1] "The Early History of Victoria: From its Discovery to its Establishment as a Self-governing Province of the British Empire." By F. P. Labilliere, Barrister-at-Law. London: Sampson Low and Co. May 1878.

The *Cumberland* sailed from Sydney on the 23rd November 1802, and on the 8th December fell in with Baudin at Sea Elephant Bay, on the east coast of King Island. Péron, the naturalist of the French Expedition tells us what followed :[1] He says : —

"Just as we had made these arrangements for the safety of our ship we saw the little schooner the *Cumberland* appear. She had come from Port Jackson and had on board Mr. Grimes, Engineer-in-Chief of the English establishment, who came by order of the Government to make a declaration to us which was as singular in form as remarkable in its object. 'It being reported,' wrote Mr. King to our commander, 'that you propose to leave some men either in Diemen's Land or on the western coast of New South Wales in order to form there a French colony, I think it my duty to declare to you, M. le Commandant, that, in virtue of the Act of 1788 for taking possession, solemnly proclaimed by England, all these countries form an integral part of the British Empire ; and that you cannot occupy any part of them without breaking the bonds of friendship which have been so recently re-established between the two nations. I shall not even attempt to dissemble, for such is the nature of my special instructions with regard thereto, that I must oppose by all means in my power the execution of the project you are suspected of being about to execute. In consequence of which H.M.S. *Cumberland* has received orders not to leave you until the officer who commands her is satisfied that your operations are foreign to any kind of invasion of British territory in these parts.'" [pp. 5, 6.]

Having delivered their message, and made the exploration of King Island noted in the Journal, the *Cumberland* sailed on her mission to Port Phillip, which they entered on the 20th January 1803. The Journal and chart show how faithfully Grimes carried out his instructions. He was undoubtedly on this occasion the discoverer of the river on which Melbourne now stands ; but, excepting the notice of his survey by the generous Flinders, his meritorious services to Australia have met with almost total neglect.

Grimes's report of the nature of the country seen round Port Phillip was considered unfavorable, and was sent home to England by the *Glatton*. Before the information reached the Government, however, Collins had been despatched—27th April 1803—to form a penal settlement at the place which had been described by Murray as resembling the scenery of Arthur's Seat and Greenwich Park.

---

[1] Voyage de Découvertes aux Terres Australes, sur les corvettes *le Géographe*, *le Naturaliste*, et la goëlette *le Casuarina* pendant les années 1800-4. Par F. Peron et L. Freycinet. Paris, 1807-16. 2 vols. 4to ; cartes, royal 4to.

The expedition was embarked on board the 50-gun ship *Calcutta*, Captain Daniel Woodriff, and the chartered transport *Ocean*, John Mertho, master. Mr. Labilliere gives a full and interesting narrative of the objects and instructions of the British Government, and of the reasons given by Collins for the abandonment of the place. It would, therefore, be superfluous to speak of them here. The prompt and energetic action of the first Australian Governor—Phillip—in searching for a more suitable spot than Botany Bay, to which he had been despatched by the British Government, had saved the eastern sea-board of Australia to Great Britain. But the bright example was lost on Collins. King sent him the report and survey of Grimes, which it will be seen (p. 24) mentions the Yarra. Indeed, Collins knew that the king's ship which had brought him hither lay at her anchors in Hobson's Bay for ten days, and filled up her water-casks with 50 tons of fresh water obtained from the river; and also that one of her lieutenants (MacCullogh) had actually walked from Sandridge to the camp near Arthur's Seat, a distance of 50 miles (Knopwood, p. 96). But, without attributing to him unworthy motives involving pecuniary gain, there can be no doubt of His Honor's having had from the outset a personal preference for Tasmania. The letters from Sir Joseph Banks to Governor King, which Mr. Rusden found in the papers of the latter, clearly show that Governor Collins before he left London intended to go to Van Diemen's Land.[1]

During the stay of Collins at Port Phillip Heads he issued from time to time a number of Orders. These were *printed* at a small hand-press set up under a gum tree on the beach, and a printed set has been preserved in London. The copy appended was made from the original MSS. now treasured in the Parliament Library of Tasmania. The date of the first of these printed Orders is given as the 16th October 1803, and it is curious to reflect that only eight months previously George Howe had issued in Sydney the first number of the first journal published in Australia, which contained the latest news from England, then eleven months old.

The third document published is the Diary of the Reverend Robert Knopwood, who was chaplain to the settlement. It commences with the departure from England, and day by day carries the narrative of events to the final settlement of Collins at Hobart Town. Hitherto, and until the publication of Mr. Labilliere's work, the only record of the voyage was to be found in the account published by the First

---

[1] Discovery, Survey, and Settlement of Port Phillip: by G. W. Rusden. Melbourne: Robertson. 1871.

Lieutenant of the *Calcutta*.¹ Its author was a man of merit, sensibility, and taste, and, despite his amusing prediction of the future of Port Phillip, his book—which is now rare—deserves a reprint. Some extracts from Knopwood's diary were given in a so-called life of William Buckley, "the wild white man,"² but that portion which is of historical value is now made public for the first time.

Many matters of curious interest respecting the inner life of the two settlements will be found in Mr. Knopwood's diary. Consequences we know are inexorable; but comment on these doings, and on the personal conduct of those who have long since passed away, may be properly left to other hands and to other pages.

Governor Collins died suddenly at Hobart Town on the 24th March 1810. It has been stated that immediately after the Governor's death two officers of the Government placed soldiers at the door of the apartment, and busied themselves in burning all his papers.³ A kindly notice of his character and a description of his funeral were written in the "Derwent Star," published on the 3rd of April 1810, by Mr. George Prideaux Harris, the Deputy Surveyor. Three copies only of this paper are known to be in existence, but it has been reproduced as a literary curiosity at the "Hobart Town Mercury" office.

The Reverend Mr. Knopwood was one of the chaplains to the fleet, and a clergyman of the old school. He was born 2nd June 1761, died 18th September 1838, and was buried in the cemetery of a little Tasmanian village named Rokeby.

Mr. Charles Grimes, Deputy Surveyor-General of New South Wales, came to that colony in H.M.S. *Gorgon* in September 1791. He succeeded Mr. Alfred Alt, the first Surveyor-General, who was invalided, and was himself succeeded by Lieutenant John Oxley, R.N., previously First Lieutenant of the *Porpoise*. In 1808 Mr. Grimes acted as the Judge-Advocate at the trial of Mr. McArthur, subsequent to the deposition of Governor Bligh.

Some particulars of the career of others of the early settlers will be found in the "Van Diemen's Land Anniversary and Hobart Town Almanac" for the year 1831, and Mr. Calder has contributed much information on this subject to the Tasmanian Press.

Captain Woodriff in November 1805 made a heroic defence of the *Calcutta* against a powerful French squadron, but was captured and

---

¹ An Account of a Voyage to establish a Colony at Port Phillip: by J. H. Tuckey. 1 vol. Longman and Co. 1805.

² The Life and Adventures of William Buckley, thirty-two years a wanderer amongst the Aborigines of the then unexplored country round Port Phillip: by John Morgan. 1 vol. Hobart Town, 1852.

³ Curious Facts of Old Colonial Days: by James Bonwick, F.R.G.S. Sampson Low. London, 1870.

long remained a prisoner at Verdun. The *Calcutta* was subsequently blown up in the affair of Basque Roads. On Woodriff's release he was made a C.B. In 1839 he was appointed to Greenwich Hospital, where he died in 1842.

Captain James Hingston Tuckey, the First Lieutenant of the *Calcutta*, an officer of merit and varied services, who wrote in a French prison and subsequently published several works connected with geography and navigation, fell a victim to African fever and anxiety in the conduct of an expedition to explore the Congo. Only a few months since Stanley accomplished what was attempted by Tuckey in 1816.

It remains to add a few particulars as to the discovery of these documents.

"The Grimes Survey and Journal" were eventually found by me last year in the archives of the Colonial Secretary's office at Sydney, after a protracted and persistent search, involving I will not say how much patience, and causing I am afraid to say how much trouble.

"The General and Garrison Order Book" of Lieutenant-Governor Collins comes from the Parliament Library of Tasmania, and was carefully copied by Mr. G. E. Collett, the sub-librarian.

"The Knopwood Diary" is in the possession of Mr. V. W. Hookey, solicitor, of Hobart Town, a family connection of one of Mr. Knopwood's executors. By Mr. Hookey's consent, a copy of it was made and presented to the Government of Victoria by Mr. J. E. Calder, formerly Surveyor-General of Tasmania, whose ardour as a collector of such matters is well and widely known, and whose name is a sufficient guarantee for the scrupulous accuracy of the transcript. All the foot-notes appended by that gentleman are marked "C."

The portrait of Collins is from a miniature, engraved for his own "Account of New South Wales." That of Captain Woodriff is taken from the painting in the possession of his family at Sydney, and for that of the Reverend Mr. Knopwood I am indebted to the Very Reverend Canon Bromby, of Hobart Town. It is copied from the original sketch by the late Hon. Thomas George Gregson, of Risdon, the first ground broken in Tasmania.

In the search for these early historical records of Port Phillip, the thanks of this colony are also due to Sir John Robertson, K.C.M.G., the late Colonial Secretary, and Mr. Henry Halloran, C.B., the late principal Under-Secretary of New South Wales; as also to Mr. R. Adams, the Surveyor-General of that province. I am besides much indebted to Mr. G. D. Hirst, acting for Mrs. Woodriff, of Sydney, as well as to Mr. Alfred Kingston, of the Public Record Office in London.

Of those who took part in the attempted colonization of Port Phillip three quarters of a century ago, but three persons are now alive, namely, the son of the Marine Sergeant Thorne above referred to, Mr. Frank Pitt of Hobart Town, and Mr. James Hobbs of Melbourne, whose portrait is given in this collection. At the age of eighty-six this gentleman lives to recall the incidents of life in the tents of Collins's Camp at the Heads, and subsequently in the turf-built huts of Hobart Town. The son of a Naval officer who was killed at the taking of Egypt, his mother, on the advice of Lord Hobart, emigrated with Collins. Mr. Hobbs, who had previously been in the Navy, joined as midshipman the King's ship then stationed at Sydney, and his recollections of facts connected with the conduct of Governor Bligh on board the *Porpoise* have become historical.[1] As a colonist, Mr. Hobbs had his share of the hardships of the early days. He did good service as an explorer, and his feats against the bushrangers lie buried in old Van Diemen's Land newspapers. He has lived to see the country pronounced by Collins *uninhabitable* become the most remarkable of England's colonies; and a handful of his countrymen, on the sea-board of a continent, spread and grow into seven great centres of civilization. In the space of the life of a man now moving in our midst, the thing has been done, and the predictions of poets, philosophers, and statesmen verified in the Australasia of to-day.

J. J. S.

Melbourne, 28th October 1878.

---

[1] Chronicle of Port Phillip: by Henry F. Gurner. Melbourne: Robertson. 1876.

J. Hobbs

PASSENGER BY THE "OCEAN."

[Born at Saltash, Cornwall, 8th April 1792.]

THE VOYAGE OF HIS MAJESTY'S COLONIAL SCHOONER "CUMBERLAND," FROM SYDNEY TO KING ISLAND AND PORT PHILLIP IN 1802-3.

A Journal of the Explorations of Charles Grimes, Acting Surveyor-General of New South Wales. Kept by James Flemming.

A JOURNAL TO AND FROM KING ISLAND,
ETC., ETC., ETC.

NOTE BY GOVERNOR KING.—The writer of this journal (James Flemming) was sent to examine the soil, timber, &c., of King Island and Port Phillip; he is very intelligent, and a man in whom I could place great confidence in his knowledge of the objects that fell to his share.—(Signed) P. G. K.—[PHILLIP GIDLEY KING.]

1802.

Tuesday, 23rd November.—Sailed from Sydney Cove on board the *Cumberland;* a fine wind after we cleared the Heads; nothing remarkable except the jolly boat drifting at night off the Five Islands.

Wednesday, 24th.—Sailed along a high shore; at night off Cape Dromedary.

Thursday, 25th.—Saw Cape Howe, between which and Ram's Head there appears several spots of clear ground.

Friday, 26th.—A gale of contrary wind; drifting all day.

Saturday, 27th.—A calm; drifting all day.

Sunday, 28th.—High wind; drifting all day.

Monday, 29th.—A fine day; opposite the same shore as on the 26th.

Tuesday, 30th.—Got past Ram's Head.

Wednesday, December 1st.—Went but a few miles.

Thursday, 2nd.—Calm.

Friday, 3rd.—Stood for Kent's Group.

Saturday, 4th.—Anchored in Kent's Group; in the morning went on shore, collected some specimens and seeds, killed some ducks and a kangaroo. One dog was bit by a snake and died. Saw many seals and sea lions. The islands are covered with a thick brush and oak.

Sunday, 5th.—Went on shore to another island; barren; caught a kangaroo. The rock is granite. Sailed from Kent's Group; a fine wind.

Monday, 6th.—High wind and heavy rain; laying-to till morning.

Tuesday, 7th.—Little wind; half knot an hour.

Wednesday, 8*th*.—Saw smoke on Elephant Island (east coast of King Island); we did not think we were so near land. At five p.m. saw two ships at anchor, the *Geographe* and *Naturaliste*, dropped anchor near them. Capt. Robbins and Grimes went on board; the *Naturaliste* sailed the same night.

Thursday, 9*th*.—Early in the morning the captain and Mr. Grimes went to the Commodore's ship and on their return heard that two vessels were lost off the "Sisters." A party of us went on shore; a fine sandy beach; we walked to what is called the Great River; there is a bar at its entrance into the sea. It is salt for a mile up when it begins to be fresh water; we did not go far up. If the trees were cleared away boats might go up it even at low tide. In our walk met with eight prisoners the French Commodore had turned out of his ship. He gave them 10lbs. of bread each; they told me that there were there more on board. It being a rough sea it was 11 o'clock before we got on board. Elephant Island is covered with seals and mutton birds.

Friday, 10*th*.—Weighed anchor and came a few miles nearer land. The captain and Mr. Grimes dined with the commodore; in the afternoon the boat went for an anchor stock. McCallum, the surgeon, and self went on shore, stayed all night at some huts belonging to the ship *Mercury's* gang.

Saturday, 11*th*.—Went a little way into the country; being in expectation of the boats coming on shore, went along the beach to the French tents. It is a fine sandy beach with several runs of fresh water; the north-east part rocky. Went on board p.m.

Sunday, 12*th*.—High wind; a great swell; no one on shore.

Monday, 13*th*.—The captain and Grimes dined at the French tents. McCallum and self went on shore in the afternoon; joined the captain and went to the huts we were at before.

Tuesday, 14*th*.—The captain went on board; McCallum and self examined the country a little way toward the sea; it is high and sandy about half a mile in deep black vegetable mould, mixed with sand; the timber small. There are the remains of some very large gum trees, but they are all rotten; the low ground is a little swampy. Mr. Grimes joined us in the evening and was informed that the captain [Robbins] hoisted His Majesty's colors behind the French tents.

Wednesday, 15*th*.—The party (seven) set off in the morning; at three miles crossed the Great River about three feet deep at low water travelled along a sandy beach. About six o'clock came to a spring of water and stopped the night; high hills and thick brush. Caught a kangaroo and three porcupines.

Thursday, 16*th*.—Went inland; at one mile found a fresh water lagoon; about 20 acres between it and the shore; the ground is high and sandy. Ascended a hill where I could see some miles. The tops of the trees appear dead and a thick brush; all the ground is sand with black vegetable mould. I went several times to the top of the hills; a white sand appears on them as far as the eye could reach; there appears to be a chain of lagoons about two miles from the sea. Came to Coomber's Bay where we stopped the night.

Friday, 17*th*.—A wet morning. Started about twelve; travelled along a rocky shore; the rain and hail annoyed us much, there being no shelter. Walked till about six o'clock and finding no fresh water came back about a mile to a spring; erected some bushes to protect us; stopped the night. Caught some kangaroo; rain and hail all night. The country barren; the shore high rocks, many of them projecting far into the sea.

Saturday, 18th.—Continued our course on the rocky shore till we came to a spring, and being told by our guide that there was no fresh water for some miles, halted. Mr. Grimes and self went to the top of a high hill where we could see ten miles. The land appeared barren, a scrubby brush, and but little grass; in bottoms are many rushes.

Sunday, 19th.—A wet morning. At noon continued our march, rain and high wind. The beach sandy; came to a salt lagoon opposite New Year's Island. Stopped the night; caught some emus and ducks.

Monday, 20th.—Mr. Grimes and men went back to continue his survey and I went along the salt lagoon till I came to a fresh-water river; traced it about two miles; came to a large lagoon. At the entrance are two small islands; it appears to be three-quarters of a mile long and three or four hundred yards wide; it is covered with bullrushes; a hill on one side, level on the other. Returned through the bush which is about half a mile from the sea. There is some tolerable grass where the brush is thin. Saw some fine trees by the river side but in every place I have seen the large trees are decaying and fresh ones springing up.

Tuesday, 21st.—The weather still wet. Made a signal for the *George's* boat to come on shore as we had no bread for some days. We moved our camp two miles further to where the boats usually land. Mr. Grimes went on board and procured us some biscuit until our vessel arrived.

Wednesday, 22nd.—The wet continuing sent a party to hunt while the others made the huts more secure. In our journey saw many sea elephants, but few seals. The elephants are in the greatest plenty at the mouths of fresh-water streams. The country round this place is hill and dale, sands and vegetable mould very light. The hunting party returned with three emus, three porcupines, and two kangaroos.

Thursday, 23rd.—Being a fine day went to shew Grimes and McCallum the fresh-water lagoon, and the wind being shifted began to expect our vessel which we did about 3 p.m. Not having seen her for eleven days we began to have serious apprehensions of her safety.

Friday, 24th.—The *Cumberland* anchored off New Year's Island. In the morning the boat came on shore, I went on board; was informed she had been drifted to Kent's Group and lay there till the wind shifted.

Saturday, 25th.—Went on the islands. Their shore is rocky, covered with seals. I came on shore with a washing party, the captain intending to follow in the morning, to proceed into the interior. On examining the specimens gathered at Kent's Group found them all damaged with wet.

Sunday, 26th.—The captain, and Mr. Grimes, and the doctor came on shore in the morning; remained at marquee all day.

Monday, 27th.—Set out at six o'clock, back the same coast we had been before. Met a hunting party sent out the day before with four

B

kangaroos and four badgers; stopped at about seven miles for Mr. Grimes to continue his survey; on his return dined. Afterwards went to a lagoon about three miles from the sea. The road to it is through a thick brush and sandy hills. There are some clear spots covered with rushes and appears at times to be flooded. Dug a spot of ground and sowed some seeds. The soil is a light black sand about 8 inches deep on the hills, and from eighteen inches to two feet in the valleys, at bottom white sand. At the end of the lagoon, next the sea, there are some forest land with large gum trees; the soil sandy, and in the marshy grounds are large fern trees with deep black soil.

Tuesday, 28th.—Went along the side of the lagoon a little way, it is of considerable extent. Afterwards divided into two parties, Mr. Grimes, the doctor, and two others to examine the lagoon; the captain, self, and two others to look into the country. The ground is alternately forest and swampy; the soil is shallow on the hills, and deep black earth in the bottoms. The wood is principally blue-gum, from two to three feet in diameter and about twenty on an acre. A little way from the beach was taken ill by drinking some bad water. Stopped some time behind the party. I soon recovered and arrived at headquarters before sunset, where I found all the others arrived about two hours before.

Wednesday 29th.—Made a signal in the morning for the boat to come on shore. Sowed some seeds, and the boat not coming, we set off after dinner, twelve in number, having been joined by one Smith, belonging to Cable's gang, and two natives from Sydney. Travelled about three miles, and being informed that we should not find water for a long way, stopped for the night. The shore is rocky, projecting a considerable way into the sea in many places. On our departure each man took thirty-two biscuits with him, as we expected plenty of game. In the evening caught three young emus, twenty-three seal, and eight kangaroos.

Thursday 30th.—One man went back to the tent with the emus, and we proceeded along the shore. Crossed a fine stream of water and several springs. I am of opinion that the springs issuing from the hills come all from lagoons in the interior. We were joined in the afternoon by the man sent back in the morning. This day caught four emus, three badgers, three porcupines, and a kangaroo. The shore appears the same as on the preceding day.

Friday 31st.—Set out at six o'clock. At about three miles parted, the captain, self, and three others into the country; Mr. Grimes, the doctor, and the other five proceeded to survey the coast. At about a mile from the sea found a small spot of grey loam. Proceeded up a run of water the ground swampy; came to the head of it at about half-a-mile, the ground rising a little. Travelled about three miles over a level country, the timber being chiefly gum and tea-tree; the soil sandy. There have been very large trees, most of which have fallen. The standing timber is from 60 to 100 feet high, and from one to three feet in diameter. Returned to the beach nearly the same road we went, and, after dinner, went to the stream of water seen on the 30th ult. Went up it a little way, and stopped the night.

1803.

January 1st (Saturday).—Started early in the morning to examine another stream seen as above. The brush was so thick that we could not proceed. It goes up between hills, as far as we could discern, three or four miles. There is a little waterfall near the beach. Returned back, and stopped the night.

Sunday 2nd—Set off at eight o'clock up another stream. There is a considerable current for about a mile, when it became dry at bottom, soon afterwards water, at about three miles swampy, about 18 inches deep of water, and very thick of trees; the water began to extend a considerable width, and, being so very thick of brush, left the swamp and went over some dry ground for about a mile and came to a lagoon. Came up with it at the west end. It appeared to turn to the right and left at the east end and three-quarters of a mile long, but could not distinctly see its form. From thence to the sea, about four miles, is a very thick brush, with many fallen trees, which make travelling nearly impossible. The land dry and sandy, and many large gum trees. At five o'clock came to the place we set out from, and stopped the night.

Monday 3rd.—Started at six o'clock, and made straight for headquarters, where we arrived between nine and ten o'clock a.m. Made a signal for the boat to come on shore, which soon arrived. Went on board for some necessaries, and came back to the tent in the afternoon.

Tuesday 4th.—A party of the crews of the *Cumberland* and *George* were coming on shore for blubber. The surf being very strong, two of the men belonging to the latter were drowned; six more were in the water, but got safe out. The men who perished were Cato, late gardener to Mr. Palmer, and Emmanuel, late gunner on board the *Anne*. The day was spent in finding them and sending them to the New Year's Island to be buried.

Wednesday 5th.—Went with the captain and two others to the lagoon seen on the 20th ult.; traced it from end to end. At top there is a small run of water comes into it down a sandy hollow. Went on the top of a hill and ascended a tree; the appearance—dead-topped gum trees, sandy hills, and thick brush. It is with the greatest difficulty that one can pass through it. Returned in the afternoon, and found Mr. Grimes and party returned. From what I was informed they had not been so far as they intended to have gone when they set off.

Thursday 6th.—Made a signal early in the morning for the boat to come on shore, as we wanted some necessaries previous to our setting off into the country. The boat not coming, remained at marquee all the day.

Friday 7th.—Continued the signal in the morning, and, it not coming, the captain went on board in the *George's* boat in the evening, which came on shore for some men that had come from Elephant Bay. They informed me that the French commodore had sailed about eight days before, and that he had lost two anchors and a launch. Rain and thunder p.m., with high wind most of the night.

Saturday 8th.—The captain arrived early in the morning, and, it being a showery day, remained at the marquee all day.

Sunday 9th.—At nine o'clock the captain, self, Harry, and a seaman set off with an intention to cross the island. We went along the shore to the stream of water we were at on the 2nd inst. Went to the lagoon we had been at before; we came to it at another place than we had previously been at. It appeared much larger, and fuller of tufty grass, the brush being very thick round it, and the water only knee deep. We ventured through it. It was nearly the same depth all the way over, which we supposed to be about two miles. It is full of tufty grass and bull-rushes, of a circular form. We afterwards kept an easterly course through a level country, sometimes dry, at others swampy. Trees small and very high, except some very large gum trees. It rained most of the day, which made it very disagreeable travelling. Marched till sunset, and it was with difficulty we could make a fire.

Monday 10th.—Started at four o'clock in the morning. Met with some fine land, the soil more strong and of a loamy nature. Went over some miles of it—some of a reddish, other of a grey cast. The trees are very high. I measured a gum tree that appeared lately fallen; 100 yards clear stem, and between five and six feet diameter. As near as I could judge there are about 20 per acre. The others small and straight. The poles are only two or three feet apart, very high and straight, from six to eighteen inches in diameter, of various sorts; high fern and sword-grass; a fine deep black soil. Passed a spot of moory ground, where we saw some badgers and kangaroos.

Tuesday 11th.—Started at six; continued our course. The country nearly as on the preceding day. At about two or three o'clock came to a swamp, with some very high fern trees. A little further came to a small stream of water. Traced it a little way, but finding it did not run directly in our course, the captain left for about a mile, when we fell in with it again. It was considerably larger, and I supposed it to be the head of the Great River, which runs into Elephant Bay. We traced it by crossing several times, there being many trees fallen across it. At about two or three miles from the place we first discovered it the water became salt, where the river is wider and fit for a boat to pass, between which and the beach are several small islands; on each side a tract of clear marsh, one side green, the other dead rushes; the side of the marsh next the sea hilly, the other level forest land. Saw many swans and ducks, and at six o'clock arrived at the mouth of the river in Elephant Bay. I suppose it may be about five miles from the place we first fell in with it to the bay. The same night we went to Cooper's, and stopped the night, being very tired and hungry.

I was informed that the French commodore took on board four of the prisoners which he landed on our arrival and one Lyons, an Irishman.

Wednesday 12th.—Set out at six o'clock, along the shore. Walked till four o'clock, when we shot a kangaroo. Sat down to broil it, but, the brush taking fire around us, was obliged to move a little further, where we made another fire; and it was our intention to have stopped the night, but, the wind being high and the smoke troublesome, about eleven o'clock the captain set fire to the bush, and we marched on towards the marquee, where we arrived at four o'clock in the morning.

Thursday 13*th.*—Remained at head-quarters all the day. A party went out foraging, and returned with five emus, two young live do., and a kangaroo.

Friday 14*th.*—The boat came on shore in the morning, and Dr. McCullum went on board, and I went into the country with two men to get specimens of wood.

Saturday 15*th.*—Looking over specimens and seeds; the captain taking observations.

Sunday 16*th.*—The boat came on shore in the morning, but, the wind being high and much surf, we did not go on board.

Monday, 17*th.*—In the morning two men went after some game; the boat went to the vessel with part of the luggage, and in the afternoon returned with the *George's* long boat, when we all went on board.

As far as I went round the island the hills are high and sandy for 2 or 3 three miles in, the brush very thick, and little grass. The interior is level, and in many cases swampy, with large lagoons. There is some good land in the middle of the island, but the timber is so thick and lofty that I could form no idea of its extent. The timber in general is gum-tree, mimosas of sorts, some ash, cotton bark, Banksia and Rhamnus; saw no cedar. The best place for a settlement is either in Elephant Bay or opposite New Year's Island; but as we saw but little of the interior there are perhaps better places. The shore is in every place difficult of access for vessels. Elephant oil and spars are the only articles of commerce the island produces; on the adjacent islands there are plenty of seals.

Tuesday, 18*th.*—All hands up at daylight; the Captain went sounding whilst the others were weighing anchor. At half-past nine o'clock sailed from New Year's Island, and at two saw land; supposed it to be Cape Albany (*Albany Otway*). Our company consisted of eighteen, the captain having taken on board Smith and Jones, who had been with us since our arrival on the island. This day had my provision served out by myself.

Wednesday, 19*th.*— Out of sight of land; a calm. At five p.m. saw land; at nine came to anchor.

Thursday, 20*th.*—In the morning off high land; the hills high and verdant. The trees inward appeared large. There appeared an opening like a small river to the eastward; at noon a valley with gentle rising ground, behind which the timber appeared large. At eight o'clock anchored in PORT PHILLIP; hot winds most of the day.

Friday, 21*st.*—Weighed anchor early in the morning, and came further into the bay; dropped anchor.[1] The Captain, Mr. Grimes, doctor, and myself went on shore, and walked across a neck of land to the sea,[2] whilst the carpenter repaired the boat. The land is a light,

---

[1] Near Point King (Sorrento).   [2] "London Bridge."

black-sand pasture, thin of timber, consisting of gum[1], oak, Banksia and thorn. Saw the scaites of some lagoons, all dry except one salt one; the land is about a mile and a half over; came on board in the afternoon.

Saturday, 22nd.—All hands up at daylight. The captain went sounding; on his return Mr. Grimes, doctor and self, two marines and two assistants to the surveyor went on shore; as we went on met with two huts, apparently built by Europeans; a little farther met with fresh water in a swamp[2] about fifty yards from the beach; farther on a small run of water. The country level; timber as the preceding day. Saw three natives at a distance; they made off as we approached them.

Sunday, 23rd.—Early in the morning the same party as yesterday, with the addition of the captain, went on shore; we ascended a high hill;[3] the land good until we got near the top, where it is stony. On the north and south sides of the hill there are from 2,000 to 3,000 acres of good land, a specimen of which is taken. Mr. Robbins and self went to the top of a hill;[3] it appeared fine land at a distance, but only stones and short brush as we approached it; saw Western Port distinctly from the top of it; we supposed it to be about five miles from the beach. Returned through an extensive swamp.[4] On the side of the hill met with two dingles with some fresh water in deep holes. Mr. Grimes and the others took another way at the bottom of the first hill; we found them on board at our return. The country all newly burnt. Caught plenty of fish; a shark took a mariner's jacket out of the boat.

Monday, 24th.—At seven o'clock the same party as on the 22nd went to continue the survey. At three miles a swamp, several runs of water, only one good, and all blocked up at the beach. The rest of this day's journey hills, rocky land,[5] light black sand, fine grass, and the trees low and scrubby. Several dingles on the side of the hills; found a little water in two holes.

Tuesday, 25th.—Having a sore foot stopped on board. Mr. Grimes and party went on shore at the usual time, and continued the survey till about two o'clock. From what the doctor informed me the land as on the preceding day; looked over seeds and specimens, &c.

Wednesday, 26th.—The Captain, Grimes, doctor, self, and three seamen set off for Western Port; at two miles a swamp[6] without trees, and fine grass; over a swell another of the same sort. Found no water till we came near the Port; saw some ducks, which was a sign of water; made to the place; it was salt, but I went a little further up and found it fresh. I stopped there with one man, and the Captain, Mr. Grimes, and another went on to the Port;[7] they got into a swamp and did not reach the beach in two hours; they returned, and after dinner we returned back the course we came. Previous to our reaching the water the doctor was so fatigued for want of water that he could not go on; he was left with a man, gun and compass, to make the best of his way back to the vessel. He sent the man off to the

---

[1] Golden wattle. —— [2] Wannaeue (Boneo) Swamp. —— [3] "Arthur's Seat." —— [4] Wannaeue Swamp.——[5] Western slopes of "Arthur's Seat" Ranges.——[6] "The Big Swamp."——[7] Between Sandy Point and Hastings.

vessel for water with the gun and compass, and he moved from the place where we left him. On our arrival found the man but not the Doctor, and it being dark nothing could be done till morning.——

Thursday, 27th.—When four men set off to the place where he was left, they found his fire but he was gone. After searching all the day they arrived in the evening without him.

Friday, 28th.—In the morning two parties went different ways in search of the Doctor; in an hour after they were gone saw the Doctor walking on the beach, when a boat was sent to bring him on board. Immediately three muskatoons were fired to bring the parties back, but they did not hear them, and they returned in the afternoon. Thunder, high wind, some drops of rain, and excessively hot for two days past.

Saturday, 29th.—At eight o'clock Mr. Grimes, self, and four others went on shore to continue the survey from the 25th. There is a small river[1] where we began; a little further some fresh water; crossed several dingles, all dry. At about two o'clock came to fresh water; it appears to be a considerable stream[2] in wet seasons. I went but a little way in the country being alone. The land is a light, black sandy soil, timber small and low, the shore rocky, iron-colored stone,[3] but sand when broken.

Sunday, 30th.—The same party as yesterday went on shore at eight o'clock. About a mile from the fresh water there is a deep gully;[4] I crossed it about half a mile from the beach; it appears to run a great way into the country. I ascended a hill[5] where I could see eight or ten miles, hills without trees, narrow valleys with scrubby brush. The soil black, gavelly sand; at a mile-and-a-half from the beach a run of fresh water to a lagoon. Came to a river;[6] it was salt; traced it to the beach; crossed it up to the knees about a mile farther; went in about a quarter of a mile found a fine fresh water river about 30 feet wide, and deep enough for a boat; Mr. Grimes took the bearings of it; traced it six or eight miles;[7] it runs in a parallel line with the sea. Fell in with a body of natives, fourteen men, besides women and children; they pointed to us to follow the ship; I gave them some biscuit; some of the men gave them some old hats and a handkerchief; they followed us a considerable way, seemingly asking for more. There are some huts on the side of the river. The land[8] sandy, with shell bottom; wood small. At five o'clock got on board.

Monday, 31st.—It looked like a wet morning; we did not go out early. At ten o'clock the Captain, Grimes, self, and two mariners, went on shore; crossed a neck of land about half a mile over; went along the beach a little way and ascended a hill; the country appearing very barren. Returned to the vessel about one o'clock.[9]

Tuesday, February 1st.—The same party as before went on shore about seven o'clock to continue the survey from 30th. There is a slip of trees from four to six chains from the beach within which is poor sandy land with short brush, and no trees inwards for several miles.

---

[1] Balcombe's Creek. —— [2] The Tanti (Schnapper Point). —— [3] Mount Martha. —— [4] Davey's Gully. —— [5] Back of Frankston. —— [6] Cannanook. —— [7] About four miles. —— [8] The Long Beach. —— [9] The Long Beach and Carrum Carrum Swamp.

In the afternoon the country more woody and land something better. The day very hot, and found no water. Saw two large emus.

Wednesday, 2nd.—At the usual time the same party as yesterday, with the addition of the doctor, went on shore ; for about a mile the land dry, a light sandy soil ; afterwards a large swamp,[1] with three lagoons in it, all dry. The land appears to be covered with water in wet seasons. Came to a salt lagoon about a mile long and a quarter of a mile wide ; had not entrance to the sea. Soon afterwards came to a large river ;[2] went up it about a mile when we turned back and waited for the boat to take us on board. The ground is a swamp on one side and high on the other.[3] Saw many swans, pelicans, and ducks. Were obliged to go up to our middle to get to the boat, and got on board between five and six o'clock. Rain and thunder in the night.

Thursday, 3rd.—At six o'clock the captain, Mr. Grimes, self, and five seamen went in the boat up the Great River ; at between two and three miles it divided into two ;[4] we took the left hand stream at half-past eight o'clock. The land became high, where we landed and went on a hill. The soil a reddish loam from ten to fifteen inches deep. Saw a large lagoon at a distance. Went over the hill to a large swamp.[5] Soil black, eighteen inches, with blue clay at bottom. No trees for many miles. Came to the boat and proceeded on ; passed two dingles ; no water ; came to a third where we found some water, where we dined and proceeded on. Opposite this the land is stony soil, stiff blue clay, and no trees only some straggling oaks by the side of the river. We went up the river till we came to rocks ;[6] could not get the boat over ; crossed it at a place the natives had made for catching fish. It was still salt though a great fall ; went about two miles on the hills which are level at top and full of stones, the land very bad, and very few trees, and appeared so to the mountains, which appeared clothed with timber. On our return back came to the river a little higher up and found it excellent fresh water, where it divided and appeared deep enough for a boat. Just as we got to the boat it began to thunder and rain. Stopped a little time and came back till we could procure wood to make a fire, and it being sunset stopped the night.

Friday, 4th.—Started at six and came to the branch we passed before, at the entrance the land swampy ; a few miles up found it excellent water, where we saw a little hill[7] and landed. The time dinner was getting ready Messrs. Robbins, Grimes, and self went on the hill, where we saw the lagoon[8] seen from the hill where we first landed. It is in a large swamp between the two rivers ; fine grass, fit to mow ; not a bush in it. The soil is black rich earth about six to ten inches deep, when it is very hard and stiff. It is better farther back. About two miles further went on shore again ; the land much better and timber larger. Soil black, ten to fifteen inches deep ; bottom sand or gravel. I went to the other side where the ground was the same ; went

---

[1] Carrum Carrum.——[2] The Yarra Yarra River.——[3] About Footscray.——[4] The Saltwater and Yarra Rivers.——[5] Moonee Ponds.——[6] Solomon's Ford.——[7] Batman's Hill ; now levelled and a part of the station of the Victorian Railways.——[8] Batman's or West Melbourne Swamp.

in about two miles; it began to rain. I returned to the boat and after dinner we all got on board and arrived on board the vessel at dusk. Saw a canoe and two native huts.

Saturday, 5th.—Early in the morning the captain went with some casks for water to the place we were at the preceding day; they returned in the evening. Mr. Grimes and the doctor were on shore but returned in about an hour.

Sunday, 6th.—The captain, Mr. Grimes, and self went up the river opposite to the place that the survey was left off on the 2nd.[1] The Captain sounded the mouth of the river; the other party along the shore. I went up a creek[2] about a mile and a half; it was salt, and ended in a swamp; a run from the plains comes into it in wet weather. There is a few trees by the sea side; behind, a level plain to the mountains. Soil six inches deep of stiff black earth, white clay at bottom, and many large stones. The country appears the same for fifteen or twenty miles.

Monday, 7th.—Early in the morning the party that went up the river before with the doctor went up to the little hill[3] we had been at on the 4th, when we stopped to breakfast; proceeded on to a creek,[4] where we dined. Saw some natives. The land in general is a fine black soil, ten to eighteen inches deep. Timber; gum, Banksia, oak, and mimosa of sorts, but not large except the gum. The river appears to rise to the height of eight or ten feet at times by wreck on the trees. Went alternately into the land on both sides the river; it continued nearly of the same quality. The greatest part of the land is above the floods. Proceeded on till sunset; stopped the night.

Tuesday, 8th.—Sowed some seeds by the natives' hut, where we slept. Continued our course up the river; the land high; rocks by side of the river; it is a freestone, the strata on edge. Came to a fall,[5] where we could not get the boat over. We went inland a little way. It is stony, about six inches black stiff soil, white clay at bottom. Mr. Robbins got up a tree; saw it to be gently rising hills, clothed with trees, for ten or fifteen miles. A little above the fall there is a small island, and the river divides in two. The timber in general is gum, oak, and Banksia; the two latter are small; the gum two to four feet diameter, and from ten to thirty feet high; on some of the low ground they are something larger. We were not more than half a mile from the river. Returned back, and crossed a neck of land 330 paces over[6] whilst the boat went round. Came to our old station at the large lagoon. I went about two miles inland and fell in with seven natives. I saw Messrs. Robbins, Grimes, and McCallum, at the lagoon. From the hill saw the vessel; returned to the river, and after dinner set out for the vessel, where we arrived about seven o'clock; the land at two miles inland is of a better quality than the specimen.

Wednesday, 9th.—Continued the survey from the mouth of the river.[7] The land for two or three miles is a gentle rise from the beach, which is muddy, with large stones; the land stiff clay, the stone appearing at top; a little further, near the beach, a swamp light black sand, white

---

[1] Footscray. —[2] Stony Creek. —[3] Batman's Hill. —[4] Gardiner's Creek. —[5] Dight's Falls. —[6] Studley Park.—[7] Williamstown.

shells at bottom. There is a slip of trees about half a mile from the beach, then a clear level plain to the mountains, which I suppose to be fifteen or twenty miles. Passed two inlets of salt water. Got on board at two.

Thursday, 10th.—At six o'clock the same party went on shore. The slip of trees by the beach continued about a mile, when the shore became more high, about eight or ten feet above high water mark; we proceeded on for four or five miles, and the wind being contrary we observed the vessel "bring to," and we walked back and got on board about three o'clock. Several nautilus shells picked up.

Friday, 11th.—At eight o'clock the captain, doctor, self, and carpenter, went on shore. We observed a hill at a distance and made to it; we crossed the two runs seen [1] on the 9th; one ends in a swamp, the other salt water where we crossed it, the country very level, some plains, stony, and much water to lodge in it in wet weather. Went to the top of the hill; it is stony; could see about ten miles around us a level plain [2] with a few straggling bushes. The face of the ground is one-third grass, one-do. stone, and one-do. earth, mostly newly burnt. Returned back nearly the same course, and found some brackish water in one of the runs we crossed before. Got on board about three o'clock.

Saturday, 12th.—Anchor up at sunrise; proceeded up the bay opposite to the place where the survey was left off on the 10th,[3] the vessel being about the middle of the bay. We crossed over in the boat to the other shore. The party consisted of the captain, Mr. Grimes, the doctor, self, and seven seamen and marines—in all eleven, with four days' provisions; got on shore at five o'clock. I went on the top of a hill, where the land is good and fine pasture from ten to eighteen inches deep, fine black earth with white sandy clay or gravel bottom. The timber small and the same as before-mentioned. Came up with the doctor, and we went about two miles in, the country appearing the same.

Sunday, 13th.—Set out at six o'clock, the captain and three men in the boat, the rest on shore. The land and timber is of the same quality for several miles, and there are five dingles, which are runs of water in wet seasons, but all dry. The shore became swampy. Crossed the mud up to the knees; it continued low and muddy a considerable way. We stopped and dined opposite to a salt lagoon; started soon after, having but little water. The swamp continued for some miles farther, when I saw a high point of land, which I crossed, and it being near sunset stopped the night. We dug for water, but it was salt; we had not half a pint per man.

Monday, 14th.—Continued our course as soon as it was light. A large swamp two or three thousand acres, a brush of saltwort. Crossed two places up to the middle. Came to a fine green hill, very fine land, eighteen inches deep of rich black soil. The captain went on before in search of water, but found none. I crossed over the hill to the beach, and found an acid spring. Hailed the boat, and the surveyor came up about ten o'clock, when we breakfasted, and filled the cask and proceeded on. The land behind the hill high and woody. Came round to a

---

[1] Koroit and Skeleton Creeks.——[2] Werribee Plains.——[3] Point Cook.

river;[1] went up it about a mile in company with the doctor. At the end of the salt water found a hole made by natives; drank of it and returned back to the beach where the boat had "brought up." I went back to the hole and dug it larger, and brought some of the water. The land is not of so good a quality after I crossed the river; timber small and crooked, mostly oak and Banksia.

Tuesday, 15th.—In the morning two men went for some water; set out about eight o'clock. I went over a plain and met with a river;[2] went up about a mile and a half; it continued salt and wide. Returned to the beach, where the party was waiting for the boat to take them over; it being low water the boat could not get up; crossed it up to the middle and a little further, dined. Proceeded on round a point,[3] the land stony and no wood; came to a swamp and another river.[4] I did not go up it as it was near night. Had much difficulty to find wood.

Wednesday, 16th.—Breakfasted before daylight. The captain and crew went back to the native hole for water, whilst the others proceeded on the land. Swamps, with gentle rising stony ground; some scaites of lagoons and small runs, all dry. About two o'clock the boat came up with us; our provision was all out. We had got four geese; stopped and dressed them and walked on till sunset; a bad fire this night. Five pounds of bread per week. Passed three islands, one large and two small;[5] some mangroves on the large island, only a few scattered trees on the plain. Many swans, ducks, and luggs.

Thursday, 17th.—A bad fire and swampy beach this night. Had about 1 lb. of flour; boiled it for our breakfast for all hands. Mr. Grimes would not go any farther without provision; the captain went off to the vessel for some, and inadvertently took what water we had left with him. Mr. Grimes called him back, got the water in a camp kettle, and proceeded on about a mile. Came to a river;[6] went up it about two miles in company with the doctor, where we found excellent fresh water. There is no run above the fresh water, only some pools; it appeared to be a considerable run in wet seasons. Crossed over to the other side, and came opposite to Mr. Grimes and party, and they went round. The land was a little better by the river side, but swampy near the sea. Proceeded on to another river; it ended in a swamp about a mile up. Soon after the boat returned from the ship, when we sat down to dinner. Afterwards continued our march to another large river.[7] The boat being at hand, it took over Mr. Grimes and his party; he proceeded to the place where he left off on the 10th, and I went up the river a little way in the boat. It is the second in size we have met with. The captain did not think fit to go further, and we returned and were soon joined by the surveyor, &c. Got on board about seven o'clock.

Friday, 18th.—Anchor up at sunrise; came opposite the place we slept on the 12th inst. As we went out of the boat eleven natives met us; they were very civil. I gave one of them a biscuit; he looked at it; I took it again, eat of it, when he did the same; whatever we said

---

[1] The Werribee.——[2] The Little River.——[3] Point Wilson.——[4] Duck Ponds.——[5] Bird Rock.——[6] Duck Ponds.——[7] Cowie's Creek.

they said it after us. There was one who appeared to be their chief. They handed us their spears to look at; one of them was barbed and one with two prongs. They followed us as we went on, and Mr. Grimes seemed much frightened and hailed the boat to follow us; when the boat came up we went on board. I made signs for them to come into the boat, but they would not venture. *Two of them appeared to be marked with the smallpox.* After dinner we went on shore with an additional guard; they all met us again. Gave them some fish, a tomahawk, and an old hat; they put our hands to their breast, and looked into my haversack. The boat loitered behind us, and the sailors said that they took the lead-line and a hoe out of the boat, and some fish; got the line again but not the hoe. The land is a light sand from the point of the hill, and in some places swampy; the timber something larger, consisting of gum, oak, Banksia, and mimosa, some small pine, one half of it dead by the country being lately burnt. Got on board at dusk.

Saturday, 19th.—Weighed anchor at daylight; came opposite to the place we left last night. Dropped anchor and breakfasted. Got on shore about nine o'clock. The beach muddy; the land a swamp, timber as before. Came opposite to an island.[1] The vessel "brought to," and we went on board about one o'clock. Soon after our arrival on shore two of the natives we had seen on the preceding day came to us. They looked much at my buttons; I cut two off and gave each of them one, and some biscuit. They went with us upwards of a mile and returned. After dinner Mr. Grimes went to take some bearings, and the captain to sound.

Sunday, 20th.—All hands on board till after dinner. The captain went to sound, and arrived at dusk.

Monday, 21st.—Anchor up at daylight; dropped ditto at about seven. The captain, Mr. Grimes, and a party of seamen and marines, went on shore; we were now in sight of the entrance of the port. Mr. Robbins told me not to go on shore; it began to blow and rain, and they all came on board at two o'clock.

Tuesday, 22nd.—Weighed anchor at sunrise, and came to the opposite shore. Mr. Grimes and assistants went to finish the survey on the south-east point of the entrance; the captain to sound. They returned on board about four p.m.

Wednesday, 23rd.—Weighed anchor about seven o'clock, and came opposite to the watering place. The wooding and watering parties went on shore. I went to examine the run of water; it was dry, except a small pond near the beach. Traced the run about a quarter of a mile; it ends in a lagoon, which was dry.

Thursday, 24th.—All hands wooding, watering, and washing. I sowed a variety of seeds by the watering place; the land is light and sandy. I went towards the bottom of Arthur's Seat, and met with lagoon with fresh water. The captain and Mr. Grimes came on shore in the evening, and all hands got on board at dusk.

Friday, 25th.—About nine o'clock the captain, Grimes, and doctor went to examine a shoal and take some bearings; they came on board

---

[1] Swan Island.

about two, and in the afternoon some of the crew went on shore to finish their washing. About ten at night the man on watch observed the small boat gone; the whaleboat was immediately sent in search of her.

Saturday, 26th.—About four o'clock in the morning the party that went in search of the boat returned without her, when another party was sent at daylight. The captain saw the boat at a small distance from the vessel; weighed anchor and took her in tow, and made a signal for the whaleboat to come alongside. Dropped anchor, and after breakfast the captain and Mr. Grimes went on shore; they returned about one, and in the afternoon weighed anchor and dropped down to the Heads and took in the whaleboat.

The most eligible place for a settlement that I have seen is on the FRESHWATER RIVER [*Yarra*]. In several places there are small tracts of good land, but they are without wood and water. I have every reason to think that there is not often so great a scarcity of water as at present from the appearance of the herbage. The country in general is excellent pasture and thin of timber, which is mostly low and crooked. In most places there is fine clay for bricks, and abundance of stone. I am of opinion that the timber is better both in quality and size further up the country, as I saw some what is called ash on the banks of the Freshwater River, and the hills appear to be clothed with wood. As to the quantity of good land at the different places, I shall be better able to describe when I am favored with a sight of a chart, as I have not been permitted to see one since I came out. There is great plenty of fish in PORT KING. The country in general is newly burnt.

Sunday, 27th.—Anchor up at sunrise; cleared the Heads between seven and eight o'clock; about one off Western Port; a fine breeze in the afternoon.

Monday, 28th.—The breeze continued all night. This morning saw Wilson's Promontory, Rock Dunder (*Rodondo*), Curtis's Island, with several small islands. A fine breeze all the day; at night out of sight of land.

Tuesday, March 1st.—A calm in the morning; about noon saw land from the mast-head, supposed to be Point Hicks. Contrary wind all day.

Wednesday, 2nd.—In the morning saw Ram's Head. The shore from Point Hicks to Ram's Head is sand hills, further inland high hills covered with timber. The wind continued at north-east, and soon after twelve lay to, there being a wind and sea; out of sight of land at dusk.

Thursday, 3rd.—The wind abated in the night. At sunrise opposite to the shore we were at when the vessel lay to; a calm hazy day; could see little of the shore.

Friday, 4th.—About eight o'clock the wind shifted to the south; in the afternoon a fine breeze from south-west. Day hazy. This day Mr. Robbins called me down to the cabin to acquaint Mr. Grimes with the quality of the land and timber in PORT KING. I looked over the chart and had a glance of the chart of King's Island.

Saturday, 5th.—A fine southerly breeze at daylight; going four and a half knots, increased to five and a half. Saw no land this day; thunder and some rain in the evening.

Sunday, 6th.—A hazy morning; wind at south. About ten o'clock saw land, Cape St. George, lat. 35° 21'. At three o'clock opposite to Jervis Bay; the land high at the heads of the bay, a small island at the entrance.

Monday, 7th.—At daylight the heads of Port Jervis bearing southerly about seven or eight leagues; the land is high to Port Hacking, where it is low; at six o'clock abreast of Botany Bay; at eight abreast of the Flagstaff, and at half-past ten anchored in SYDNEY COVE.

GENERAL AND GARRISON ORDERS BY DAVID COLLINS, ESQ., LIEUT.-COL. ROYAL MARINES, LIEUT.-GOVERNOR OF PORT PHILLIP.

(*From* 16*th October* 1803, *to* 20*th February* 1804.)

Sullivan Bay, [Port Phillip], 16th Oct. 1803.

General Orders.

Parole—Sullivan. C. Sign—Woodriff.

The Commissary is directed to issue, until further orders, the following ration weekly:—To civil, military, and free settlers—beef, 7 lbs.; or pork, 4 lbs.; biscuit, 7 lbs.; flour, 1 lb.; sugar, 6 ozs. To women, two-thirds; children, above 5 years, half; and children, under 5 years, quarter of the above ration.

A copper will be immediately erected for the convenience of cooking, and persons appointed to dress the provisions, which are to be ready every day at twelve o'clock.

Half a pint of spirits is allowed to the military daily.

Garrison Orders.

A guard, consisting of 1 sergt., 1 corp., and 12 privates, will mount daily in front of the marine encampment. Officers for the duty this day, 1st Lt. Johnson; to-morrow, 2nd Lt. Lord.

The centinels at the different posts will be at all times vigilant and careful to preserve peace and good order. After the beating of the taptoo, they are not to allow any (the night watch which will be ap-

DAVID COLLINS,

Lt.-Col. Royal Marines and Lieut. Governor of Port Phillip.

From a miniature by Barber.

pointed excepted) to pass without the countersign. All prisoners taken during the night are to be sent to the quarter guard. The centinels at the landing place will not suffer any spirituous liquors to be landed at, or near their post, without a written permit signed by the Lieut.-Governor, and they are not to prevent any military or civil officer, or free settler, from going into a boat, or on board of ships at anchor in the harbour, but other persons, if employed by an officer, are to produce a pass, signed by the officer, which is to be given to the centinel, and by him to be delivered to the sergt. of the guard. The greatest attention to be paid to this order. The morning parade will beat at nine o'clock, the evening at sunset. Taptoo will be beat at nine o'clock. The orderly drum every day at one.

Sullivan Bay, 17th October 1803.
General Orders.
Parole—Calcutta. C. Sign—Woodriff.

The following working hours are established until further orders :— From sunrise in the morning (at which time the drum will beat) until noon (excepting half an hour at eight), and from one o'clock until sunset, at which time the people, wherever employed, will bring in their tools, and deposit them under the inspection of the superintendents and overseers, in such places as they shall point out.

Garrison Orders.

The officer of the day will occasionally visit the working parties, and report what he may there observe to the Governor. The centinel at the store tents is, upon no account whatever, to permit anyone but the Commissary, and the persons immediately employed under him, to enter therein (the Lieut.-Governor excepted). This is to be a standing order which is never to be disobeyed. The centinels at the landing place are at all times to preserve regularity while the stores are delivering. They are not to allow any stragglers near their post, and only such as may be under the direction of an overseer. The Commanding Officer is pleased to appoint 1st Lt. Sladden to do the duty of Adjutant, and 1st Lt. Johnson that of Quarter-master to the detachment, until further orders. Officers for duty this day, 2nd Lt. Lord; for to-morrow, 1st Lt. Johnson.

Sullivan Bay, 18th Oct. 1803.
General Orders.
Parole—Port Jackson. C. Sign—King.

The settlers and prisoners are not to make fires near the encampment, but in such places as will be pointed out to them by Lt. Johnson; the tents being all pitched, an accident happening unto one, it could not be replaced. The centinels have orders to stop all prisoners found out of their tents after 9 o'clock at night, and bring them to the quarter guard. Mr. John Ingle is appointed inspector of public mechanics and artificers, until further orders.

Garrison Orders.

The Lt.-Colonel on taking command of the detachment of Royal Marines, landed at Port Phillip, entertains a hope that they will all feel a just sense of the honorable situation in which they are placed. They have been selected by their Sovereign to compose the garrison for the protection of this infant settlement. He trusts this will stimulate them to use their best exertions, and enable the Lt.-Colonel to report to the Secretary of State that such a trust has not been unworthily placed in them. He hopes they all know that obedience to orders, sobriety, and cleanliness, form the essential points in the character of a good soldier. While he observes that these are attended to, he shall feel a pride in having them under his command, and shall hold it his duty, by every means in his power, to render their situation comfortable. He is unwilling to mention the word punishment, but it is necessary they should know his firm determination to have the strictest obedience paid to such orders as he may think proper to give from time to time for their regulation, and trusts that when at a future period this shall be joined by other detachments of their brave comrades, he shall be able with pleasure to hold up this small band as an example worthy their imitation. The officer of the day will have the charge of the guards, and once during the night will go the visiting rounds. A patrol of a corpl. and two privates will occasionally, between the relief of the centinels, go round the encampment and take up all persons that they may find after the taptoo has beat, and bring them to the quarter guard. The detachment off duty will parade for drill at seven o'clock every morning at seven o'clock (Sundays excepted), if the weather will admit. The civil and military officers wanting the countersign may have it on application to Lt. Sladden. The quarter guard to be augmented by three privates to-morrow; the additional centinel is for the preservation of two water casks at the watering place, which are appropriated solely to the use of the civil and military establishment.

Sullivan Bay, 19th Oct. 1803.
General Orders.
Parole—Survey. C. Sign—Hartwell.

The Commissary will not deliver any articles from the public stores, but between the hours of eight and nine in the morning, and one and two in the afternoon; nor is he on any account to issue anything without a written order, signed by the Lt.-Governor.

Garrison Orders.

2nd Lt. Menzies, of the Royal Marines, will disembark to-morrow morning from His Majesty's ship *Calcutta*, and join the detachment. A garrison court-martial to assemble to-morrow morning at eleven o'clock, at 1st Lt. Johnson's marquee, for the trial of such prisoners as may be brought before it. 1st Lt. Johnson, president; 2nd Lt. Menzies, 2nd Lt. Lord, members.

The prisoners to be acquainted, and the evidences warned to attend.

Sullivan Bay, 20th Oct. 1803.
General Orders.
Parole—Delivery. C. Sign—Dispatch.

This bay and the harbour in general being unfortunately full of voracious sharks and stingrays only, it is recommended to the convicts not to go into the water without the utmost precaution, and they are positively prohibited from bathing in front of the encampment.

Garrison Orders.

The garrison court-martial held this day is dissolved, and 1st-Lt. Menzies will re-embark on board His Majesty's ship *Calcutta*. The sentence of the garrison court-martial held this day, will be put into execution this evening at retreat beating.

Sullivan Bay, 21st Oct. 1803.
General Orders.
Parole—Explore. C. Sign—Tuckey.

Garrison Orders.
The detail for duty only.

Sullivan Bay, 22nd Oct. 1803.
General Orders.
Parole—Duty. C. Sign—Attention.

A general muster of all the male convicts will take place on Monday morning next, at seven o'clock. They will understand that no provisions will be issued to such as do not attend, and those who are absent will be punished. The Commissary will issue clothing to the convicts as soon as a sufficient quantity is landed from the ship. The officers and others who have been allowed convicts to attend on them, will immediately make a return thereof to the Commissary, and the superintendants and overseers of gangs will make a return to him of the people employed by them respectively, a report of which is to be made to the Governor.

Garrison Orders.

The troop will beat at ten in the morning, at which time the guard will mount, until further orders. The detachment being divided into parade companies, 1st-Lt. Johnson will take command of the 1st, and 2nd-Lt. Lord that of the 2nd parade companies.

22nd Oct. 1803.
General After Orders.

The settlers and convicts will assemble to-morrow morning in front of the marine encampment, at eleven o'clock, for the purpose of attending Divine service to return thanks for our prosperous voyage and safe arrival in this harbour. The convicts will attend as clean as their present situation will admit.

Garrison After Orders.

The detachment will parade to-morrow morning, at eleven o'clock, in front of their encampment, for the purpose of attending Divine service.

Sullivan Bay, 23rd Oct. 1803.
General Orders.
Parole—Hawkesbury.   C. Sign—Pelham.

There being already on the ground a quantity of fuel sufficient for the use of everyone here, it is positively ordered that no more timber be cut down in the neighbourhood of the encampment, for any purpose, without the Lt.-Governor's consent previously obtained.

Garrison Orders.

Sergt. Richard, sargent of the 1st parade company, having been found guilty of the crime with which he stood charged before a court-martial, was sentenced to be reduced to the pay and duty of a private centinel, but some alleviating circumstances having appeared in the course of the proceedings, and in the defence offered by the prisoner, he was recommended by the court to the clemency of the Commanding Officer, which recommendation he was pleased to confirm, and the prisoner was restored to his former situation. A review of arms and necessaries to-morrow morning after troop beating.

Sullivan Bay, 24th Oct. 1803.
General Orders.
Parole—Portland.   C. Sign—Grenville.

Garrison Orders.

Detail for duty only.

25th Oct. 1803.
Garrison Morning Orders.

This being the anniversary of His Majesty's accession to the throne, the detachment will assemble in front of the encampment, at twelve o'clock, and fire three vollies in honor of the day, after which the guard will mount at two o'clock.

Sullivan Bay, 25th Oct. 1803.
General Orders.
Parole—King George.   C. Sign—Accession.

Garrison Orders.

The detail for duty only.

Sullivan Bay, 26th Oct. 1803.
General Orders.
Parole—England.   C. Sign—Rule.

Garrison Orders.

The presence of the officer of the day being at all times indispensably requisite in the camp, he is not, on any pretence, to quit it without the knowledge of the Commanding Officer. The comfort and appearance of the military depending much upon their cleanliness, The Right Honourable the Lords Commissioners of the Admiralty were pleased to admit a certain number of women to accompany their husbands on the present expedition, for the purpose of contributing to that end, by washing for the detachment. The Commanding Officer therefore directs and appoints the following women to be so employed, and in the following manner, namely :—The wife of William Bean, pte., to wash for fifteen persons ; the wife of George Carley, pte., to wash for fifteen persons ; the wife of James Spooner, to wash for fourteen persons ; and as an ample supply of necessaries has been sent out with the detachment, he will not admit of any excuse for their appearing in a dirty, unsoldierlike manner, discreditable to themselves and to the corps to which they belong. The different packages and cases in which the marine stores and clothing are contained, are not, on any account, when emptied, to be destroyed or converted to any other use without the approbation of the Commanding Officer. The detail for duty.

Sullivan Bay, 27th Oct. 1803.
General Orders.
Parole—Melville.   C. Sign—Cochrane.

As it is evident that the care and propagation of live stock is of the greatest importance in an infant settlement, the Lieut.-Governor hopes he need not suggest to anyone the necessity of preserving what has been landed, but that there may be acquired as speedily as circumstances will allow a stock competent in itself to supply the settlement with animal food, he is under the necessity of directing that no part of the live stock belonging to individuals—sheep, swine, goats or poultry—be slaughtered or exported from the settlement until further orders, without his knowledge and approbation. A return of live stock in the possession of individuals of every description, to be delivered to the Commissary immediately.

Garrison Orders.

The detail for duty only.

Sullivan Bay, 28th October 1803.
General Orders.
Parole—Direction.   C. Sign—Order.

The prisoners being now distributed into gangs under superintendents and overseers, who are to be accountable for their labour, they are not on any occasion to be taken from these gangs, or their employment changed, but by the express direction of the Lt.-Governor. All applications for this purpose are to be made in the first instance to Mr. Thomas Clark, Principal Superintendant.

Garrison Orders.

Sergt. James McCauly is to attend and assist the Adjutant at all parades and drills until further orders.

The detail for duty.

Sullivan Bay, 29th Oct. 1803.
General Orders.
Parole—Expectation.   C. Sign—Hope.

John Blinkworth, a settler, has permission to sell a few articles of wearing apparel which he brought from England.

Garrison Orders.

The quarter-guard will not turn out more than once a day to the Lieut.-Governor unless particularly ordered.

Detail for duty.

29th Oct. 1803.
General After Orders.

The Commissary will issue the undermentioned clothing to each male convict to-morrow morning, at nine o'clock, for which purpose they will all attend at the provision stores at that hour, viz.:—1 jacket, 1 waistcoat, 1 pair duck trowsers, 1 pair breeches, 2 check shirts, 1 pair shoes, 1 hat.

Sullivan Bay, 30th Oct. 1803.
General Orders.
Parole—Addington.   C. Sign—Abbot.

The Lieut.-Governor thinks it necessary to inform the people that the clothing which was issued to them this morning is to serve them for the ensuing six months (the article of shoes excepted), and that until the expiration of that time no more will be issued to them on any account. It therefore becomes the duty of every man that regards his own comforts to take the utmost care of his clothing, and the Lt.-Governor expects that they will be at all times ready to produce them when he shall call upon them for that purpose. He has remarked that several of the tents are much dirtied and blackened at the entrance; as others are clean; this must proceed from the dirtiness of the persons themselves who live in them. He therefore gives this notice, that the next tent which he finds in that state will be instantly taken away and sent to the public stores. The overseers will attend to this order, and see that no dirt or rubbish is left in the streets of the encampment.

Garrison Orders.

A garrison court martial will sit to-morrow morning, at eleven o'clock, for the trial of such prisoners as may be brought before it.

1st Lieut. Sladden, President ; 1st Lieut. Johnson, 2nd Lieut. Lord, Members.

The prisoners to be acquainted, and the evidences warned to attend.

The detail of duty and inspection of arms and necessaries.

Sullivan Bay, 31st Oct. 1803.

General Orders.

Parole—Watson.   C. Sign—Brooks.

Garrison Orders.

The sentence of the court martial held this day to be put in execution to-morrow morning at seven o'clock.

Detail for duty.

Sullivan Bay, 1st Nov. 1803.

General Orders.

Parole—Receipt.   C. Sign—Issue.

Garrison Orders.

The Commanding Officer is obliged to direct that in future the allowance of spirits shall be mixed with three waters, and issued twice a day to the detachment. The officer of the day will taste it when mixed. The quartermaster will continue to receive the allowance daily from the Commissary, but he will take it into his charge, and see that it is mixed agreeable to the above order at the marine store tent. One sergeant and ten privates will be landed this afternoon from His Majesty's ship *Calcutta* for the duty of this garrison. The quarter master will give them directions which tents they are to occupy.

Detail for duty.

Sullivan Bay, 2nd Nov. 1803.

General Orders.

Parole—Chatham.   C. Sign—Pitt.

The Lt.-Governor directs that in future there shall not be suffered any lights in that part of the encampment occupied by the convicts after nine o'clock at night. He likewise directs the superintendents, overseers, and others, in whom a trust is placed, to use their utmost endeavors to detect the practice of gambling, which, he understands, exists among the convicts, a crime, so big in itself with their certain ruin, it is his duty to prevent by every means in his power ; and if his positively forbidding them to gamble is not sufficient, he will most certainly punish every man that has been guilty of it in opposition to his order.

Garrison Orders.

The quarter guard will consist in future of one sergt., one corpl., and eighteen privates, and a picquet of three privates, will mount every evening at retreat beating until further orders. When any of the detachment is confined in the quarter guard the quartermaster is not to issue the allowance of spirits to prisoners while confined but reserve it at the disposal of the commanding officer.

A garrison court-martial will sit to-morrow morning at eleven o'clock, at the marine mess room, for the trial of such prisoners as may be brought before it. 1st Lieut. Sladden, president; 2nd Lieut. Menzies, 2nd Lieut. Lord, members. The prisoners to be acquainted and the evidences to attend.

Detail for duty.

Sullivan Bay, 3rd Nov. 1803.

General Orders.

Parole—Townshend.   C. Sign—Sydney.

The Commissary will, on Saturday next, serve to each male convict one wooden bowl, one platter, and one spoon. As they cannot but be sensible that Government has done everything that can make their situation comfortable, the Lt.-Governor trusts they will take the greatest care of what is issued to them from time to time for that purpose.

Garrison Orders.

A written crime [sheet], signed with the name and rank of the officer giving it in, is in future always to be sent with the prisoner ordered into confinement. The sergt. of the guard will insert in his report the arrival and departure of whatever boat shall come to the landing or other place in this bay after sunset. The court-martial which sat this morning is dissolved. The proceedings will be read this evening at retreat beating.

Detail for duty.

Sullivan Bay, 4 Nov. 1803.

General Orders.

Parole—Ocean.   C. Sign—Clear.

Garrison Orders.

Detail for duty only.

Sullivan Bay, 5 Nov. 1803.

General Orders.

Parole—Collins.   C. Sign—Success.

Divine service being to be performed to-morrow morning at eleven o'clock, the convicts will attend at that hour. The overseers will muster them and see that they are decently dressed. Provisions will be issued in future twice a week, viz. :—Tuesdays and Saturdays.

Garrison Orders.

The detachment will parade to-morrow morning at eleven o'clock for the purpose of attending Divine service.

---

6 Nov. 1803.

Garrison Morning Orders.

On account of the unfavourable appearance of the weather, the performance of Divine service will not take place as ordered yesterday.

Sullivan Bay, 6 Nov. 1803.

General Orders.

Parole—Sydney Cove.   C. Sign—Expedition.

Garrison Orders.

Detail for duty to-morrow, and an inspection of arms and necessaries.

Sullivan Bay, 7 Nov. 1803.

General Orders.

Parole—Industry.   C. Sign—Profits.

A female goat, the property of Lt. Dowers, of His Majesty's ship *Calcutta*, having been wantonly kicked, and thereby killed, by some person or persons at present unknown: Lieut.-Governor is hereby pleased to promise a reward of five pounds to any person who shall come forward with such information as shall lead to the discovery of the offender or offenders herein.

Garrison Orders.

The different centinels, wherever placed, are always to demand the countersign of every person approaching their posts, and they are not to suffer any one whatsoever to pass them with any other word than the countersign.

Detail for duty.

Sullivan Bay, 8th Nov. 1803.

General Orders.

Parole—Westminster.   C. Sign—London.

Mr. Hartley having submitted a list of articles which he has for sale, with their prices, to the Lieut.-Governor, he has given him licence to sell them, and has caused the list to be made public on the order board.

Garrison Orders.

Detail for duty.

8th November 1803.
General After Orders.

The two casks at the watering place, which have been appropriated to the use of the civil and military officers, being properly prepared to be shut up during the night, the centinel at that post will be withdrawn at seven o'clock at night, and planted there at the same hour in the morning. The keys of these casks are to be lodged with the adjutant, and the persons concerned will attend to the regulation, and cause whatever water they may require to be got within the above hours.

Sullivan Bay, 9th November 1803.
General Orders.
Parole—Civic.   C. Sign—State.

Garrison Orders.

Detail for duty only.

Sullivan Bay, 10th November 1803.
General Orders.
Parole—Ellenborough.   C. Sign—Law.

The Lieut.-Governor is concerned to learn that six men have been so blind to their own welfare, as to absent themselves from the settlement, and proceed in the desperate undertaking of travelling round to Port Jackson. If such is actually the motive of their absenting themselves, they must inevitably be lost in the attempt, and nothing more will ever be heard of them, for, independent of the risk they run of being killed by the natives, it is impossible for them with any quantity of provisions they could carry, to endure the fatigue of penetrating a thousand miles through the woods of this country, for such would be the distance, which by rounding the heads of the different harbours that present themselves in their route, they would have to travel. Although caution to them is now useless, yet it may not prove so to those who remain. He therefore takes this occasion of informing them, that while admitting the probability of their succeeding and reaching Port Jackson alive, they would instantly be apprehended, and sent back to this settlement by the Governor, here to meet the punishment justly due to their rashness and offence. Samuel Lightfoot is appointed and assistant in the general hospital. A watch bell being erected, it will ring at the following hours, viz.:—At six o'clock in the morning, when the convicts will turn out for work; at eight, when they will leave off for half an hour; at twelve, when they will again leave off work; at one, when they will again return to work; again at four, and at seven when they will leave off work. The bell will ring for the last time at eight o'clock at night.

Garrison Orders.

The quarter-drum will beat for the retreat until further orders, in the evening at half-past six o'clock.

Detail for duty.

Sullivan Bay, 11th November 1803.

General Orders.

Parole—Eldon.   C. Sign—Grant.

Garrison Orders.

Detailed for duty only.

Sullivan Bay, 12th November 1803.

General Orders.

Parole—Canterbury.   C. Sign—Moore.

If the weather permits, Divine Service will be performed to-morrow, at eleven o'clock in the forenoon. In consideration of the extreme heat of the weather, the Lieut.-Governor appoints the following as the hours of labour until further orders.—From five in the morning, at which time the bell will ring, until eight o'clock; from half-past eight until twelve, and from two until seven in the evening.

General Orders.

The detachment will assemble for the purpose of attending Divine Service, to-morrow, at eleven o'clock in the forenoon; and the guard will, on Sundays, mount at nine o'clock in the morning, until further orders.

Detail for duty only.

Sullivan Bay, 13th November 1803.

General Orders.

Parole—Markham.   C. Sign—York.

Garrison Orders.

The quartermaster will employ the tailor belonging to the detachment, and such other tailors as the Commanding Officer may appoint, in altering the clothing that became due in June last. The suits are to be fitted to the men, and made up according to the pattern established by the Admiralty. Each suit when finished is to be labelled, and put into the care of the quarter-master, until the whole are completed, when they will be issued. This work will be put in hand on Monday. A review of arms and necessaries, to-morrow morning as usual, after which the articles of war will be read.

Detail for duty only.

Sullivan Bay, 14th November 1803.
General Orders.
Parole—Porteus.   C. Sign—London.

Garrison Orders.
Detail for duty only.

Sullivan Bay, 15th November 1803.
General Orders.
Parole—Good voyage.   C. Sign—Mertho.

Garrison Orders.
Detail for duty only.

Sullivan Bay, 16th November 1803.
General Orders.
Parole—Barrington.   C. Sign—Durham.

A copper being erected near the watering place for the cooking provisions, and proper persons appointed to attend it; the Lieutenant-Governor prohibits the making of fires for cooking the convict's provisions, in any other part of the encampment except on the beach near the Carpenter's hut, where another copper will be put up for the accommodation of the people at that end of the encampment. The superintendents will attend to this regulation.

Garrison Orders.

The tents of the marine encampment will be struck for an hour at a quarter past one o'clock this day, during which time they will be swept and cleaned. This regulation will take place in future on Wednesdays and Saturdays at the above hour, if the weather permits.

16th Nov. 1803.
General After Orders.

The convicts will all assemble to-morrow at eleven o'clock in the forenoon, in front of the Encampment, when His Majesty's Commission appointing the Lt.-Governor of this settlement will be read.

After Garrison Orders.

The detachment will assemble to-morrow at eleven in the forenoon on the Parade, when His Majesty's Commission appointing the Lt.-Governor of this settlement will be read, after which the detachment will fire three vollies.

17th Nov. 1803.
Garrison Morning Orders.
The troop will beat this morning at eleven o'clock, and the guard will mount at two.

Sullivan Bay, 17th Nov. 1803.
General Orders.
Parole—Punishment. C. Sign—Justice.

Garrison Orders.
Detail for duty only.

Sullivan's Bay, 18th Nov. 1803.
General Orders.
Parole—Winchester. C. Sign—North.

The surgeon will send a return to the commissary, on the morning of each provision day, of the number and the names of sick convicts under medical treatment, for whose use he will issue the following ration, which will be drawn by the surgeon and served out to them in such proportions as he shall direct: Beef, 3½ lbs. or pork, 2 lbs.; biscuit, 7 lbs.; flour, 1 lb.

Garrison Orders.
Detail for duty only.

Sullivan Bay, 19th Nov. 1803.
General Orders.
Parole—York. C. Sign—Ely.

Divine service will be performed to-morrow at eleven o'clock in the forenoon, and every Sunday that the weather may be sufficiently favorable. The convicts are expected regularly to attend without any further orders.

Garrison Orders.
The detachment will parade for divine service to-morrow at eleven o'clock in the forenoon, and every Sunday that the weather may be sufficiently favorable.
Detail for duty.

Sullivan Bay, 20th Nov. 1803.
General Orders.
Parole—Worcester. C. Sign—Hurd.

Garrison Orders.
A review of arms and necessaries to-morrow at troop-beating as usual. A garrison court-martial will sit to-morrow morning at eleven o'clock, at the officers' mess-room, for the trial of such prisoners as

may be brought before it. 1st-Lieut. Sladden, president; 1st-Lieut. Johnson, 2nd-Lieut. Lord, members. The prisoners to be acquainted, and the evidences warned to attend. The duty of the day will, until further orders, be taken weekly. The officer of the week will attend at morning and evening parades, and have the charge of the guard going the rounds, if, as heretofore, done by the officer of the day. All the officers will attend on Sundays, and at the review of arms and necessaries, and whenever the whole detachment is assembled on any service more particular than a common parade. Officer for the ensuing week, 2nd-Lieut. Lord.

Sullivan Bay, 21st Nov. 1803.
General Orders.
Parole—Caution. C. Sign—Duty.

The Lieut.-Governor having received such information from the commander of His Majesty's ship *Calcutta* as leads him to suppose that a large body of natives is at no very great distance from the settlement: and as it is very doubtful for what may be their motive for coming on this side of Arthur's Seat, he thinks it necessary to caution the convicts and other persons against going in that direction any distance along the beach in search of fish in their leisure hours. He hopes that the punishment inflicted on Thursday last on the five delinquents who had absconded will have its weight with all those who witnessed it. If any should still intend to quit the settlement in the same manner, he will call to their observation the wretched appearance of Hangan and his two associates, who returned to their duty on Friday night, by whose account they will find that when engaged in a perilous undertaking of that nature they cannot trust even one another, these people all declaring that while they were sent to procure water for the whole party those who remained took that opportunity of absconding with the provisions which they had left in their care, perfectly indifferent as to what might prove their fate. Such treachery must excite the honest indignation of every well-disposed mind, and the Lieut.-Governor thinks that that alone should be sufficient to deter others from associating in so rash and hazardous an enterprize. If they imagine that the masters of ships in quitting this port will receive any persons on board without the Lieut.-Governor's licence, let them be undeceived by his assurance that the owners and masters of ships sent out to this country are bound by their charter parties to Government in such heavy penalties, if known to take away one individual without a certificate that he has permission to do so, that it cannot be their interest to incur the forfeiture of them. He therefore hopes that he shall not hear any more of absconding from the settlement.

Garrison Orders.

The commanding officer is concerned to be under the necessity of establishing the following drill for the non-commissioned officers. On Wednesday from six until seven in the morning; on Saturdays from two until three in the afternoon. The sentence of the court-martial which sat this morning will be put in execution to-morrow morning at seven o'clock. The court is dissolved. Detail for duty.

Sullivan Bay, 22nd November 1803.

General Orders.

Parole—Harmony.   C. Sign—Cecilia.

Garrison Orders.

Detail for duty only.

Sullivan Bay, 23rd November 1803.

General Orders.

Parole—Hereford.   C. Sign—Butler.

Garrison Orders.

The Commanding Officer is surprised to observe the unsteady appearance of the men at the evening parade. This can only proceed from their determination to evade the regulations which he adopted in the hope of preventing this unsoldierlike appearance, that he complains of in them, and which if persisted in will compel him not to increase the quantity of water, but reduce the quantity of spirits which is at present allowed them. Detail for duty.

Sullivan Bay, 24th November 1803.

General Orders.

Parole—Cornwallis.   C. Sign—Coventry.

Garrison Orders.

Detail for duty only.

Sullivan Bay, 25th November 1803.

General Orders.

Parole—Landaff.   C. Sign—Douglas.

Garrison Orders.

Detail for duty only.

Sullivan Bay, 26th November 1803.

General Orders.

Parole—Dampier.   C. Sign—Rochester.

Garrison Orders.

The detachment will parade for Divine Service to-morrow morning at eleven o'clock in the forenoon. Detail for duty.

Sullivan Bay, 27th November 1803.
General Orders.
Parole—Courtnay.   C. Sign—Exeter.

A general muster of all the convicts will be taken on Tuesday morning, the 29th inst., previous to the provisions being served; and as some regulation of the several messes will take place, those who neglect attending at that time will not receive any provisions. The permission given to the sawyers to work in their own time for individuals is withdrawn. As the reeds which are to be found in the vicinity of the settlement may be wanted for public purposes the Lieutenant Governor forbids their being taken by anyone whatsoever, until the use for which they are wanted shall have been submitted to him. Several pieces having of late been frequently discharged very near the camp, all firing of musquets or other arms (military duties excepted) is prohibited within one mile round the encampment.

Garrison Orders.

A review of arms and necessaries to-morrow at troop-beating. Detail for duty.

Sullivan Bay, 28th November 1803.
General Orders.
Parole—Carlisle.   C. Sign—Vernon.

Garrison Orders.

A Garrison Court-martial will assemble to-morrow at eleven o'clock in the forenoon, for the trial of such prisoners as may be brought before it.

1st Lieutenant Sladden, President.
1st Lieutenant Johnson ⎱ Members.
2nd Lieutenant Lord   ⎰

The prisoners to be acquainted and evidences warned to attend. Detail for duty.

Sullivan Bay, 29th November 1803.
General Orders.
Parole—Sutton.   C. Sign—

The Commissary will issue at ten o'clock to-morrow in the forenoon, one wooden bowl, platter, and spoon to each of the military and their wives, and to each free woman belonging to the prisoners.

Garrison Orders.

The quartermaster will furnish the Commanding Officer, with the names of such men of the detachment who have received slops since their landing, with an account of the articles which may have been issued to each.

The sentence of the Garrison Court-martial, held this day, to be put in execution to-morrow morning at six o'clock.

The court is dissolved.

Detail for duty.

Sullivan Bay, 30th November 1803.

General Orders.

Parole—Caledonia.   C. Sign—St. Andrews.

It having been mentioned to the Lt.-Governor, that many of the people not adverting to the consequences, are daily bringing birds' nests into the encampment, containing either eggs, or young unfledged birds. He thinks it necessary to prohibit a practice at once so cruel and destructive; any person found offending against this order will be punished. It appearing by the proceedings of a Court-martial, held yesterday, that two of the convicts, and one of their wives had purchased articles from a soldier belonging to the detachment of Royal Marines, the Lieutenant-Governor informs them that they are not to have any dealings or transactions whatsoever, with the military, who have not anything of their own to dispose of, and assures them that he shall always consider the purchasers of such articles as greater offenders than the sellers, and deal with them accordingly.

Garrison Orders.

The Commanding Officer hopes that no one of the detachment under his command, but such an unsoldierlike character as Thomas Hodgeman, would be concerned in any dealings or transactions with the convicts. They must perceive that the bad consequences that ever must and will attend such disgraceful conduct, and which he trusts none of them will ever be guilty.

Detail for duty.

Sullivan Bay, 1st Dec. 1803.

General Orders.

Parole—Randolph.   C. Sign—Oxford.

The Lieut.-Governor expecting the arrival of ships in this harbour, and being desirous of preventing as much as possible the clandestine introduction of spirits into the settlement, and the irregularities which must ensue, if once such an evil is admitted, directs that there shall in future be no other landing place than the one opposite the eastern angle of the battery in Sullivan Bay for boats belonging to ships, or vessels of any description, except when on business of particular emergency, it should be absolutely necessary for them to have communication with the settlement, and which could not be effected at the established landing, they may in such case be permitted to go round to the adjoining bay, where the sentinel will suffer them to land. The sentinel at the battery will, on perceiving a boat proceeding round the eastern point of the bay, immediately acquaint the officer of the guard therewith, who will communicate the same to the Lieut.-Governor. And no boat is to come to or go from the landing place after the taptoo has beat upon any account without his knowledge, or in case of his absence the knowledge of the officer second in command. This is to be considered a standing port order.

Garrison Orders.

Detail for duty only.

Sullivan Bay, 2nd Dec. 1803.

General Orders.

Parole—St. David's.   C. Sign—Murray.

His Majesty having been graciously pleased to appoint the following persons to compose the Civil Establishment of this settlement, they are to be observed as such accordingly, viz. :—

Lieut.-Colonel Collins to be Lieut.-Governor.
Revd. Richard* Knopwood to be Chaplain.
Capt. Benjm. Barcauld to be Judge Advocate.†
Mr. Wm. J'anson to be Surgeon.
   „ Mattw. Bowden to be first Asst. Surgeon.
   „ Wm. Hopley to be second   „
Mr. Leond. Fosbrook to be Deputy Commissary.
   „ George Prid. Robert Harris to be Deputy Surveyor.
   „ Adalarius Wm. Hy. Humphrey to be Mineralogist.
   „ Thomas Clark to be Superintendant.
   „ Wm. Patterson to be Superintendant.

All persons who have received tools from the Public Store are forthwith to bring them to the carpenter's shop for the purpose of their being marked, after which they will be returned to them ; and whatever tools are found upon anyone not marked, after Saturday the 10th inst., will be seized and delivered to the Commissary.

Garrison Orders.

Detail for duty only.

Sullivan Bay, 3rd Dec. 1803.

General Orders.

Parole—Fairweather.   C. Sign—Return.

The biscuits being nearly expended, the Commissary will on Tuesday next the sixth instant, issue the following weekly ration until further orders, viz., to civil, military, and free settlers :—

7 lbs. beef, or	6 oz. sugar,
4 „ pork,	1½ pints of peas.
6 „ flour,	

The usual proportion of the above ration to woman and children.

---

* Richard in original by mistake.——† This gentleman did not come out to P.P.

Garrison Orders.

The detachment will parade at eleven o'clock to-morrow in the forenoon, for the purpose of attending Divine Service. The guard will in future mount on Sundays at eight o'clock in the morning. The troop will beat as usual at ten, and the Church drum at eleven in the forenoon. Detail for duty.

Sullivan Bay, 4th Dec. 1803.

General Orders.

Parole—Alexandria.   C. Sign—Egypt.

Garrison Orders.

Such tools as are in the possession of the detachment, whether for public or private use, will be sent to-morrow to the carpenter's shop to be marked, pursuant to the General Orders of the second instant. The Quartermaster will see this done. Detail for duty, and an inspection of arms and necessaries.

Sullivan Bay, 5th Dec. 1803.

General Orders.

Parole—Amsterdam.   C. Sign—Holland.

Garrison Orders.

Detail for duty only.

Sullivan Bay, 6th Dec. 1803.

General Orders.

Parole—Arcangel.   C. Sign—Russia.

Garrison Orders.

Detail for duty only.

Sullivan Bay, 7th Dec. 1803.

General Orders.

Parole—Babelmandel.   C. Sign—Athens.

Garrison Orders.

Detail for duty only.

Sullivan Bay, 8th Dec. 1803.

General Orders.

Parole—Batavia.   C. Sign—Bengal.

The provisions being issued on Tuesdays and Saturdays, the people will work on those days during the following hours, viz.:—On the Tuesday from five in the morning until eleven, and from two until sunset. And on the Saturday from five in the morning until eleven, from which hour they will not be employed for the public again until Monday morning. The Lieut.-Governor, observing that not more than half the convicts attended the performance of Divine Service last Sunday, thinks it necessary to inform them that he expects the attendance of every one who is able to appear; and that if they neglect this necessary duty, he shall direct the Commissary to put those who shall absent themselves upon two-thirds allowance provisions for one month.

Garrison Orders.

Detail for duty order.

Sullivan Bay, 9th Dec. 1803.
General Orders.
Parole—Excursion.   C. Sign—Western Port.

Garrison Orders.

One sentinel being withdrawn, the picket will not mount again until further orders.   Detail for duty.

Sullivan Bay, 10th Dec. 1803.
General Orders.
Parole—Arthur Seat.   C. Sign—Good Look-out.

Garrison Orders.

The Quartermaster will not in future issue the daily allowance of spirits to any of the detachment who may be under medical treatment. The detachment will parade at eleven o'clock to-morrow in the forenoon for the purpose of attending Divine Service.

Sullivan Bay, 11th Dec. 1803.
General Orders.
Parole—Berlin.   C. Sign—Bengal.

Garrison Orders.

Detail for duty, and an inspection of arms and necessaries.

Sullivan Bay, 12th Dec. 1803.
General Orders.
Parole—Expectation.   C. Sign—Success.

Garrison Orders.

The quarter drum for the retreat will beat at a quarter before seven until further orders.
Detail for duty.

Sullivan Bay, 13th Dec. 1803.

General Orders.

Parole—Grose.　C. Sign—Paterson.

Garrison Orders.

Detail for duty only.

Sullivan Bay, 14th Dec. 1803.

General Orders.

Parole—Good conduct.　C. Sign—Approbation.

The commander of His Majesty's ship, the *Calcutta*, having signified to the Lt.-Governor his intention of sailing for Port Jackson, on Sunday next, the detachment of Royal Marines belonging to that ship, at present doing duty in this settlement, will be returned to her to-morrow. The Lt.-Governor feels a pleasure in saying that, during the time they have been under his orders, they have conducted themselves in every respect like good soldiers, and he regrets that the present situation of public affairs will not admit of his making any requisition for their being annexed to the detachment of the same corps now on service in the colony, which it was his intention to have done. He is also much gratified in being able to mark with his approbation, and hold up as an example worthy the imitation of their fellow-prisoners the meritorious conduct of John Rawlinson, Urias Allender, Christopher Forshas, Wm. Thomas, James Price, and David Wakefield, which since their return from Port Jackson has been reported to him by Mr. Collins, who had the charge of the boat in which they were employed. They may rest assured that he will not lose sight of the service which so creditably to themselves they have performed.

Garrison Orders.

The detachment of Royal marines belonging to His Majesty's ship, *Calcutta*, will be ready to re-embark on board that ship to-morrow.

The morning drill will, until further orders, commence at six in the morning, and in the afternoon at half-past one.

Detail for duty.

Sullivan Bay, 15th Dec. 1803.

General Orders.

Parole—Arrival.　C. Sign—Francis.

Garrison Orders.

Detail for duty only.

Sullivan Bay, 16th Dec. 1803.

General Orders.

Parole—Buffalo.　C. Sign—Kent.

Garrison Orders.

	S.	C.	P.
For guard to-morrow	1	1	9
Picquet this evening	0	0	6

16th Dec. 1803.
General After-orders.

The Lieut.-Governor is under the necessity of directing that the people who are employed in the preparations which are carrying on for removing the settlement, do continue to work to-morrow after receiving provisions, and on Sunday. This extra labor shall be made up to them at a future time, and he hopes he shall not find himself disappointed in his expectations of their loading the store-ship with the same spirit and activity that they manifested when her cargo was delivered.

Sullivan Bay, 17th Dec. 1803.
General Orders.
Parole—Breslau.   C. Sign—Boston.

Garrison Orders.

	S.	C.	P.
For guard to-morrow	1	1	9
Picquet this evening	0	0	6

In consequence of the general After-orders of yesterday, the detachment will not parade to-morrow for Divine service.

Sullivan Bay, 18th Dec. 1803.
General Orders.
Parole—Woodriff.   C. Sign—Calcutta.

Garrison Orders.

A review of arms and necessaries to-morrow morning as usual. For the duty of the ensuing week 1st Lieut. Johnson. Detail of guard for duty.

Sullivan Bay, 19th Dec. 1803.
General Orders.
Parole—Derwent.   C. Sign—Bowen.

Garrison Orders.

Detail for duty only.

Sullivan Bay, 20th Dec. 1803.
General Orders.
Parole—Brest.　C. Sign—Bristol.
Garrison Orders.
Detail for duty only.

Sullivan Bay, 21st Dec. 1803.
General Orders.
Parole—Port Dalrymple.　C. Sign—Flinders.

The Commissary will immediately make a return to the Lieut.-Governor of the numbers of all descriptions of people in the colony, distinguishing them as civil, military, free settlers, free women, and prisoners, in order to enable him to make a distribution of them for the first embarkation in the *Ocean* transport for Van Dieman's Land.

The master of that ship having having informed the Lieut.-Governor that he shall be ready to receive the cargo on Friday morning, Mr. Clark, the superintendent, will select two able gangs of fifteen men each, under the overseers Joseph Meyers and John Whitehead, who are to attend every day at the store and the jetty, and assist in removing the provisions, &c., to the boats. The Commissary will make such preparations at the store as will prevent any delay occurring in the removal of the various articles under his charge. Mr. Ingle will attend at the beach, and take the utmost care that none of the bale goods, dry provisions, or cases of tools and ironmongery receive any damage by the water. The superintendant, Patterson, will attend at the stores and direct the gang placed there. The Lieut.-Governor expects to see the same regularity and order preserved in these gangs that he noticed while the ships were unloading. All tools that are in the possession of individuals are to be forthwith sent to the public store, in order to their being packed up. The Commissary will issue to each person in the settlement (women and children excepted, to whom he will serve only the usual proportion), one pound of raisins on the provision day next before Christmas, on which day Divine service will be performed in the forenoon, if the weather permits.

Garrison Orders.

The quartermaster will take the necessary measures for having the stores in his charge ready for embarkation when called upon for that purpose. He will number or otherwise mark all the marquees and tents at present occupied by the detachment, in order to their possessing the same again wherever they may be landed. Detail for duty.

Sullivan Bay, 22nd Dec. 1803.
General Orders.
Parole—Buenos Ayres.　C. Sign—Cadiz.
Garrison Orders.
Detail for duty only.

Sullivan Bay, 23rd Dec. 1803.
General Orders.
Parole—Calais. C. Sign—Cairo.

Garrison Orders.
Detail for duty only.

Sullivan Bay, 24th Dec. 1803.
General Orders.
Parole—Humphery. C. Sign—Collins.

Garrison Orders.
The detachment will parade to-morrow at the usual hour to attend Divine service. Detail for duty.

Sullivan Bay, 25th Dec. 1803.
General Orders.
Parole—Canary. C. Sign—Cambridge.

Garrison Orders.
A review of arms and necessaries to-morrow morning as usual. For the duty of the ensuing week 1st Lieut. Johnson. A garrison court-martial will assemble to-morrow morning at eleven o'clock, at the mess-room, for the trial of such prisoners as may be brought before it.

1st Lieut. Sladden, president; 1st Lieut. Johnson, 2nd Lieut. Lord, members.

The prisoners to be acquainted and evidences warned to attend. Detail for duty.

Sullivan Bay, 26th Dec. 1803.
General Orders.
Parole—Cape of Good Hope. C. Sign—Cape Horn.

A daring robbery having been committed on Sunday morning in the Commissary's tent, and the sick having been at the same time meanly plundered of their provisions in their tents by some person or persons at present unknown, the Lieut.-Governor calls upon all the well-disposed persons in the settlement to aid and assist in bringing the offender or offenders to justice; and he is hereby pleased to promise to procure from His Excellency the Governor-in-Chief a conditional pardon for any prisoner who shall bring forward and prosecute to conviction any person or persons who have been guilty of these outrages. The Lieut.-Governor, in the most positive manner, forbids the prisoners from going to the sea shore after crayfish between sunset and sunrise; and as they will in future be regularly mustered during the night, any person found absent from his tent will be severely punished, unless he can satisfactorily account for such offence. The following persons are established as a night watch and patrol until further orders. They will apprehend and lodge in the quarter-guard all such suspicious persons whom they may meet between the above-mentioned hours; the principal of the watch reporting in the morning his proceedings during the night to the Revd. Mr. Knopwood :—Wm. Thomas Stocker, Principal; John Sculler, Patk. McCarty, James Taylor, John Flinders. It is recommended to the prisoners to be careful in securing their provisions from depredation during the night, as no loss so occasioned can in future be made good from the stores. The surgeon will furnish a return of the expenditure of medicines and hospital stores and of the actual number of persons who have been under medical treatment from the day of our landing to the 31st instant, both inclusive. The Commissary will also make a return of the quantity of provisions and clothing issued by him within the above period.

Garrison Orders.

The persons of those who are appointed as a watch during night by the General Orders of this day being well known to the sentinels they will, on challenging them and being answered "Night watch," not demand the countersign, but let them pass on, being satisfied that they are the persons so appointed, and the sentinel and guard will at all times give them such assistance as they may require for the apprehension of offenders. The sentence of the Court Martial held this day will be put in execution to-morrow morning at six o'clock.

Detail for duty.

Sullivan Bay, 27th Dec. 1803.

General Orders.

Parole—Vigilance. C. Sign—Attention.

The indulgence which was granted to certain convicts of erecting and residing in huts without the encampment having been abused, the Lieut.-Governor is under the necessity of directing their being pulled down, and the owners thereof immediately classed to tents. The Commissary will issue the provisions to the prisoners (such persons only excepted as the Lieut.-Governor may point out) daily until further orders; the serving hour to be at seven o'clock in the evening, when the people leave off work. This measure is adopted to prevent their being robbed at any time of a quantity of provisions, of which they would feel the loss.

Garrison Orders.

The quartermaster will give in a return the 31st of this month of all stores received by him from the Commissary for the use of the detachment; the return will specify the expenditure, receipt, and remains. A Garrison Court Martial will assemble to-morrow, at eleven in the forenoon, at the mess room for the trial of such prisoners as may be brought before it:—1st-Lieut. Sladden, president; 1st-Lieut. Johnson, 2nd-Lieut. Lord, members. The prisoners to be acquainted and the evidences warned to attend. The commanding officer is concerned to observe the shameful conduct of several of the soldiers of the detachment. Drunkenness is a crime that he never will pass over, and to prevent as far as in him lies their disgracing themselves, and the royal and honorable corps to which they belong, by incurring the censure of Courts Martial, he directs that in future their allowance of watered spirits shall not be taken to their tents, but drank at the place where it is mixed, in the presence of the officer of the day. If this regulation shall be found insufficient he assures them that the first man who is found guilty of drunkenness by a Court Martial shall never again receive the allowance of spirits.

Detail for duty.

Sullivan Bay, 28th December 1803.
General Orders.
Parole—Carthagena.   C. Sign—Charles Town.
Garrison Orders.
Detail for duty only.

Sullivan Bay, 29th December 1803.
General Orders.
Parole—Constantinople.   C. Sign—Dantzic.

Garrison Orders.
The quartermaster will immediately cause to be dug a pit, at a convenient distance from the southernmost part of the marine line, to be used by the detachment as a privy, and they are on no account to use any other. Earth is to be thrown into it every morning. The Court Martial which sat this morning will meet again to-morrow at eleven o'clock in the forenoon. The sentence of the Court Martial which sat this morning will be put in execution this evening at retreat beating.

Detail for duty.

Sullivan Bay, 30th December 1803.
General Orders.
Parole—Plymouth.   C. Sign—Portsmouth.

Garrison Orders.
The garrison Court Martial is further adjourned until eleven o'clock to-morrow, when it will again assemble as before directed. The corporal who goes with the relief will be very particular in attending to the orders which are given by the sentinels to each other, and sergeant of the guard will occasionally visit and learn from what orders they have received.

Detail for duty.

Sullivan Bay, 31st December 1803.
General Orders.
Parole—Chatham. C. Sign—Sheerness.

The Lieut.-Governor is under the necessity of directing that the business of loading the *Ocean* be not suspended until that is completed. The people will therefore work the remainder of this day and Sunday. It has never been his wish to make that day any other than a day of devotion and rest, but circumstances compel him to employ it in labor. In this the whole are concerned, since the sooner we are enabled to leave this unpromising and unproductive country the sooner shall we be able to reap the advantages and enjoy the comforts of a more fertile spot, and, as the winter season will soon not be far distant, there will not be too much time before us wherein to erect more comfortable dwellings for every one than the thin canvass coverings which we are now under, and which are every day growing worse. Several people applying to him daily for shoes, he informs them that on the arrival of the whole at the new settlement shoes shall be served out to all those who have not lately been supplied with new ones, and advises them to take care of those they have now got, not wearing them until they are past mending, which some of them have done. He cannot but pity the delusion which some of the prisoners labour under, in thinking that they can exist when deprived of the assistance of Government. Their madness will be manifest to themselves when they shall feel, too late, that they have wrought their own ruin. After those who have absconded he shall make no further search, certain that they must soon return or perish by famine.

Garrison Orders.

The detachment will not parade for Divine service to-morrow. They will not on that or any other day absent themselves from the camp without the permission of the officers of their companies. The court-martial which sat this morning is dissolved.

Detail for duty.

Sullivan Bay, 1st January 1804.
General Orders.
Parole—Prosperity. C. Sign—England.

Garrison Orders.

The troop will beat to-morrow at nine o'clock, at which time the guard will mount. The sentence of the court-martial which sat yesterday will be put in execution to-morrow morning at seven o'clock. A review of arms and necessaries to-morrow at troop beating, after which the Articles of War will be read. A garrison court-martial will assemble at the mess-room for the trial of such prisoners as may be brought before it at eleven o'clock in the morning. 1st Lieut. Sladden, president; 1st Lieut. Johnson, 2nd Lieut. Lord, members. The prisoners to be acquainted and evidences warned to attend.

Detail for duty.

Sullivan Bay, 2nd Jany. 1804.
General Orders.
Parole—Westminster. C. Sign—London.
Garrison Orders.

The garrison court-martial which sat this day is dissolved. The sentence of the garrison court-martial which sat this day will be put in execution at 7 o'clock to-morrow morning.

Detail for duty.

Sullivan Bay, 3rd Jany. 1804.
General Orders.
Parole—Bristol. C. Sign—Hull.
Garrison Orders.

The Commanding Officer is willing to believe that the unsoldierlike behaviour of the prisoners Rae and Andrews will never be imitated by any of the detachment. He feels it necessary to point out to them that it is the duty of all good soldiers to discountenance such a proceeding and report it to their officers, as their concealing it may be attended with consequences very fatal to themselves, as well as injurious to the service of their sovereign, to whom every man has sworn and owes allegiance.

Detail for duty.

Sullivan Bay, 4th January 1804.
General Orders.
Parole—Liverpool. C. Sign—Dover.
Garrison Orders.

Detail for duty only.

Sullivan Bay, 5th January 1804.
General Orders.
Parole—Falmouth. C. Sign—Penzance.

Some danger having been apprehended from the fires which have been lately in the vicinity of the encampment, the Lieut.-Governor directs the settlers and others who have cooking places in the rear thereof to extinguish their fires at nine o'clock at night; and, as these places will be visited after that hour, any person who may be found acting contrary to these orders will be reported in the morning.

Garrison Orders.

The officer of the week will daily visit the tents at the hour at which the men dine, and inspect the state of the provisions and the mode of cooking, observing at the same time that such economy is used by them as to ensure a proper proportion of the ration for each day.

Detail for duty.

Sullivan Bay, 6th January 1804.
General Orders.
Parole—Topsham.   C. Sign—Exmouth.

Garrison Orders.
Detail for duty only.

Sullivan Bay, 7th January 1804.
General Orders.
Parole—Knopwood.   C. Sign—Sladden.

Garrison Orders.
Detail for duty only.

Sullivan Bay, 8th January 1804.
General Orders.
Parole—Sidmouth.   C. Sign—Teignmouth.

Garrison Orders.
The arms and necessaries of the detachment will be inspected to-morrow at troop beating. As the Commanding Officer proposes that half of the detachment shall proceed with the first embarkation for the new settlement, the quartermaster will immediately send half of the stores under his charge on board the *Ocean*.
Detail for duty.

Sullivan Bay, 9th January 1804.
General Orders.
Parole—Brixham.   C. Sign—Torbay.

Garrison Orders.
Detail for duty only.

Sullivan Bay, 10th January 1804.
General Orders.
Parole—Norfolk.   C. Sign—Norwich.

Garrison Orders.
The arms belonging to the detachment being frequently in want of repair, which can alone proceed from the carelessness of the men, the Commanding Officer forbids their being taken to pieces for the purpose of cleaning but by the consent of the officer under whose inspection they are placed, and in the presence of a non-commissioned officer, who will take care that no part of the arms is unnecessarily removed. These

are to be kept at all times ready for service, and he is certain that if this order is strictly attended to the arms will not be in such frequent want of repair; and he shall in future direct stoppages to be made for the repair of such arms as shall appear to him to have been damaged by carelessness; nor are they on any account to be taken out or used but on duty. He is concerned to observe that some of the non-commissioned officers are so extremely inattentive to their duty as to bring the men to the parade in a slovenly and unsoldierlike state. It is their peculiar duty to inspect the men on the beating of the quarter-drum and to report them to the officer of the company when they find their appearance to be unmilitary. He should feel much regret at bringing a non-commissioned officer to a court-martial, but as the service cannot be carried on without they attend to their duty, so shall he feel it his to have only good and attentive men in that very useful class of soldiers. It is again ordered that none of the detachment off duty quit the camp without having first obtained leave from the officer of the company to which they are classed.

Detail for duty.

Sullivan Bay, 11th January 1804.

General Orders.

Parole—Good news.   C. Sign—Hope.

Garrison Orders.

Detail for duty only.

Sullivan Bay, 12th January 1804.

General Orders.

Parole—Margate.   C. Sign—Broadstairs.

Garrison Orders.

The quartermaster will complete the detachment with leggings, and will take care that the whole of the new clothing is completed by the 18th instant. The adjutant will practise the men at firing with powder on Monday and Tuesday next, for which purpose the quartermaster will prepare a dozen rounds of blank cartridges for each man.

Detail for duty.

Sullivan Bay, 13th January 1804.

General Orders.

Parole—Kingsgate.   C. Sign—Ramsgate.

Garrison Orders.

Detail for duty only.

Sullivan Bay, 14th Jany. 1804.

General Orders.
Parole—Canterbury.   C. Sign—Sittingbourne.

Garrison Orders.
The detachment will not parade for Divine service to-morrow morning. Detail for duty.

Sullivan Bay, 15th Jany. 1804.

General Orders.
Parole—Chatham.   C. Sign—Dartford.

Garrison Orders.
The detachment off duty will parade for drill at six o'clock to-morrow morning if the weather is fair. The officers will attend. The arms and necessaries will be inspected at troop beating. Detail for duty.

Sullivan Bay, 16th Jany. 1804.

General Orders.
Parole—Oxford.   C. Sign—Henley.

Garrison Orders.
Detail for duty only.

Sullivan Bay, 17th Jany. 1804.

General Orders.
Parole—Abingdon.   C. Sign—Woodstock.

Garrison Orders.
The detachment will parade at half-past eleven in the forenoon to-morrow, and at twelve o'clock fire three volleys, it being the anniversary of the day upon which Her Majesty's birth is kept. The quarter-master will issue the new clothing to the detachment, who will wear it to-morrow. Detail for duty.

Sullivan Bay, 18th Jany. 1804.

General Orders.
Parole—Queen.   C. Sign—Charlotte.

Garrison Orders.
Detail for duty only.

Sullivan Bay, 19th Jany. 1804.
General Orders.
Parole—Gibbs.　C. Sign—Crane.

Garrison Orders.
Detail for duty only.

Sullivan Bay, 20th Jany. 1804.
General Orders.
Parole—Riches.　C. Sign—Baker.

The Lieut.-Governor hopes the return of Danl. McAllenon will have convinced the prisoners of the misery that must ever attend those who are mad enough to abscond from the settlement. To warn them from making an attempt of a similar nature they are informed that, although this man left his companions on the fifth day after their departure hence, they all began to feel the effects of their imprudence, and more of them would have returned had they not dreaded the punishment which they were conscious they deserved. Their provisions were nearly expended, and they had no resources. They lived in constant dread of the natives, by whose hands it is more than probable they have by this time perished, or if this should not have happened, how is it possible that strong hardy men who were always able to consume even more than the liberal allowance of provisions which is issued to them, can exist in a country which nowhere affords a supply to the traveller. The Lieut.-Governor can by no means account for this strange desertion of the people; were they ill-treated, scantily fed, badly clothed, or wrought beyond their ability, he should attribute it to these causes, but as the reverse is the case, he is at a loss to discover the motive. He thinks it necessary to advise them not to harbour or supply with their provisions any people who may quit the settlement, as it is his fixed determination to punish them with greater severity than he would the infatuated wretches themselves. He is concerned that the several prisoners who are now absent must be left to perish, as by McAllenon's account they are beyond the reach of every effort he might make to recall them to their duty. Divine service will be performed on Sunday next if the weather permits.

Garrison Orders.
Detail for duty only.

Sullivan Bay, 21st Jany. 1804.
General Orders.
Parole—Wilson.　C. Sign—Adams.

Mr. Wm. Nicolls is appointed a Superintendent of Convicts, and is to be observed as such, he will take upon him the direction of the carpenters belonging to the colony. Samuel Gunn will direct the department of shipwrights, and John Fell will assist the storekeeper in the issue of stores and provisions. Lieut. Sladden, the Revd. Mr. Knopwood, and G. P. Harris, Esq., will meet on Monday morning at eleven o'clock, at the mess-room, to hear, and determine, such complaints as the Lieut.-Governor shall cause to be laid before them for that purpose. The Revd. Mr. Knopwood, Mr. Bowden (assistant-surgeon), and A. W. H. Humphrey (mineralogist), will hold themselves in readiness to embark on board the *Ocean* store ship with the Lieut.-Governor.

Garrison Orders.

A detachment consisting of 1 subn., 1 sergt., 2 corpls., 1 drumr., and 20 privates will hold themselves in readiness to embark on board the *Ocean* store ship. Officer for this duty 2nd Lieut. Lord. Detail for duty.

Sullivan Bay, 22nd Jany. 1804.

General Orders.

Parole—Lady Nelson. C. Sign—Symonds.

Garrison Orders.

An inspection of arms and necessaries to-morrow morning as usual. Detail for duty.

Sullivan Bay, 23rd Jany. 1804.

General Orders.

Parole—Enderley. C. Sign—Champion.

In future when any materials for repairing or making shoes are issued by the Commissary the shoes so made or repaired are to be brought to the store, where they will be delivered by the storekeeper to the person for whom they are designed. This Regulation is to be invariably observed.

Garrison Orders.

The detachment of Royal Marines which have been ordered to hold themselves in readiness for embarkation will embark at the jetty tomorrow after guard mounting on board the *Ocean*. Boats will be ready to receive them and their baggage. The commanding officer, hoping that the punishment already inflicted on the prisoners James Read and Robert Andrews will deter them from such unsoldierlike conduct in future, is pleased to remit the remainder of the punishment which they were sentenced to receive, and directs them to be released and return to their duty. He trusts that this lenity will be accepted by them as it ought, and that, when he shall be joined by that part of the detachment which he is constrained to leave behind him, he shall receive such report of their conduct from Lieut. Sladden as will enable him to meet them with satisfaction. Detail for duty.

Sullivan Bay, 24th Jan. 1804.
General Orders.
Parole—Fawcett.   C. Sign—Ellen.

Garrison Orders.
Detail for duty only.

Sullivan Bay, 25th Jan. 1804.
General Orders.
Parole—Brook.   C. Sign—Carr.

The Lieut.-Governor proceeding to Van Dieman's Land with the first embarkation, the direction of the remaining part of the Civil and Military Establishment is left with the officer next in command, 1st-Lieut. Wm. Sladden of the Royal Marines, who is to be observed as such.

Garrison Orders.
Detail for duty only.

Sullivan Bay, 26th Jan. 1804.
General Orders.
Parole—Embarkation.   C. Sign—Ocean.

Garrison Orders.
Detail for duty only.

General Orders.
Ship *Ocean*, Port Phillip, 27th Jan. 1804.

The whole number of prisoners embarked in the *Ocean* (the officers' servants excepted) will be distributed into three divisions, one of which will be upon deck at a time in the same manner as seamen are divided into watches, and for the same period of time. The several overseers who are with the people will see that the watches are regularly relieved; and the watch or division upon deck, during either day or night, must not upon any account go below until relieved. They will at all times give such assistance towards carrying on the duty of the ship as may be required of them by Captain Mertho, or any of his officers. The division which is upon deck during the morning watch will wash and clean themselves upon the forecastle, and as these several regulations are calculated for their health and convenience the Governor expects a due observance of them. The three men who were on board, late belonging to the 25th Foot, will be classed one to each watch, and will perform the same duty which they were entrusted with at Sullivan Bay.

[From a sketch by T. G. Gregson, Esq., of Risdon.]

D. Woodriff.

CAPTAIN OF H.M.S. "CALCUTTA."

[*From a painting in the possession of his family at Sydney.*]

Head-Quarters, Sullivan Cove, Derwent River, 20th Feb. 1804.

General Orders.

Parole—Derwent River.   C. Sign—Sullivan Cove.

The storekeeper will issue the following weekly ration until further orders, viz.:—To civil, military, free settlers, and prisoners, 7 lbs. beef or 4 lbs. pork, 7 lbs. flour, 6 ozs. sugar; to women, two-thirds; children above five years, half; and children under five years one-fourth of the above ration. The issuing days for provisions will be in future Tuesdays and Saturdays. The military will receive half-pint of spirits daily as before.

Garrison Orders.

A guard consisting of two corpls. and six privates will mount daily in front of the line of military until further orders. One corporal and three privates will be detached from the guard to the island, for the purpose of furnishing a sentinel for the protection of the store tents. This sentinel will not suffer anyone to approach his post after sunset except the Lieut.-Governor, or any person sent with a written authority from him, and the visiting officer. No boat is to land at the island after sunset, and any boat approaching the island after that hour is to be kept off until directions are received from the Lieut.-Governor. A picquet of three privates will join the guard every evening at sunset.

[*The remainder of the Orders relate to Tasmania.*]

JOURNAL OF THE REVEREND ROBERT KNOPWOOD, A.M.

[*24th April* 1803 *to 31st December* 1804.]

A JOURNAL OF THE PROCEEDINGS of His Majesty's ship "CALCUTTA," *olim* "WORLEY CASTLE," commanded by Dan. Woodriff, Esqr., Capt., between the 24th April 1803 to the arrival in Port Phillip Harbour, New South Wales, Sunday, October the 9th 1803. This log is kept from 1 a.m. to 12 p.m., by the Reverend Robert Knopwood, A.M., Chaplain to the Settlement.

OFFICERS ON BOARD H.M. SHIP "CALCUTTA," SUNDAY, APRIL 24, 1803.

Dan. Woodriff, Esqr., Pst. Capt., Royal Navy.

James Tuckey	...	...	1st Lieut.	John Houston	...	...	5th Lieut.
Richd. Donovan	...	...	2 ,,	Richd. Wright	...	...	Master.
Nicholas Pateshall	...	...	3 ,,	Edward Brumley	...	...	Surgeon.
Wm. — Dowers	...	...	4 ,,	Edward White	...	...	Purser.

E

Royal Marine Forces:

C. Menzies, 1st-Lieut. | J. M. McCulloch, 2d-Lieut.

Master's Mates: Stone and Gammon.

Midshipmen:
Vernon, Stevens, Harcourt, Vicary, Armstrong, Woodriff, Wiseman.

NAMES OF THE OFFICERS of the Civil Establishment going to the intended SETTLEMENT of Pt. Philip, New S. Wales.

			£	s.	d.
Lieut.-Colonel His M. Royal Marine Forces.					
David Collins ... ... Lieut.-Governor ... ... Calcutta			450	0	0
			250	0	0
Revd. Robt. Knopwood ... Assistant Chaplain ... Calcutta			182	10	0
			146	0	0
Ben. Barbold (did not come out) } Deputy Judge Advocate			182	10	0
			146	0	0
Wm. J'anson ... ... Ast. Surgeon ... ... Calcutta			182	10	0
			91	5	0
Mathew Bowden ... ... 2d „ ... ... Ocean Passengers			91	5	0
Wm. Hopley ... ... 3d „ ... ... Ocean Pa.			91	5	0
Leonard Fosbrook ... ... Deputy Commissary ... Ocean Pa.			91	5	0
G. P. Harris ... ... Deputy Surveyor ... ... Ocean Pa.			91	5	0
A. W. H. Humphry ... Mineralogist ... ... Ocean Pa.			91	5	0
Thom's Clark } Wm. Patterson } ... ... Superintendants of Convicts Ocean Pa. (£50 each)			100	0	0

Royal Marine Officers:

R.	Lieut.-Col. Collins	...	Passenger on board H.M. ship *Calcutta*.
	Wm. Sladden	...	1 Lieut. Ocean Pa. [*passenger.*]
	J. M. Johnson	...	2 „ H.M. ship *Calcutta*.
	Edward Lord	...	3 „ Ocean Pa.
	Serjents ... 3.	...	Corporals ... 3.
	Drummer ... 1.	...	Fifer ... 1. ... Privates ... 39.

NOTE 1.—On a fly-leaf, Knopwood says that the number of convicts who sailed for Port Philip was 307, which figures are misprinted in old Tasmanian almanacs 367. The wives of 12 of the convicts accompanied their husbands. Some of the soldiers also had their wives with them.—C.

NOTE 2.—To the list of officials above given by Knopwood, Collins, in a return to Governor King, dated at the Heads, 5th November 1803, adds the names of John Ingle and William Parish as overseers.

FREE SETTLERS.—" List of persons who have obtained Lord Hobart's permission to proceed to Port Phillip, 5th April 1803."—[*Labilliere.*] :—

" NAMES.	OCCUPATIONS.	REMARKS.
Mr. Collins ...	Seaman.	
Edwd. Newman	Ship Carpenter.	
Mr. Hartley ...	Seaman.	
Edward F. Hamilton.		
John J. Gravie.		
Mr. Pownall.		
A Female Servant.		
Thos. Collingwood	Carpenter.	
Duke Charman.		
John Skilhorne	Cutler.	
Anty. Fletcher	Mason.	
T. R. Preston	Pocketbook Maker."—[ED.]	

H.M. Ship *Calcutta*, Spit Head, Sunday, April 24, 1803.

Sunday, 24. Wind W.S.West. A.M.—At nine unmoord ship, and sent a boat for Lieut.-Col. Collins at Portsmouth; at twelve the boat returnd with the Governor of New South Wales. P.M.—20 minutes past 1, weighd anchor and stood for St. Hellens. Fresh breezes and squally. At half-past 2 anchord at St. Hellens, in company with the *Ocean* transport, Cap. Merthow.

Monday, 25. Wind N.W.; P.M. S.W. A.M.—At 9 Lieut. Huston and self went on shore at St. Hellens, on the Isle of White. At 11 H.M. Ship *Calcutta* fird a gun for our boat. Half-past weighd anchor and made all sail. Lieut. Chesterman of the 9th Regt. left the ship. At 1 p.m. we got on board the *Calcutta*; 2, fresh breezes and hazy. The *Ocean* in company.

Tuesday, 26. Wind S.W.West. A.M.—At 10 fresh breezes and clear, the *Ocean* transport in company. P.M.—do. WR.[1] Several strange sail in sight. At 3 off the Isle of White; at 4 strong breezes with dark threatning wr., Needles Point N.N.E. 7 or 8 miles ¼. Finding the breeze from the west freshning bore up for the Needles. At 5 cross the Bridge; at 6 came too with the best bower in 10 fthm. in Yarmouth Roads. Hust Castle west. Sions Tower, Limington, upon the New Forest, N. Mrs. W. (Woodriff) lives there, the Capt. and sons went on shore. Half-past 6, the *Ocean* transport anchord in the road.

H.M. Ship *Calcutta*, at anchor, Yarmouth Roads, Isle of White, April 27, 1803.

Wednesday, 27. Wind N.N.E. A.M.—Steady fresh breezes and clear. At noon Capt. Woodriff returnd on board. P.M.—Half-past 12, weighd and made all sail, the *Ocean* in company. Half-past 1, crossd the Bridge (a very dangerous passage). At 5 do. wr. Half-past 5, observd a frigate laying at anchor off Weymouth. Capt. W. and Coll. Col. dind in the ward room with the officers.

Thursday, 28. Wind N.E. b. N. A.M.—At 9 spoke a French fishing boat and got some Mackrell. At 10 hove too; sent a boat on board the ship *Bowen*, from Biddiford bound to London. At noon the Lizard Light House N. 3 lgs. P.M.—Fresh breeze and clear. At 7 we took our departure from England, the St. Agnes or Scilly Light House N.N.E. ½ E. about 5 lgs. dist. Several strange sail in sight.

Friday, 29. Wind N. b. W. A.M.—Fresh breeze and cloudy. At 10 observd 1 strange sail in sight. P.M.—do. WT. The *Ocean* in company.

Saturday, 30. Wind N. b. W. A.M.—Fresh breeze and cloudy, with a swell from the north. P.M.—At 6 spoke the *Ocean*; at 10 squally and a heavy swell.

Sunday, 1 *May*. Wind N. b. W. A.M.—Fresh breeze and cloudy. At 6 saw a brig to windward; 10, musterd at quarters; a very high

---

[1] Wr., for weather; morn., for morning; aft., for afternoon; eve., for evening.

sea and squally. P.M.—do. wr. At half-past 10 burnt a blue light to the *Ocean;* at 12 fird a gun and burnt another light; a very heavy swell from the N.W.

H.M. Ship *Calcutta* at sea. May, 1803.

Monday, 2. Wind S.W. A.M.—Three-quarters past 2, strong gales and squally, with a heavy sea from the N.W. At 6 down top-glnt. yards. At 10 observed the *Ocean* to the leeward. At halfpast bore down to her. P.M.—Half-past 3 very strong breezes and squally. At 4 shew our colours to a French ship standing to the N.E. At 5 a heavy swell, the sea so high and the motion so great that chief of the officers were obliged to sleep in the ward room; the dead-lights to the cabins were obliged to be put in. At 5 very heavy seas following the ship.

Tuesday, 3. Wind S.W. b. W. A.M.—At 4 strong gales, with a heavy swell and rain. At noon strong breezes and cloudy. P.M.—Do. wr. At 7 more moderate; no cabin windows open to day. At half-past 10 departed this live, Ann Stoker, a convict's wife.

Wednesday, 4. Wind N.N.W. A.M.—Fresh breeze and a heavy swell from the northward. P.M.—10 minutes past 4, committed the body of Ann Stoker to the deep. Half-past 5, observed a ship and brig to the leeward; the cabin windows open this day.

Thursday, 5. A.M.—Moderate breezes; at 10 2 strange sail in sight. Half-past 10, departed this life John Thomas, a convict. P.M.—At 2 committed the body to the deep.

Friday, 6. Wind N.N.E. A.M.—Fresh breezes and cloudy; 11, saw a strange sail; a large ship to the N.W. P.M.—At 4 a Danish ship passed us; we shewd each others colours. At 8 more moderate and clear.

Saturday, 7. Wind north. A.M.—Moderate wr., with small rain. Half-past 4, departed this life Stephen Byrne, a convict. Half-past 11 committed the body to the deep. At 12 do. wr. P.M.—At 7 light winds; 3 sail in sight.

Sunday, 8. Wind N.N.E. A.M.—Light breezes and clear wr. At 10 mustered by divisions. Half-past, performed divine service to all the convicts (304), besides their wifes and children, and the ship's company. Capt. Woodriff, Col. Collins, and all the officers in full uniform on the quarter deck. P.M.—Do. wr.

Monday, 9. Wind N.E. b. E. A.M.—Light airs and clear wr.; caught 3 hork bill turtles. P.M.—Do. wr., inclining to a calm; gave the turtle to the sick convicts.

Tuesday, 10. Wind N.E. A.M.—Light airs inclining to a calm. P.M.—Caught 2 turtle.

Wednesday, 11. Wind N.E. A.M.—At 6 a calm; at 9 do. wr.; at 10 exercisd the marines with cartridge. P.M.—Do. wr.; at 8 this day we caught 14 turtle as before.

Thursday, 12. Wind vble. A.M.—A calm, and clear. P.M.—At 11 sprung up a breeze.

Friday, 13. Wind N. by W. A.M.—Light airs and fine wr.; sailmakers employd making awnings. P.M.—Employed variously.

Saturday, 14. A.M.—Light airs and clear. At 4 p.m. a calm. Half-past 7 sprung up a breeze from the S.W. This eve. at 6 we observed a very fine steady breeze come—the trade winds.

Sunday, 15. Wind N.W. A.M.—Fresh breezes 30 minutes past 9. We passed a brig standing to the eastward at 10. Musterd at quarters. Quarter-past performed Divine Service, as before. At half-past 11 saw the high Peak of Teneriffe at 15 lgs. dist., S.W. by W. At 1 P.M. the N.E. point of land dist. at 12 lgs.; the snow was very plain upon the Peak. At 9 we were very near the S.E. point of land.

Monday, 16. Wind E.S.E., at 8 vble., half-past 8 N.E. A.M.—At 7 light airs and variable, standing for Santa Cruz Roads, bearing west 8 or 9 miles. At 8 a whale past very near the stern of the *Calcutta*. At 9 a boat from the Town of Santa Cruz, with the Port Captain, a Spanish officer, came on board. At 10 he went on shore. At 11, Capt. Woodriff and Col. Collins went to the Governors House, &c. Don Joseph de Purlesque, Governor General of the Canary Islands, and a Lieut.-General in the Spanish Service. P.M.—At 1 came to an anchor in Santa Cruz Roads with the best bower, when moored ship in 16 fthm. with the following bearings—East point of land E. by N. ¾ N.; the south point of Santa Cruz Bay, on with the south east of the Island S.W. ¼ S.; northern church spire W. ⅞ S.; north round tower in the bay on with the high peak near do.; likewise the boundry of the bay N. by E. The pier head on with the southernmost church spire bearing S.W. by W. off the shore ⅓ a mile. Found riding in the bay a Spanish man of war brig and many merchant ships. At 2, Capt. W. and Col. Colls. returned on board.

H.M. Ship *Calcutta*, at anchor, Santa Cruz Roads, Teneriffe, May 1803.

Monday, 16. At 3 the *Ocean* came to an anchor. At 5 Capt. Woodriff, Col. Collins and self went on shore to Mr. Armstrong's, the British Agent, &c., &c. He lives as you enter the town on the right, opposite the Mall. The landing place was commodious being formed by a stone pier, with steps, alongside of which two boats at a time may lay with ease and take in their fresh water, which comes down by a tank from the town. We *landed on the very place where Lord Nelson lost his arm*, it appeared to have fallen nearly into a state of ruin. There were several peices of connon laid by the side; but none mounted. They were repairing it before we came away. From the pier you enter the town by a gate at which stands a guard; to the left is a large battery, Fort St. Phillip, which leads round to the High street. At the tower end was observed a light well-finished monument of white marble, commemorating the marvellous appearance of the image or bust of Our Lady at Candelaria to the Guanches, the Aborigines of the country, who were thereby converted to Xtianity, 104 years before the preaching of the Gospel. The four sides of the monument bore long inscriptions to this effect; and it was erected at the expense of Don Bartholomi de Montagnes, perpetual Captain of the Royal Marine Castle, at Candelaria :—

In the centre of this street were a stone bason and fountain. (*Here it was that the British Seamen and Marines were repulsed when they attacked Santa Cruz with Lord Nelson*), from which the inhabitants were supplied with very good water, conveyed from the neighbouring hills by wooden throughs, supported on slight posts and reaching quite to the town. At the head of the street, near the Government House or Requisition, stood a large Cross; and at a small distance the Governor's House and the Church of St. Francis; annexed was a monastery of Franciscans. At this church we see a grand funeral of one of the Franciscans, the corpse was carried on a bier, the face and feet exposed, they were a long time performing burial service; and when they deposited the body in the grave, which is first prepared with a coffin to receive it, is let down by fillets, and a paul coverd over, to prevent your seeing a quantity of lime thrown on the face and body. We were informed that the body remained there only a few days, then taken up, and put into a charnal-house adjoining to the church. The hills on the N.E. part of this island is surrounded by inaccessible mountains. There were not any fortifications upon the commanding ground above the town; but at each end of the bay stood a fort between which were erected 3 or 4 circular redoubts, connecting with each other by a low parapet wall, wearing the appearance of a line of communication between the forts; but few cannon in the works. There is a very curious cave called Beggers, on the S.W. side about a mile and a-half from the town, likewise an aqueduct. The road there is bad, being loose stones that bore all the appearance of cinders. The new roads that they are making to Bonavista is broad and good. They were cutting the barley and Indian wheat, both of which were good crops. The sea breezes generally sets in about 10 from the N.E. side of the island and blows to 5 or 6 in the eve. Frequently there is a tremendous surge at the pier, when the wind is at east, that it is not possible to land. The land breeze sets in from the W. which continue till 7 or 8 in the morn. The altitude of the Peak itself we were informed, was 15,396 feet, only 148 yards short of 3 miles.

The Peak of Teneriffe, which the Dutch make their first meridian is said to be three miles high, in the form of a sugar loaf, and is situated on an island of the same name near the coast.—Vide Guthrie. Geog., page 659.

Tuesday, 17. A.M.—Employed variously. P.M.—Fresh breezes and clear. I went to see the town and the church, Nostra Seniora de Consion. At 3 returned on board. We caught a great number of mackrell on board. 5 Spanish officers from the Man of War brig dind with us.

Wednesday, 18. Wind vble. N.E. A.M.—Fresh breezes and hazy. At 11 the Spanish Man of War brig left the Bay. We turned up our hands and gave them three cheers; they returnd it. P.M.—I went on shore and into the fields, which appeard very bad land. They cut the corn with a sickle, than place it upon a large round of stones, where it lays some days, than take it to the store houses in the town. The Governor's daughter, Mr. and Mrs. Armstrong and family, with the harbour-captain, drank tea with Capt. Woodriff; they were very much pleasd with the ship. At 6 they went on shore.

Thursday, 19. A.M.—Moderate breezes. P.M.—Prepared for sailing. This being the great Festival of Assencion, the Spanish flags were hoisted on all the forts and the ships in the bay. At 10 I went on shore with Capt. Woodriff, Mr. Tuckey, and some officers, to see High Mass performd, first at the Church at St. Francis. They than went to the Great Church, Nostra Seniora de Consion, where the High Mass was perform'd, and all the principal inhabitants attended at the alter, which was highly decorated; in this church were two small British flags, which were taken when Ld. Nelson attacked Santa Cruz in 1799. The man who shew: the church was particular in telling us of the bravery of their troops, and of the colours being taken. One of our officers observd to him that they were very right in taking such great care of them, for that Lord Nelson very likely would *call for them again soon*.—Mr. Wright, Massiter (?).

H.M. Ship *Calcutta*, at sea, May 1803.

Friday, 20. Wind E.N.E., N.E. A.M.—At 8 made the signal with a gun for all officers to repair on board. Employd getting ready for sea. P.M.—20 past 2, weighd and made all sail, the *Ocean* in company. At 4 Santa Cruz N. by E. 12 miles. At 6 the Mountain Peak W.N.W. ¼ N. 5 lgs. We see the Peak this eve. at very high perfection.

Saturday, 21. A.M.—At 4 fresh breezes. Employed stowing the anchors. P.M.—Do. wr. and clear.

Sunday, 22. A.M.—Steady fresh breezes and clear. At 10 must. (mustered) by divisions; half-past performed Divine service, all on deck. P.M.—At 2 we passed the Tropic of Cancer. Lat. observd 26–10 N. Long. 17–17 W.

Monday, 23. Wind N.E. b. E. A.M.—At 9 steady fresh breezes and clear. P.M.—do. wr. At 6 with a swell from the N.E.

Tuesday, 24. A.M.—Fresh breezes and clear. P.M.—do. wr. At 6 observd a brig standing to the northward.

Wednesday, 25. Wind S.W. b. S. A.M.—At 7 saw the Island of Sal, and made the signal to the *Ocean* for land discovered. A very remarkable high mount, bearing S. by W. ½ W. At 12 Point of Sal, ¾ N. 3 lgs. Moderate and fine wr.

[A sketch of the Isle of Sal, from H.M. Ship *Calcutta*, May 25, 1803, bearing E. by S. ½ S.]

Thursday, 26. Wind S.W. b. S. A.M.—Half-past 6, S.E. point of St. Jago, W.S.W. Island of Mayo, east. At 7 stood close round the east point of Praya Bay. At 30-past 7 bore up, flagstaff at first N. by E. 2 or 3 miles; east point of Fraya Bay, on with the Peak of Island Fugo. West. P.M.—Moderate and clear. The evenings are dark at half-after 6.

[A sketch of the Island of St. Jago and Praya Bay.]

St. Jago is inhabited by the Portuguese, the largest, most populous, and most fertile of the Cape de Verd Islands in Africa. It lies 13 miles west of Mayo, and abounds with high craggy mountains, particularly on the left of the town. Here are *stock birds*, and fruit of all kinds, and very cheap. The Flagstaff and Governor's House are situated on the S.E. side of the harbour, which has a long train of battery by the side of the hill. The houses are very small. We observd a large convent from the town.[1] Before the town is a small Island calld Quails.

Fugo.

One of the Cape de Verd Islands, in the Atlantic Ocean. It is a volcano, and burns continually. You see it very plain from St. Jago. It is much higher than any of the other mountains, and seems to be a single one at sea. The Portuguese who first inhabited it brought negros with them, and a stock of cattle; but now the chief inhabitants are blacks, of the Romish religion.

Friday, 27. Wind N.E. A.M.—Moderate and hazy. P.M.—do. wr.

Saturday, 28. Wind N.N.E. A.M.—Light breezes, made and shortend sail occasionally. At half-past 11 read the articles of war to the ship's company, and punishd Edward Westwood, a colonial marine, with twenty-four lashes for neglect of duty—sleeping on his post over the convicts. P.M.—do. wr.

Sunday, 29. Wind N.E. b. N. A.M.—At daylight a brig in sight to the N.W.; light breezes and clear. At 10 musterd by divisions; half-past performd Divine Service. Whit Sunday I dind with Capt. Woodriffe, Col. Collins. P.M.—do. wr.

Monday, 30. Wind N.N.E. A.M.—Light breezes and clear. P.M.—2, do. wr.; at 8, continual lightning; 35 past 9, squally with rain and lightning.

Tuesday, 31. Wind S.E. b. S. A.M.—At 4 light winds with rain and lightning; at daylight saw a sail S.E.; 15 past 8, spoke *The Telegraph*, belonging to the Honble. the East India Company; down jolly boat and sent an officer on board; we sent letters by her to England; she came from Bengal bound to England with dispatches; at 12, fresh breezes and heavy showers of rain. P.M.—Continual hard rain; at 7 more moderate.

Wednesday, 1 [*June*]. Wind S. b. W. A.M.—At 7, light airs, inclining to a calm. P.M.—do. wr. Employd variously.

Thursday, 2. Wind S.E. b. S. A.M.—Light airs and clear. P.M.—Employd variously, the *Ocean* in company.

Friday, 3. Wind S.W. b. S. Ther. 83. A.M.—Moderate and clear; at 9, musterd the ship's company at quarters, and exercisd the great guns and small arms, fird several shot. P.M.—At 4 light airs with rain; at 6 caught 2 dolphins.

Saturday, 4. Wind S.W. b. S. Ther. 84. A.M.—At 9 moderate and clear; at 11 observd a very large waterspout to the north, dist. 4 miles; at half-past rain, with a fresh breeze. P.M.—Clear wr.

Sunday, 5. Wind, S.E. A.M.—Fresh breezes; at 11, squally, with rain; at half-past 9 musterd at quarters; 10, heavy, dark weather, could not do duty to-day. P.M.—do. wr., clear at intervals.

NOTE.—Between the entries of Thursday, the 26th of May, and that of the next day, two pages are left unwritten on, on one of which is given a curious sketch of Praya Bay, &c.; and on the other a sketch map of the track of the *Calcutta* between the Cape de Verd islands. [C.]

Monday, 6. Wind S. A.M.—Moderate breezes; at 11, squally, with rain at intervals. P.M.—At 6 do. wr., with rain and lightning. In this latitude before you have the squalls in generally lightning before the rain, and it looks very awful.

Tuesday, 7. Wind S.E. A.M.—At 11 observd a strange sail to the S.W. stearing northward; half-past squally, with a heavy swell and hard rain. P.M.—do. wr. at intervals.

Wednesd., 8. Wind, S.E. b. S. A.M.—Fresh breezes and cloudy; at noon, squally with rain. P.M.—At 5 saw a ship to the northward; shew our colours to her.

Thursday, 9. Wind S.E. A.M.—Moderate breezes and clear. P.M. —At 2 saw a brig to the S.W. standing to the N. ward; at 4 t. kd. a strange sail S.E. by E.; 45 minutes past 4 set top gl'nt. sails; 03 past 5 up courses and hove too, boarded the *Emereld*, from the River Gabon (in Africa), bound to Liverpool with gold dust, ivory, &c., &c. Gabon River, the S.W. cost of Africa, is a large river that falls into the ocean from the eastward, within the island of St. Thomas, directly under line or the equator. At half-past 11 we crossd the equinoctial line or equator, lat. observd 35.*

Friday, 10. Wind S.E. b. S. A.M.—Steady fresh breezes and clear; at 10 Old Neptune came on board. Such persons as had never crossd the line were compelld to undergo the ridiculous ceremonies of shaving, &c., which those who were privileged were allowed to perform. P.M.— The day was conducted with much myrth; at 3 moderate and clear wr.

Saturday, 11. Wind S.S.E. A.M.—Moderate breezes and cloudy; 30 past 10, saw a sail to the S.W., standing to the windward, set t. gl'nt. sails. P.M.—do. wr.; at 1 shortend sail and boarded *Rio Nova* from Africa to Demarara with 325 slaves, men and women; took three men out of the above ship for mutiny, and confined them; quarter before 3 in boat and made all sail; we got parrotts, &c., from the ship; half-past 11, Mary Wiggins was deliverd of a son, wife of a Colonial marine.

Sunday, 12. Wind S.E. A.M.—Steady fresh breezes, and clear; 30 past 9, musterd by divisions; 10 performd divine service to all the convicts, &c., &c., as before. P.M.—40 past 5 spoke the *Ocean*; enquired after the health of the people; was informd they were all well, but that Mr. Hartley, a settler, had behaved ill on board. The evenings are dark at 6, nor light till near 6 in the morn.

Monday, 13. Wind S. b. W. A.M.—Moderate wr.; at 9 releasd and sent to duty the three men from the *Rio Nova*. P.M.—do. wr., *Ocean* in company.

Tuesday, 14. A.M.—At 8 moderate and cloudy; at noon a fresh trade wind, with pleasant wr. P.M.—do. wr.

Wednesday, 15. Wind E.S.E. A.M.—Fresh breezes and cloudy; at 4 squally, with rain and lightning. P.M.—do. wr. at intervals.

---

* It is impossible to understand what these figures mean, the ship having crossed the line only half an hour before noon of this day; but possibly the next day's latitude, in minutes, written in the wrong entry, is intended by them. They are copied exactly. The *Friday's* entry, however, seems to prove that she did not cross the line on the 9th, so it may be Thursday's latitude, North. [C.]

Thursday, 16. A.M.—Moderate breezes. P.M.—do. wr.; employd variously, *Ocean* in company.

Friday, 17. Wind S.E. A.M.—Fresh breezes and cloudy. P.M.—do. wr.; employd variously and rounding the cables; at 10, squally with rain; a large ball of fire seen from the clouds.

Saturday, 18. Wind S.E. A.M.—At 2, heavy squalls, with rain and lightning, and swell from the southward. P.M.—At 4 more moderate. It is dark so early that we are obliged to beat to quarters of an eve at half-past 5.

Sunday, 19. Wind S.E. A.M.—Moderate breezes and cloudy; at 10 musterd the ship's company; half-past, performd divine service to all the convicts and ship's co. P.M.—do. wr. and clear; at 4 observd 7 whales about the ship.

Monday, 20. Wind S. b. E. A.M.—Moderate breezes and clear wr. P.M.—30 past 4, saw a ship in the S.W. standing to the windward; 30 past 7, the strange sail passed us to leeward.

Tuesday, 21. Wind S.E. b. S. A.M.—At daylight saw a brig to windward; at 9 observd a ship to the S.W. standing to the S. ward. P.M.—Light winds; shew our colours to the strange ship. In England the sun rises 58 minutes before 3, here not till a quarter after 6 in the mor.

Wednesday, 22. Wind S.E. b. E. A.M.—At 8, light breezes, with fine wr.; p.m. at 2, calm and clear; at 11, moderate breeze, with rain; half-past, squally; in top gl'nt. sails, down jib.

Thursday, 23. Wind E. b. N. A.M.—Moderate breezes and cloudy. P.M.—do. wr., the *Ocean* in company.

Friday, 24. Wind N. E. A.M.—Squally, with frequent showers. P.M.—Moderate breezes and cloudy.

Saturday, 25. A.M.—Fresh breezes, with frequent flashes of lightning at 2; at 5, rain and lightning, violent; 30 past 7 sounded, no ground, 90 fthm. P.M.—Squally, with rain.

Sunday, 26. A.M.—Fresh breezes and cloudy, with a high sea that we could not perform duty to-day. P.M.—Fresh breezes and cloudy with rain. At 10 pas 10 we observed the clearest night rainbow ever seen to the south; at 10 it was squally with rain. Lat. obsd. 22—16 S., long. 38·33 W.

Monday, 27. A.M.—At 4 fresh breezes and squally. P.M.—Moderate wr.; at 2 sounded in 35 fthm., fine sand, bent the best bower cable. At 5, Cape Trio W.S.W. ½ S. about 6 leags.

Tuesday, 28. Wind S.E. b. E. A.M.—At daylight, Cape Trio W. b S. the neermost pt.; at 8 moderate and cloudy. At noon light breezes, neermost Eat of the land (a round hill) W. ¾ N. Cape Trio W. b. N. ¼ N. 4 lgs. neermost isle; off do. N. b. W. Lat. obs. 23° 04′ S. P.M.—Light airs with pleasant wr. At 12 F.S.M. sails; Cape Trio N.E b. E. 4 lgs.

Wed. 29. Wind E. by N. A.M.—At 4 light airs and cloudy. At 8 down jib; Cape Trio W. b. N. ¾ N. about 6 or 7 lgs. At noon Cape Trio E. b. N. ¾ N. just in sight from the poop; enterance of Rio Janeiro Harbour W.N.W. distant off 4 lgs.

H.M. Ship *Calcutta*, at anchor at Rio Janeiro, June 30, 1803, South America, Sth. Pacific Ocean.

Wed. 29. Wind E. b. N. P.M.—At 30 past 1 sprung up a breeze from the S.E.; made all possible sail for the harbour of Rio Janeiro. At 4 passd the outer islands; found Island Rondo and Flat Island of Rio Janeiro in one W.S.W.; Maya and Paya in one N.E. b. E. and S.W. b. W. At 6 passed Gamba Isld. At 7 a light breezes; *Pahoon* (the pilot) came on board and took charge of the ship. At 8 passed Santa Cruz Fort. At 30 past 9 came too with the best bower in 17 fthm. abrest the palace. *Patronmore, the Harbour Master.*

Thursday, 30. Wind varbl. A.M.—Light airs and variable; at daylight had the following bearings: Sugar Loaf S. b. E., spire of the Benedictine Convent West, Isle of Enchardos, on which is the ruins of a monastery, N.W. ¼ W., Fort Santa Cruz S.E. ⅛ S., and a large white building on the opposite side of the harbour N.E. ¼ E. Found here the Honble. Company's Ship *Lord Castlereigh* (Capt. Robinson) and an English whaler, a Portuguese line-of-battle ship and a number of merchantmen. P.M.—Do. wr. Mr. McDougal was the first mate in the *Ld. Cas.*, and very intimate with my friend Lieut. Colin McDonald, Royal Navy. Lat. obsd. 22° 52′ S.

Friday.—The Town of St. Sebastian (or as it is more commonly named the Town of Rio de Janeiro, which was in fact the name of the river forming the bay, on the western side of which was built the town) is large. The palace of the Viceroy stood in the Royal Square, of which, together with the public prison, the *Mint* and the *Opera House*, it formed the right wing. The Hospital, which had formerly been a Jesuit's Convent, stood near the summit of the hill at the back of the town. Senor Ildefonse (he was frequently with our party, and din'd with Capt. Woodriffe, Col. Collins, Mr. Tuckey and self at John Rodriguers Pereson de Almeida; Mr. Mordaunt, lives at the same house). Senor Ildefonse was the principal surgeon in the place. He studied in England. The English surgeons are held in high reputation. The town of Rio de Janeiro was said to contain not less than 100,000 souls, of which 40,000 are slaves brought from the Coast of Ginnea. With these people of both sexes the streets are constantly filld, scarcely any other people being seen in the day. Ladies and gentlemen were never seen on foot in the streets during the day, those whose business led them out being carried in close chairs, the pole of which came from the head of the vehicle and rested on the shoulders of the chairmen. The language spoken here by the white people was Portuguese. The eclesiastics in general could converse in Latin—they pronounce it very differently to the English pronunciation. The Negro slaves spoke a corrupt mixture of their own and Portuguese language. The town was well supplied with water, which was conveyed into it from a great distance by means of an aqueduct (or carioca) which, having to cross a road or public way, was raised upon a double row of lofty arches; from this aqueduct the water was received into stone fountains, constructed with capacious basins; here the inhabitants have their linen washed by their slaves, near the Convent of the Antonian monks. We also observed several large and rich convents in the town. The chief of these were the Benedictine and the Carmelite; one dedicated to St. Antony, another to our Lady of Assistance, and another to Sta Theresa; the two last were for the reception of nuns. The Convent D. Ajuda, or of Assistance, received as pensioners, or boarders, the young ladies having lost their parents, who were allowed to remain, conforming to the rules of the convent, until married, or otherwise provided for by their friends. The whole of the churches are under a bishop, whose palace was in the town, a short distance from one of the principal convents (Benedictine). To a stranger nothing could appear more remarkable than the innumerable religious processions which were to be seen at all hours in this town. At the close of every day an image of the Virgin was borne in procession through the principal streets, the attendants arrayed in white surplices, and bearing in their hands lighted tapers, chanting at the same time praises to her in Latin; to this, as well as to all other religious processions, the guards turned out, grounded their arms, kneeled, and shewed the most submissive marks of respect, and the bells of each church or convent in the vicinity of their progress sounded a peal while they were passing, and people assembled at their windows. Every church, chapel, or convent being under the auspicies of some tutelary saint, particular days were set apart as the festival of each, which were opened with public prayers, and concluded with processions, music, and *fireworks*. During several hours after dark, on these solemn festivals, the inhabitants are seen walking to and from the church, dressed in their best habiliments, accompanied by their children, and attended by their slaves and carriages. We were informed that they never permitted any base metals near their alters, all their vessels, &c., being of the purest gold or silver. At the corner of almost every street in the town was observed a small alter, dedicated generally to the Virgin, and decorated with curtains and lamps, before these alters, at the close of every evening, the Negroes assembled to chant their vespers, kneeling together in long rows in the street. The tradespeople of the town have adopted a regulation which must prove of infinite convenience to strangers as well as the inhabitants; we found the people of one profession or trade dwelling together in one, two, or as many streets as were necessary for their numbers to occupy. Houses here were built, after the fashion of Santa Cruz, with a small wooden balcony over the enterance; to the eye accustomed to the cheerful appearance of glass windows a certain gloom seemed to pervade even their best and widest streets, the light being conveyed through window frames of close lattice-work. The women of Rio De Janeiro, being within the tropics, do not possess the best complexions, but their features were expressive; the eye dark and lively; the hair was dark, this they mostly wore with powder, strained to a high point before and tied in several folds behind. The mines, the greatest source of revenue to the Crown of Portugal and in the government of this place, the great cause of jealousy both of strangers and the inhabitants, were situated more than a week's journey hence, except some which had been lately discovered in the mountains (the Organ Hills) near the town. Sufficient employment was found for the Mint, at which was struck all the coin that was current here besides what was sent to Europe. The dimond trade had been for some time taken into the hands and under the inspection of Government, but the jewellers' shops abound with topazes, chrysolites, and other precious stones. The barracks for the troops appeard to be commodious and to be kept in good order. A small number of cavalry were always on duty, employed in the antichamber of the palace, or in attending the Viceroy either on days of parade or in his excursions into the country. A captain's guard of infantry with a standard mounted every day at the palace. The present Governor's name is Don Joseph Ferdanez du Portugal—he had been Viceroy at Rio de Janeiro two years and a half. An officer from each regiment attended every evening at the palace to take orders for the following day, which were delivered to him by the Adjutant of Orders, who himself received them directly from the Viceroy. At the palace every transaction in the town was known, and so strict was the search for deserters from the ships, when reported to the guard at the palace, they were almost certain of getting the men by the next morn. In addition to the centinels, every regiment and every guard sent parties through the streets patroling the whole night for the preservation of peace and good order. During our stay the wifes of the convicts were allowed to take clothes to wash with them on the Island of Enchados, a small island with an old monastary on it to the W.N.W. of the town. The ladies and gentlemen we observed were continually walking of an evening quite late, especially when any of their festivals were. Both males and females were early taught to dress as men and women. We see a hoop on a little donna of four years old, and a bag and a sword on a sesnor of six. This appearance we observd as much as that of the saints and virgins in their churches being decorated with powdered perraques, swords, laced clothes, and full dressed suits. The Convent of Sta Theresa we were informed was the strictest of any; there were eighteen young people there which had taken the veil and they were not allowd to see any one but their nearest relations. The priests were not permitted to see them. The chapel was very neat, it stood upon the hill near the aqueduct. The Convent De Adjuda.—This I frequently visted, where I conversed with a very beautiful young lady named Antonia Januaria. Her polite attention I shall not easily forget, having received great friendship from her, and should I ever return there again shall be happy to see her. [*The next page is left blank.*]

H.M. Ship *Calcutta*, at anchor, Rio Janeiro, July 1, 1803.

Friday 1. Wind S.E. A.M.—The people employd at the rigging. At 8 sent an officer on shore to the Viceroy. At 9 saluted the fort with 15 guns which was returnd with an equal number. P.M.—Moderate wr. and clear.

Saturday 2. Wind vble. A.M.—Received fresh beef and vegetables. P.M.—The men employed variously. I dind on board the *Lord Castlerey* with Mr. Huston.

Sunday 3. Wind vble. A.M.—At 10 musterd the ship's company; at half-past performed Divine Service. P.M.—A large party dind with us from the *Ld. Castlerey*.

Monday 4. Wind vble. A.M.—Moderate, with small rain. I dind on shore with Capt. Woodriffe and Coll. Collins at Mr. John Rodriguez Pereson de Almeida, and met a party there. P.M.—Do. wr.

Tuesday 5. A.M.—Light breezes and variable. P.M.—A large party dind with us.

Wednesday 6. Wind vble. A.M.—Moderate wr. with small rain. P.M.—I dind on shore at Doctor Iscrado, the first phisician in the town—he spoke English. A party of ladies visited the *Calcutta* at 11 a.m.; an in the eve we gave a large ball to all the ladies and gentlemen on board the *Ld. Castlerey*. The officers going out in *Lord Castlerey*, East Indiaman, Capt. Robertson, they were all at the ball, viz., Colonel Vigars, Company's Service, Major Medley do., Lt.-Col. Monticsor and lady, 22nd Light Dragoons, Capt. Broom do., Capt. Muntchason, Capt. Dick, Lieut. Futton, Lieut. Martin, 8th Dragoons. Ladies—Mrs. Robinson, Mr. and Mrs. Broadberk, a cadet, Mrs. Brock, Miss Mutchason, Miss Asgill, and Miss Mac-card. Mr. Macloud, the first mate, a friend of Mr. Macdonald, of the Royal Navy, who was in H.M. Ship *Resolution* with me.

Thursday 7. Wind vble. A.M.—I went on shore. Saild the *Lord Castlereigh*, East Indiaman. P.M.—Sea and land breezes. In the eve I went to the opera of Neinha.

Friday 8. Wind vble. A.M.—Moderate and clear. I went on shore and see the town and convents; I see a very beautiful girl at the Convent D. Yuda, from her I received fruits, &c.

Saturday 9. Wind vble. A.M.—Do. wr. This morn Col. Collins, Lieut. Huston, and self went to breakfast at the Monastary of Fransiscans with Pater George Bunden, he was an Englishman and had been there a long time; he shew us all the Convent which was very grand. Received fruit, fresh beef, water, &c., for the ship's company and convicts. P.M.—Continuel lightning.

Sunday 10. Wind vble. A.M.—At 9 I went on shore, and see High Mass performed at the Monastary D. Fransiscans, and I visited the Convent D. A. Juda and see the *charming* girl Antonia. In the eve a large party of officers and self went to the play-house and see the Poor Soldier performed; the Vice Roy was there, attended by his aidecongs and the Governor of Angora (or Angore), and the house very crouded. During the day I visited the Carmelite and many chappels. Col. Collins, Lieut. Dowers, Lieut. Huston, and self dind at the English hotel in the square. We see the Negros dansing—not less than 4,000 people—on the plain to the W. of the town.

Monday 11. Wind vble. A.M.—Mr. M. Culloch, Mr. Johnson, and self went a shooting on shore; saw many curious birds. We dind at Mr. Davises on the E.S.E. point of the harbour as our ship layd; in the eve we returned. P.M.—At 8 some lightning.

Tuesday 12. Wind vble. A.M.—Light breezes and clear; the men employed variously. P.M.—Do. wr.

Wednesday 13. A.M.—Do. wr. and winds. At 6 departed this life James Carman, a seaman. Received various stores, &c. P.M.—Do. wr. and clear. At 4 committed the body to the deep.

Thursday 14. Wind vble. A.M.—Received fresh beef, &c., for the ship's company and a quantity of fruit. P.M.—Light breezes and clear.

Friday 15. Wind vble. A.M.—Light breezes and variable; people employd variously. P.M.—Received fresh beef, &c., &c.

Saturday 16. A.M.—Light breezes and clear. At 8 made signal for all officers, &c., to repair on board. Weighd the stream. Received a quantity of provisions on board.

Saturday, 16. P.M.—Light breezes. People employed variously.

Sunday, 17. A.M.—Light breezes and clear. At 6 hove short; at 10 weighd, with a light breeze from N.N.W.; *Ocean* in company, and made all sail. At 11.30 past falling calm; came too with a small bower, in 20 fathm., soft ground. About 17 miles down, bearings as follows :—St. Cruz fort, S.S.E.; Sugar Loaf, S. ¼ W.; Isle Cobras West, Handels Islands, and William Guillons S.W. b. W.

I visited D. Ajuda for the last time [1]

½ mile. The Carmelites had a great feast this day in the eve, great fire works. Capt. W. Col. Coll., Lieut. Huston, and self, on shore, and returned late on board with the Capt., &c., &c.   *   *   I see Antonio this eve at 5, and we took leave of each other with Regret. Vale!

Monday, 18. Wind vble. A.M.—Rain, with a moderate breeze from the southward. P.M.—Squally. People employed variously. Remarks :—Captain Woodriffe, Lieut. Dowers, Huston and self, went on a shooting party on the side of Bong Voyage. We took our cold dinner, and dined at Mrs. * * * * , where there were 5 daughters. At 6 P.M. we got on board. Mr. Maudaunt, a Bengall merchant, came on board to take a passage to the Cape.

Tuesday, 19. Wind vble. A.M.—Light breezes and clear. At 7 made signal to weigh with a gun. A pilot came on board. Weighd and made all sail. With a light breeze from the N ward, at 9 passd Fort Santa Cruz; at noon, Calm Flat Island, S.S.W.; Isle Redondo, S.W. ½ S.; Sugar Loaf, N.W. ¼ W.; Outermost Island, to the eastermot,[2] E. ¼ S.; Laye [3] Island, on with the Isle Cobras, N.W. ⅓ W.; Fort Santa Cruz, N.N.W., in 15 fm. of the nearest shore ¼ mile.

H.M. Ship *Calcutta*, at Sea, July, 1803.

Wind calm. P.M.—Calm and clear. At 30 past 1 a light breeze sprung up from the eastward; at 4, moderate breezes; Sugar Loaf, N. ¼ W., 6 or 7 Lgs.; at 7, burnt a false fire, which was answ'd by the *Ocean*.

E. b. S.—20 minutes of two we closd the Convent de Ajuda, and at 3 the St. Benta and the Isle of Cobra.

Town of St. Sebastian	W.
River Rio Janeiro	N.E. b. N.
Land breeze	N.W.
Sea breeze	S.E.

Cross'd the Tropic of Capricorn, Nostra Sentiora de Concessione, D. Ajuda.

---

[1] This interlineation is just as it stands in the original.
[2] Probably eastermost.——[3] Indistinct. [C.]

					° ′
Lat. observed	...	...	...	24·42 South.
In account	...	...	...	24·42
Long.	...	...	...	42·47 W.

Wednesday, 20. Wind East. A.M.—At 2 we passd the Tropic of Capricorn; at 8, moderate and cloudy. P.M.—Frequent showers; down top glnt yards, and secured the booms, &c., &c.

Thursday, 21. Wind S. b. E. A.M.—Fresh breezes and cloudy wr. P.M.—Do., wr., the *Ocean* in company. The stock we bought at Rio de Janeiro as follows:—Turkeys, 36, at 6s. a peice; capons and fowls, very fine, 13 dozen, 4s. a couple; ducks, very large, 68, at 4s. a couple; geese, very good, 4, at 6s. a couple; pigs, very good, 13, at 4d. a pound, and a very great quantity of fruit and vegitables.

Friday, 22. Wind E.N.E. A.M.—Steady fresh breezes and cloudy. P.M.—Do., wr., the *Ocean* in company.

Saturday, 23. Wind E.N.E. A.M.—Fresh breezes and cloudy. P.M.—At 7, hazy wr., with small rain.

Sunday, 24. Wind N.E. b. E. A.M.—At 8, moderate and cloudy; 10, musterd by divisions, and performed divine service, though it was very cold. P.M.—Fresh breezes and clear wr., and smooth water.

Monday, 25. Wind north. A.M.—Fresh breezes and cloudy wr. P.M.—Do. wr. At 4 made signal to the *Ocean*, No. 278; with compass signal, E. b. S., to the *Ocean*. Altered the course 1 point to port. At 12, strong breezes and squally

Tuesday, 26. Wind north. A.M.—Steady fresh breezes and cloudy. At noon do. wr. Employed working up junk. We observed many pendany[1] birds and thers,[2] though not less than 1000 miles off the nearest shore. This day we finished our port wine [3] of Teneriff. P.M.—Made No. 30 with compass signal, east to the *Ocean*. Altered our course. At 6, do. wr.

Wednesday, 27. Wind N. b. E. A.M.—At 4, fresh breezes and cloudy. P.M.—Do. wr., with rain.

Thursday, 28. Wind west. A.M.—Strong breezes with hazy wr. P.M.—At 9, up foresail and set the fore stay sail for the *Ocean* to keep up. At 12, squally with frequent flashes lightning. A very bad night. The ship laboured very much for want of sail.

Friday, 29. Wind W. b. S. Thermometer at half past 8 A.M. 53. A.M.—At 1, heavy squalls, with hard rain. At 4, unsettled wr., ship still under the mn. top sail on the cap. The ship very uneasy for want of sail. At noon, squally with rain, and obliged to have both the ports and scuttles fastened down, to prevent the sea breaking into the cabin, it ran so high. We were scudding all day under a fore storm staysel. P.M.—Strong breezes and cloudy, with a heavy sea following, and ship labouring very much for want of sail.

Tristin de Cunha, lat. 37.5 S., long. 11.29.30 W.

Saturday, 30. Wind W. b. N. A.M.—At 8, more moderate; breezes and cloudy. P.M.—Fresh breezes and cloudy. At 6, squally. 7, strong

---

[1] The final letter may be either *g* or *y*, the rest of the word is quite distinct.—— [2] *Others* probably.——[3] Two indistinct words here. [C.]

breezes with heavy squalls. At 12, do. wr.; a very bad night. The *Ocean* in her station. At 4, the *Calcutta* labouring very much for want of sail.

Sunday, 31. A.M.—30 past 1, hard squalls, with heavy rain, lightning, and thunder, and a very heavy sea running. At 2, do. wr. 30 past 8, the *Ocean* not in sight, and the ship labouring very much for want of sail. At noon, fresh breezes and hazy. P.M.—1, squally wr. At 7, strong breezes with heavy squalls. At 9, do. wr., with lightning. At 11, do. wr., and continual lightning very severe. A very heavy sea. I was up the middle watch, the weather so bad.

Monday, August 1. Wind N.N.W. A.M.—Strong breezes with hard squalls and a very high sea. At 4 P.M. heavy squalls with rain, the sea so high that it came over the poop of the ship on the larboard side. At 8, squally. 12, more moderate.

Tuesday, 2. Wind N.N.W. A.M.—At 4, do. wr. At ½-past 2 saw the land, S. b. E. At 8, moderate and fair, east of Tristin De Cunha. From S.W. to S. b. E. off the nearest shore, about 3 miles, an island on with the nearmost point of Tristian de Cunha, S.W. half West. At 9, up top glnt yards [*not up since the* 20 *of July*]. At noon, moderate breezes and clear. The peak of Tristian de Cunha, N. ½ W., about 10 miles. P.M.—At 9, squally, with unsettled weather.

Wednesday, 3. Wind S. b. E. A.M.—At 4, squally with rain. At noon, fresh breezes and do. wr. P.M.—At 6, more moderate and cloudy.

Thursday, 4. Wind N.W. b. W. A.M.—Moderate breezes and fair weather. P.M.—At 6, do. wr. and clear.

Friday, 5. Wind S.S.W. A.M.—3, fresh breezes and passing squalls. At noon, do. wr. P.M.—At 2, moderate and hazy.

Saturday, 6. Wind west. Calm. Thermomiter at 50. A.M.—Moderate and cloudy weather. At 5, squally; made and shortend sail accordingly. P.M.—At 2, moderate and clear. At 4, inclining a calm. At 6, perfectly so. When we were at quarters, which we beat to regularly of an eve; at ¼ after fresh breezes, and at ¾ strong breezes with heavy squalls. In so short a time we all remarked the sudden great change of the weather: the weather so cold we were all obliged to have our winter dress on.

Sunday, 7. Wind west, W. b. S. A.M.—Fresh breezes and cloudy. 10, musterd by divisions, and strong breezes with squalls. P.M.—1, squally with rain.

Monday, 8. Wind S.W. A.M.—At 4, fresh breezes and cloudy. At 8, more moderate. P.M.—At 6, carried away the fore topmast studding sail in a squall. A very large whale came past the ship quite near us.

Tuesday, 9. Wind S.S.W. A.M.—At 8, moderate breezes and squally, with frequent showers. ½-past, shortened sail and hove too, down boat, and sent in search of John Bowers, who fell overboard and was drown'd. 30 past 9, up boat and made sail. At 11, found the fore yard badly sprung. Employd unbending the fore sail and preparing to lower the yard down. P.M.—Moderate breezes with fine weather. At 2, got the fore yard down, fore and aft the quarter deck; carpenters employed fishing do. At 8, carpenters employd as before. At 12, moderate weather; the carpenters employed at the fore yard.

F

Wednesday, 10. Wind S.W. A.M.—6, fresh breezes with squalls, and small rain ; carpenters employed as before about the fore yard, and the armorer making hoops for, &c. At noon, fresh breezes and cloudy; carpenters employd on the yard forward for going aloft, and preparing to sway it up. At 8, do. wr. This eve, 30 past 6, swayd the fore yard up. At 8, do. wr. ; this eve we observed the 2 wite Magelene Clouds, which are seen in this hemisphere, at the S.S.W. of the Cape. They were discovered by Mr. Magelene, circumnavigator of the globe.

Thursday, 11. Wind S.E. b. E. A.M.—At 3, moderate breezes, with squall at intervals. P.M.—Moderate and fine weather. Swayd the main yard higher up. At 5, moderate and cloudy. 9, sounded no ground, 80 fthm.

Friday, 12. Wind E.S.E. A.M.—At daylight saw the land last, from E. b. N. to N.N.E. 15 past 7, bore up and made sail. Cape St. Agulhas S.E. b. E., about 5 lgs. Employd clearing away to bend the cables and getting away things ready for anchoring. 30 past 11, beat to quarters, and got all the guns clear ready for action. At noon, moderately clear; a remarkable cape S.E., Cape of Good Hope N.W. $\frac{1}{2}$ W., Fals. Cape N. $\frac{3}{4}$ W., dist. 4 or 5 miles. P.M.—Moderate breezes and clear, standing for Simons Bay. At 30 past 4 shortend sail, and brought up with the best bower in Simons Bay, 10 fthm., fine sand, when moor'd as follows :—Roman Rock east, Noahs Ark S.E., Round Tower Battery S. b. E., Wharf W. b. $\frac{1}{4}$ S. ; a remarkable house on the W. side of the Bay N. b. W. $\frac{1}{4}$ W., dist. off Wharf about 1 mile.

H.M. Ship *Calcutta* at anchor in Simon's Bay, extreme point of Africa.

Saturday, 13. Wind varble. A.M.—At 9, saluted the battery with 11 guns, which was returned by (Round Tower Battery) with an equel number. Found an English whaler and two ships riding in the bay under Dutch colours. P.M.—Moderate and variable. People employd as requird. I dind on shore with Mr. Maudaunt, &c., &c.

Sunday, 14. Wind vble. A.M.—Light breezes and variable. Receivd 25 butts of water, and fresh mutton 724 lb., and soft bread for ships company and convicts. P.M.—People employd variously. Mr. Maudaunt, —Brumley, Lieut. Patishall, L. Donovan, Lieut. M.Culloch, and self, went to Cape Town, and dind at Hudsons hotel.

Monday, 15. Wind vble. A.M.—Receivd fresh beef and mutton for the ships company and convicts. P.M.—Fresh breezes. Employd variously. Sailed the English whaler.

Tuesday, 16. Wind varble. A.M.—Receivd 842 lb. of fresh beef and 400 lb. of soft bread. Receivd 7 British seamen (volunteers   ). P.M.—Moderate and fair. Arrived the *English whaler*, Captain Gardner. People employed watering, &c.

Wednesday, 17. Wind vrble. A.M.—Receivd 350 lb. fresh beef and mutton, and 400 lb. of soft bread, for the ships comp. P.M.—Moderate and fair weather. We returnd from Cape Town.

Thursday, 18. Wind varble. A.M.—Receivd 724 lb. fresh beef and mutton, and 450 lbs. of soft bread. P.M.—Moderate and fair. People employed as most necessary.

Friday, 19. Wind varble. A.M.—Receivd 394 lb. of fresh beef and mutton, and 600 lb. of soft bread, for the ships company and convicts. P.M.—Moderate, with unsettld wr. Arrived a ship, under Dutch colours. John Henry Cashman, a convict, this afternoon stole Mr. Brumleys gold watch, and robd Mr. Mac Donals pocket book of 4 dollers. At 6 this eve jumpd overboard, with an intention of getting on shore. He was discovered, and boats sent to pick him up, but before they got to him he went down and was dro'nd. The above lad was servant to Mr. Right the Master.

Saturday, 20. Wind vable. A.M.—Receivd 783 lb. of beef and mutton and 600 lb. of bread for the ships company and convicts. P.M.— Moderate and fair wr. Employd variously. This morn I went out a shooting. Saw some wild deer, but could not get a shot at them. Mr. Hutter and 2 officers, Mr. Patishall, were of the party. We see the print of a tigers paw very fresh, and of wolfes before us. I killed a brace of partriges. Receivd stock for the colony.

Sunday, 21. Wind vble. A.M.—Receivd 840 lb. of fresh beef and mutton for the crew and convicts, and 450 lb. of soft bread. P.M.— Receivd hay, &c., for the colony.

Monday, 22. Wind varible. A.M.—Employed getting ready for sea. Receivd 600 lbs. of fresh beef and mutton and 200 lbs. of soft bread for the crew & convicts. P.M.—Light airs and hazy wr.

Tuesday, 23. Wind vble, N.W. A.M.—Moderate and fine wr. At 5, unmoord ship and hove short. At 8, made the signal for all officers, &c., to repair on board. P.M.—Light airs and variable. At 3, a light breeze from the N.W. 30 past 3, weighd and made all sail, a boat towing ahead. At 6, anchord in 13 fthm. with the following bearings: —Noahs Ark, at S. ¼ W.; the Roman Rock, S.E. b. E. ; Pauls Bay, S. ¼ E. ; and the center of Simons Town.[1] At 9, rain and continual lightning.

Wednesd., 24. Wind easterly, S.E. A.M.—Light airs, inclining to a calm with rain. P.M.—Fresh breezes and thick hazy wr. with rain. At 4, weighd and stood in under the stay sails. At ½ past 5 anchord with the best bower in 10 fthms.—the Roman Rock S.E. b. E., Noahs Ark S.S.E. ¼ E., and the Wharf S.S.W. ¾ W.—veerd to a cable At 8, much lightning.

Thursday, 25. Wind N. A.M.—Strong breezes. At 11 more moderate, and made the signal for sailing. At noon, weighd and made all sail; fresh breezes & hazy. P.M.—Fresh breezes and hazy wr. At half-past noon, passd thro' between the Roman Rock and Noahs Ark. At 2, saw a brig, N. b. W. Employed stowing the booms. At 4, Cape Point N.W. b. W., and Fals Cape E. b. S. At 5, Cape Fals. N.N.E., 4 or 5 lgs.

H.M. Ship *Calcutta* at Sea, August, 1803.

Thursday, 25. On our departure from the Cape it was naturally for us to indulge at this moment a melancholy reflection which obtruded itself upon the minds of those, who, we, settlers at Pt. Philip. The land behind us was the abode of a civilized people, that before us was the residence of savages. When, if ever, we might again enjoy the

---

[1] No omission here, the same longitude probably applying to both. [C.]

commerce of the world was doubtful and uncertain. The refreshments and the pleasures of which we had so liberally partaken at the Cape and Simons Bay were to be exchanged for coarse fare and hard labour at Pt. Philip, and we may truly say all communication with families and friends now cut off, we were leaving the world behind us to enter on a state unknown.

Friday, 26. Wind west. A.M.—At 10 saw a large ship to the N.E., standing to the northward. P.M.—Moderate breezes and cloudy.

Saturday, 27. Wind S.E. b. E. A.M.—At 2, strong breezes and squally, with heavy rain and lightning. Furld the top sails at 8. Strong gales with a heavy swell from the south. No observation. P.M.—Strong gales and squally weather. At 5 more moderate.

Sunday, 28. Wind S.S.W. A.M.—Strong breezes with rain and hazy wr. this 24 hours. Strong southerly current. Lat. obsd. 37° 16 S. P.M.—Strong breezes, squally, with rain. At 9 H. 49 M. 57 SEC., P.M., the time keeper, No. 8, stoppd. At 11, the ship laboured very much, the sea very high.

Monday, 29. Wind N. b. W. A.M.—At 3, down mizen stay sail. Ship working very much and making mutch water in the fore sail room; also the boatswains, gunners, and carpenters store rooms. At 8, more moderate, with a large head sea. Got all the sails and other stores on deck to dry. At 12, one of the timbers of the head earlings broke, and all the guard irons and rails washd away. P.M.—Fresh breezes and squally, with rain. Lat. 37·05 S.

Tuesday, 30. Wind S. b. W. A.M.—At 3, mod. breezes and clear wr. P.M.—Light breezes and clear. At 11, squally with rain. Lat. obsd. 36-15. S.

Wednesday, 31. Wind east. A.M.—Fresh breezes and clear. Employed variously. P.M.—Fresh br. and cloudy. At 4, observed a great many whales about the ship, and a strong current running, N.E. b. E., 2¼ knots per hour. Lat. obsd. 36·51 S. About 300 miles from Simons Bay to the E. b. South.

Thursday, September 1, 1803. Wind east. A.M.—Fresh breezes and clear. Many whales near the ship. At 9, do. wr. P.M.—Steady breezes. Lat. obsd. 38.31. S. Wind unfavourable.

Friday, 2. Wind E. b. S. Strong breezes and squally wr. At noon, do. wr. P.M.—At 6, do. wr. Wore ship; took in 1 reef. At 7, strong winds and squalls; under 3d reefd f. sails and storm stay sail. Lat. obsd. 40°. 41. S.

Saturday, 3. Wind S.E.b.E. A.M.—Fresh breezes and hazy wr. at 8. Found the chain pumps to be choked by reason of a quantity of tar having got down into the well; got them up, and cleard them. No observation. P.M.—Strong breezes with squalls and rain, with a very high sea.

Sunday, 4. Wind E.S.E. A.M.—At 7, in jib-boom, to ease the bowsprit and ships bow; observed the knees of the head to work very mutch. At 9 took in the sprit-sail yard; on deck the ship making a great quantity of water. At noon, strong breezes and hazy; lying to under treble reefd M. T. sail. P.M.—Strong gales and squally wr., with heavy rain at 4. At 8 more moderate. No observation; a very high sea.

Monday, 5. Wind S.S.E.　A.M.—Strong breezes, with squalls at intervals. Variation, 28° 04 west at noon; under storm stay-sails, and wore to the N.E. It is unusual to have the wind so long at the S.E., the wind generally.—Lat. obsd., 40° 30 S. Not more than 500 miles from Simons Bay. A high sea, and had a very bad night. P.M.—Squally wr., with rain. At 30 past 1 saw a sail in the eastern; at 2, standing to the south; at 5 past 4 observd that the strange sail had wore to the north; made the private signal to her. At 5 the carpenter reports more defects in the knees of the head. We thought the strange sail was the *Ocean* transport.

Tuesday, 6. Wind W.N.W.　A.M.—Moderate wr.; at 7 saw the strange sail E.S.E. 3 or 4 leagues, running to the eastward; at noon the strange sail S.E. Lat. obsd., 39.47 S.　P.M.—Moderate breezes and cloudy wr., with rain at 4. Lost sight of the strange sail in the S.E.

Wednesday, 7. Wind S.b.W., S.b.E.　A.M.—Fresh breezes and light squalls. Lat. obsd., 39° 13 S.　P.M.—Moderate breezes and cloudy weather; took in and made sail, as required.

Thursday, 8. Wind S.S.E.　A.M.—Fresh breezes, with continual rain. No observation. P.M.—Do. wr., with lightning from the N.West.

Friday 9. Wind E.N.E., variable south; calm, W.b.N.　A.M.—Fresh breezes, with rain. P.M.—Do. wr. at 4; at 3 continual lightning; 30 past 11 squally, with hard rain. Lat. obsd., 36° 43' south.

Saturday, 10. Wind S.W.b.W.　A.M.—Steady fresh breezes and clear. At 9 punishd. Thoms Fitzgerald (a convict) with 3 dozen lashes for theft. P.M.—Do. wr.; at 10 much lightning to the N.W. Lat. obsd., 36 28 S. This day we got a fair wind.

Sunday, 11. Wind W.S.W.　A.M.—At 3 strong breezes, with rain; ½-past 3 heavy squalls, with lightning; at 8 fresh breezes, with rain; at 10 do. wr.　P.M.—Steady fresh breezes. Lat. 36° 41 S.

Monday, 12. Wind W.b.S.　A.M.—Fresh breezes and cloudy wr. P.M.—Moderate breezes and clear wr.

Tuesday, 13. Wind S.W.　A.M.—Squally, with heavy rain; at noon pleasant wr. P.M.—Moderate breezes, with squalls at intervals.

Wednesday, 14. Wind variable to the west. A.M.—Light winds and clear wr. P.M.—Do. wr. The prisoners beds, &c., were taken up to air, and prison smoaked.

Thursday, 15. Wind north-east. A.M.—Light airs, inclining to a calm; at 30 past 9 departed this life Jeremiah David; at 30 past 11 committed the body of the deceasd to the deep, with the usual ceremony. P.M.—Moderate and clear wr.; at 11 strong breezes and hazy wr.

Friday, 16. Wind N.E., N.N.E.　A.M.—At 4 do. wr.; at 11 strong breezes and hazy wr. P.M.—Fresh gales and squally wr., with a heavy head sea; at 2 set the fore top sail, close reefd; at 8 squally, in the fore top sail.

Saturday, 17. Wind N.N.E.　A.M.—At 2 fresh gales and squally weather; at noon do. wr.; set the main top sail and F. top mast stay sail.　P.M.—At 1 strong breezes and hazy wr.; at 4 do. wr.; at 11 do. wr.

Sunday, 18. Wind N.b.E.　A.M.—Fresh breezes and squally weather; at 6.30 past out 2d reef top sails, and made sail; at 10 fresh breezes; ½ past musterd at quarters. P.M.—Moderate and fair wr.

Monday, 19. Wind N.N.E. A.M.—Steady fresh breezes. P.M. do. wr.; the armorer employed making stentions for the launch.

Tuesday, 20. Wind N.b.E. A.M.—Fresh breezes and squally at ½ past 1; at 3 in top glnt. sails at ½ past 5 steady breezes; at 11 steady fresh breezes. Lat. obsd., 37 55 south. P.M.—Fresh breezes and cloudy wr., and squally at intervals; hands up all night * for land. The islands of St. Paul and Amsterdam. At 11 strong breezes and cloudy; this night we passed between the two islands of *St. Pauls* and *Amsterdam* Island in the Indian Ocean. It lies in lat. 37 deg. 56 mins. S., and long. 77 deg. 22 min. east. Amsterdam Island, in the Indian Ocean. to the N. of St. Pauls Island, is in lat. 36° 40 min. S., and long. 77 6 min. E.; 75 deg. 15 min. E. per book.

Wednesday, 21. Wind N.N.E., westerly, S.b.W.; at 5 south; do. 11 do. A.M.—At 1 strong breezes and hazy wr., with rain; at 8 observd the tiller rope to be much chaf'd and worn, rove a new one; at 11 passd a quantity of rock and sea weed; thick hazy wr. P.M.—Fresh breezes and hazy wr.; at 3 a calm; at 4 fresh breezes; at 5 in top gallnt. sails and 3d reef of the T. sails; 30 past 5 stowed the jib; at 9 fresh breezes, with rain and squally wr. 37 55 lat. obsd.

Thursday, 22. Wind south, S.S.W., W.b.S. A.M.—At 1 fresh breezes and squally, with constant rain; at 3 furld the top sails; at 4 strong gales and squally; at 7 more moderate; at noon fresh breezes. P.M.— Moderate breezes and cloudy wr.; at 10 do. wr.

H.M. Ship *Calcutta* from St. Pauls towards New South Wales, 1803.

Friday, 23. Wind N.W.b.N., N.W. A.M.—At 1 fresh breezes and squally wr.; 30 past 1 in lower studing sails; 30 past 6 handed the M. sail; 30 past 7 took in the fore top gallant; at 8 furld the mizn T. sail; 30 past 10 in 3d reef of the fore top sail; at noon fresh gales and hazy wr. Lat. obsd., 38 22 S. P.M.—Strong breezes and squally wr.; at 15 past 2 in M. T. gall. sail, took in 3d reef of the M. topsail; at 6 fresh gales and heavy wr., with rain; at 30 past 9 out 3d reef of the M. T. sail, and out M. top gallt. sail; at 11 strong gales, and very high sea from the N.W.b.W. The equinoctial gales as the sun pass the equator.

Saturday, 24. Wind N.W., west. A.M.—At 2 fresh gales and clear wr.; at 6 out 2d reef of M. T. sail; 20 past 9 took in M. top gallt. sail, and lowered the M. T. sail on the cap, out all reefs of do. to dry; at 30 past 10 in 1st reef of the M. top sail and set it. Employd working junk. The sun this morn at 8 A.M. crossd the equinoctial line. Lat. obsd., 38 28 S.; the difference of time between us and Greenwich is 6h. 12m. 20s. later than we are. P.M.—Strong breezes and squally wr., with rain and a large following sea; at 2 do. wr.; at 5 in second reef main top sail, and set the jib and stay sail; at 9 shipd a great quantity of water at the 3d port from aft on the larboard side, and filled the gun room and cockpit; at 11 squally, with hard rain; at ½ past observd a very clear rainbow; 12 more moderate. 215 miles last 24 hours.

---

* An indistinct word here, probably the equivalent of *looking* or *seeing*. [C.]

Sunday, 25. Wind W.b.S. A.M.—At 6 set treble reef fore top sail, unbent the main top; at noon squally, in main top sail. P.M.—At 2 fresh breezes and squally, with rain.

Monday, 26. Wind W.N.W. A.M.—At 5 fresh breezes and cloudy wr. P.M.—Fresh breezes and squally, with constant rain; took in the studing sails; at 6 fresh breezes, with thick hazy wr.; at 10 split the main top sail, close reefd the sail.

Tuesday, 27. Wind W.S.W. A.M.—Fresh breezes and hazy wr. P.M.—Strong breezes and cloudy.

Wednesday, 28. Wind N.W. A.M.—Cloudy unsettled wr.; at 6 rove new top glnt. sheets. P.M.—Employd securing the cutwater with strappings, &c.

Thursday, 29. Wind N.W.b.W. A.M.—Fresh breezes and hazy wr.; 9 this morn we perceivd the water much smoother than usual, and we are within the south point of New Holland; at P.M., Mic. Day, the Captain and Col. dind with us off of 2 geese, &c.; and the first day that we could set steady at table since we left the Cape. Lat. obsd., 38° 49 S. Distance off of the South Cape of New Holland, 200 miles.

Friday, 30. Wind north, N.b.E. A.M.—Fresh breezes and cloudy wr. We obserd, though the wind blew very fresh, the water was smooth, by reason of being within the Southern Cape of New Holland; dist. 300 miles. P.M.—Strong breezes and squally; at 4 in top glant. sails and 2d reefd the top sails; 30 past 6 close reefd, and furld the mizn T. sails, stowed the M. top stay sails, continual strong winds.

Saturday, October 1. Wind N.E.b.N., W.N.W. A.M.—Stowed jib, strong breezes and squally wr., with rain; 30 past 5 double reefd the mizen S. sails and top glnt. sails and M. T. mast stay sails; at noon strong breezes and cloudy. P.M.—At 1 fresh gales and squally weather; at 10 do. wr.

Sunday, 2. Wind north. A.M.—Fresh breezes and squally; at 9 the carpenters employd stowing the booms; at 6 moderate breezes and cloudy. P.M.—Do wr. employed stowing the booms.

Monday, 3. Wind N.W.b.N. A.M.—Fresh breezes and squally wr. Departed this life Christ. Smith (a convict). P.M.—30 past 6 committed the body to the deep with the usual ceremony.

Tuesday, 4. Wind W.N.W. A.M.—Light breezes and cloudy; at 11 squally wr.; sailmaker employd at the main sail. P.M.—Fresh breezes and squally, with rain; at 5 under double reef top sails; at 6 hard gales.

Wednesday, 5. Wind W.b.S. A.M.—Strong gales; under double reef top sails; sailmaker employd repairing the main sail. P.M.—Light breezes and clear wr.; made and shortend sail as requisite.

Thursday, 6. Wind N.N.W. A.M.—Light breezes and cloudy. Tryd soundings; no ground at 60 fthms.; bent best bower cables; at noon fresh breezes and cloudy; double reef the top sails. P.M.—Strong breezes and squally wr.; took in 3d reef the F. sails. At 8 sounded at 90 fthms.; running under F. and M. top sails and fore T. mast stay sail. People looking out all night for land. Blowing very hard, and high sea.

Friday, 7. Wind S.S.W. A.M.—Strong breezes; sounded; found no ground at 70 fthms. At noon light airs and clear. P.M.—Light breezes and hazy wr.; 20 past 1 down jolly boat, sounded, found no ground at 300 fthms.; at 7 took in top glant. sails; at 8 calm, with a heavy swell from the S.W.

Saturday, 8. Winds vble. to the N.E., W.N.W., W.b.S. A.M.—Light breezes and cloudy. At 1 double reefd f. sails; at 8 fresh breezes; set the top gal sails at 10. Made the land a head S.E.b.E. 8 leags.; sounded in 52 fms., brown sand and gravel; bent the small bower cable. Tack'd ship to the west, the N.West. Extremity of Kings Island at N.E., and the southern do. at S.E.b.E. 3 remarkable sand hills E.N.E., east, and E.b.S. Sounded in 53 fms., coarse brown sand and gravel; off the shore 8 or 9 miles. Obserd the sea to break northerly on the N. end of New Year Island, a small island that joins Kings. Lat. obsd., 39° 50 S. P.M.—Fresh breezes and squally wr.; at 1 tkd. ship to the north; at 3 strong breezes, with heavy squalls. Split the main topsail, and down top glnt. sails. At 4 hard squalls, a very heavy west swell, and the sea going over the poop; at 7 sounded, found no ground at 45 fms.; at 8 up F. sail; sounded 37 fathms., brown sand; at 11 blowing very hard, and ship labouring very much; at 12 strong gales, and a very high sea beating against us.

Sunday, 9. A.M.—Wind W.N.W., W.b.S. Strong gales and squally. Sounded in 40 fathms. Carried away the larboard tiller rope. At 30 past A.M., set fr. stay sail. At 30 past 1 set f. sail. Sounded in 40 fathms—coarse brown sand. At 5, saw the land about Port Phillip to the N. b. E. The land near the entrance of the harbour appeared low land, and at a distance very beautiful.[1] Seal Island, S.E. ½ E., and *Whales Point*, W. b. S. (named so by Capt. Woodriff, the head being very much like one): it is on the larboard side as you enter the harbour. At 15 past 10 we anchord with the best bower in 6 fathms; found laying here the *Ocean* transport, which arrived on Friday the 7 of Oct. When moord ship we had the following bearings:—The east side of the enterance West, and the east end of the long island N.E. ½ E. off the south shore, 1½ mile. A very fine country to appearance, but no water but salt lakes—

```
              N.
              |
West.—————————|—————————East.
           The | Ship.
         Where | we laid.
              South.
```

P.M.—Fresh breezes and clear wr. Employed clearing away the booms, &c. Out launch at 4. Moord ship with the small bower to the west-

---

[1] "The face of the country bordering on the port is beautifully picturesque, swelling into gentle elevations of the brightest verdure, and dotted with trees as if planted by the hand of taste, while the ground is covered with a profusion of flowers of every colour; in short, the external appearance of the country flattered us into the most delusive dreams of fruitfulness and plenty.

"The soil (except in a few places where marl is found mixed with vegetable mould) is invariably sandy, and its blackness proceeds from the ashes of the burnt grass, which has everywhere been set fire to by the natives. The proportion of sand varies, and in some spots the soil may be sufficiently strong [to produce vegetables, and perhaps Indian corn; but it may safely be asserted that (*excepting a few acres at the head of the port*) no

ward. Capt. Woodriff and Lieut. Governor Collins went on shore on the south side of the island. At 6 they returned. Could not find any fresh water. They reported the soil to be very bad, and the trees small, unfit for the use of H.M. Navy. The Bay is very large, more so than any I ever see, but the enterance does not exceed a mile and a half, though from the camp, S.W. to the N.E. of the Bay, it is not less than 60 miles to the fresh water lake. At 10 it blew a very hard gale of wind. It was very fortunate for us that we arrived at our destination in the morn. 12, do. wr., with very hard squalls.

H.M. ship *Calcutta* at Anchor in Port Phillip Harbour, New South Wales, October 1803.

Monday, 10. Wind S.S.E. A.M.—At 10, Lieut. Patteshal, Mr. White, and self, went on the south side of the Bay, opposite the ship, and many miles in and round the opposite shore, but could not find any water but what was very brackish that we could not drink. The land was very bad, light soil, and a great many of the trees blown up by the roots, which appeared to have taken very little root. Not any of the natives did we see, but many hutts, in which were cockle shells and muscle. We see a few birds, parrots and a couple of quails; not the least vestige of any quadrupedes or fish. Along the shore we returnd by no means satisfied with the country. The Capt. and Governor went on shore and found no water that was good, but a small run near Arthers Seat, the east side of the Bay.[1] When we arrived here it was in the spring, the month of April[2] 1803.

Tuesday, 11. Wind S.S.E. A.M.—The same party and self went on shore to the island in the middle of the Bay, now called Signet [Mud] Island, where we see a great number of black swans. I was the first that killd one on the island. We kill 3, and caught many alive, and caught many pelicans, and some sea birds. Capt. W. and the Gov., with Mr. Tuckey, went on the west side of the Bay to procure water. Could not find any. Three of the natives were friendly with them, and gave Mr. T. a spear. The information that the Governor, &c., gave was by no means favourable, for want of soil, water, and trees. The difference of time with us and England is nine hours forty three minutes: we are so much forwarder than they are.

Wednesday, 12. Wind westly. A.M.—Fresh breezes and cloudy. Sent a party on shore cutting grass, and another watering. At 7, the Capt. and Col. Collins, and 1 Lieut., Mr. Tuckey, went to the northern part of the Bay to procure water, and see the same three natives. The Colony Surgeons report the water procured by sinking tubs as wells to be good and fit for use. The Capt. gave one of the natives a blanket. They attended them some time. At 15. past 11. the Captain and

spot within five miles of the water will produce wheat or any other grain that requires either much moisture or good soil. On some of the highest elevations an arid sea-sand is found, giving nourishment to no other vegetable than heath and fern. The basis of the hills consist of very coarse granite, which is here found in every stage of formation, from grains scarcely adhering, and crumbling into sand between the fingers, to the perfect stone which almost defies the chissel."—[*Tuckey*, p. 157.]

[1] This day died John Skilhorne, free settler. The first death.—*Ed.*
[2] "I presume he means the equivalent of April of the northern hemisphere."—[*C.*]

officers returnd, but found no water fit for use. Sent the carpenter and some men to look for wood on shore.

Thursday, 13. Wind S.W. A.M.—Fresh breezes and cloudy. Sent the small launch for water. The same party of officers went to survey the S.E. part of the Bay and watering place. The carpenter returnd from on shore, where he had been to search for wood to secure the head and knees of the ship. Had not seen any fit for that purpose. At 15. past 1. confind Lieut. Donovan to his cabin pr order of Capt. Woodriff, for his being absent from the ship whilst he was on shore.[1]

Friday, 14. Wind west, vble, calm. A.M.—Fresh breezes and cloudy weather. Sent the Master up the harbour to sound for a conveniant place to remove the ship for delivering the colonial stores, &c. At 30. past 9 he returnd, and reported good anchorage 3 or 4 miles further to the eastward. At 10, cleard hawsr. Sent on there a party of the Colonial Marines, also convicts, with Lieut. Johnson, to pitch some tents. They carried the equipage and live stock. P.M.—Light breezes with rain. At 30 past 1 unmoored ship and hove short on the small bower. Loosd the T. sail. At 15 past 2 weighd and made sail. At 30 past 3 light airs with rain. Found the tide too strong for the wind. Anchord in 13 fthms. with the small bower, west end of the long island, N.E. b. N., and the S.E. head of the enterance W. ¼ N., off the shore 1 mile & ¼. Calm at 4. The carpenter reports 2 of the planks in the counter started. Caulkers caulking the poop waterways. At 7 in the morn Mr. White and self went on shore on the south side of the Bay, and walked far into the country. We see the kangaroos and some parretts, but could not kill any. We walkd to the watering place. The water through the casks was good, and the information from the 4 men that were there that it agreed with them. At 5 returnd on board.

Saturday, 15. Wind E.S.E. A.M.—Light breezes, inclining to a calm. At 30 past 8 hove short on the f. bower. Loosd sails. *Ocean* transport under weigh. At 9, weighd and made sail. Sounded from 6 to 18 fthms. At 15 past 10 crossd the shoal north of
Point in 4 fthms. At 30 past 10 anchord in 7 fthms.; fine sand. At noon, strong breezes and cloudy; the *Ocean* at anchor east of us, 1 mile distance. Employd sounding [sending] the colonial stores on shore. Where we lay we can see the camp, distance from us 4⅓ miles. P.M.—At 30 past 3 moord ship with the best bower to the westward, the camp bearing S.E. ¼ S., the entrance of the port west, and Seals Beach open, and Arthers Seat E. ½ N. Nearest distance off shore 1¼ mile in 5 fathms water. Employd fitting the launch for surveying the harbour.

Sunday, 16. Wind S.E. A.M.—Moderate and clear weather. At 30 past 8 sent the launch with the first Lieut., Mr. Tuckey, attended by 2[2] civil officers, Mr. Harris, Mr. Collins, and Mr. Gammon, of the colony, and a 6 oard cutter, victuald for 8 days, to survey the Bay from

---

[1] NOTE.—From this time Mr. Knopwood seems to have had some difficulty to accommodate himself to the seasons of this hemisphere, and frequently adopt the spring and summer months of the north for the spring and summer ones of Australia; but he has generally run his pen through them, though not always; but wherever he has left the errors standing I shall not follow him.—[*C*.]

[2] This figure is exactly copied. It appears to have been 3 originally, but 2 is written *over* it very plainly.—[*C*.]

the camp northward, if possible to assertain a more eligable situation for forming a settlement. At 9, employd landing the convicts with their baggage. At 11, the Capt. and Colonel went on shore to direct the landing, &c., of the prisoners. P.M.—At 2, completed the landing of the marines and prisoners with their baggage.

Remarks in Sullivan Bay and Hobert Camp, Port Phillip, New South Wales, October 1803.

Monday, 17. Wind eastly. A.M—Fine pleasant wr. Employd delivering the hospital stores. At 10 I went to the camp to see about my marquee, and gave orders for its being completed for me. At 4 P.M. the Capt. and Colonel went on shore; the Colonel slept there for the first time. At ½-past 4 the Master returnd from surveying, and found a good channel in the E.N.E. direction. I remaind on board as a visitor.

Tuesday, 18. A.M.—I remaind on board till 10, then went on shore to the camp to order about my marque; returnd on board to dine.

Wednesday, 19. A.M.—At 9 went on shore and sent all my things to the camp. Waited upon the Governor. At 11 got my marquee in order, and slept there for the first time. The convicts employd variously; many of the officers searching in the country for water and soil. P.M.—At night Lieut. Sladden confind Sarjent Sarjent for drunkenness and in conduct.

Thursday, 20. A.M.—At 9 Lieut. Menzies, of the Royal Marines, came to the camp to set at the court martial on the prisoner Sarjeant Sargant. At 11 the court commenced. At 2 P.M. it finishd, and the report carried to the Governor. I dind at the mess with the officers. At 6 the officer of the R. Marines, Lieut. Sladden, red the sentence of the court martial, which was that Sarjeant Sarjant be broke and put into the line as a private; but, on account of his prior good conduct, that he be recommended to the Governor, who reproved him and reinstated him.

Friday, 21. A.M.—At 50 past 7 the launch and cutter returnd from surveying the harbour, having last night arrived in the N.W. point of the bay, where they have discoverd a straigh, an apparent passage towards the sea, which the first Lieut., Mr. Tuckey, intended to have explored, but was driven to the southward during the night by a tide or current from the apparant straigh; and at daylight, finding himself near the ship, returned on board. At 11 Capt. Woodriff and Lieut. Tuckey came to the camp, who produced to the Governor a chart, the survey about 90 miles round the bay from Arthers Seat (the highest hill on the east of the bay); and had landed in several places to observe the soil, trees, and to obtain water. The report was—the soil bad, trees very small, and but little water; nor could they get any fish. Lieut. Houston and Midshipman Mr. Vernon (son of the Bishop of Carlisle), dind with me. In the eve I went on board H.M. Ship *Calcutta* to tea and sleep.

Saturday, 22. A.M.—At 7 Mr. Tuckey, the first Lieut., and two boats went to survey from the N.W. point of the bay. In the eve I return to the camp. Lieut. MacCullough, of the Royal Marines, slept at my marquee. Mr. Tuckey, Mr. Gammon, Mid. Mr. Collins, Mr. Harris—

the two last gentlemen belong to the colony—they found a fresh water river on the N.E. poind of the bay, where they pitched their tent for the night.[1]

A Private Remark given me from Mr. Harris and Lieut. Tuckey of H.M. ship *Calcutta*.

Sunday, 23. A.M.—At 8 they observd three of the natives, who approach them. Mr. Tuckey gave them fish, bread, and many preseants; they were much pleasd and friendly. At 10 Mr. T. and Mr. Collins went across the bay, about 5 or 6 miles, with a boats crew, leaving Mr. Harris and Mr. Gammon & 2 men to take care of the tent, and make observations on shore. The three men, seeing Mr. T. go away in the boat, they likewis went away. Early in the afternoon they returnd with a great many of them; and at 2 P.M. they in the boat coming back observd 70 in a party. Mr. Tuckey called to them, at which they hastened to the place where the tent was. On Mr. T. coming up he found Mr. Gammon surrounded; and the chief at that time seized Mr. G., who calld out to Mr. T. to fire on them. Mr. Harris was surrounded at the tent; and the blacks were taking what they could from the boat. Mr. T. fird over them; they ran away a small distance, but soon approachd again with the king (who wore a very elegant turban-crown),[2] and was always carried upon the shoulders of the men. Whenever he desired them to halt, or to approach, they did it immediately. Mr. T. fird over them a second time, at which they removed to a very small distance. Those about the king, to the number of 50 or 60 were all armed. The blacks finding that none were wounded, and that the number were approaching, and the second in command was going to throw his spier at Mr. Tuckey, gave orders to shoot him, as an example; they fird, and Innis killed him, and another wounded; they all fled. The number of savages were not less than one hundred and fifty. Had not Mr. Tuckey fortunately came up with the boat, no doubt but they would have killd Mr. Gammon and Mr. Harris and the 2 men, and have eat them. We have great reason to think they are canibals.

Remarks at Sullivan Bay and Hobert Camp, Port Phillip, New South Wales, 1803.

Sunday, 23. A.M.—At 11 the whole of the camp assembled, and the Governor at the head of the Royal Marines, with officers, to hear divine service, which was performd in the square of the parade before all

---

[1] "On the eastern side of the port, twenty-eight miles from the entrance, a stream of fresh water empties itself into the port [*Cannanook?*]. This stream runs through an extensive swamp, and appears to be a branch from a large river at the northern extremity of the port, which the shortness of time and badness of the weather prevented our examining [in the boats]. The bed of this stream is covered with foliaceous mica, which our people at first conceived to be gold dust, and thence expected they had discovered an *Elsaledorado*."—[Tuckey, p. 160.]

[2] In "The Life and Adventures of William Buckley" (published at Hobart Town in 1852), who was an absconder from Collins' party in 1803, and lived amongst the Port Phillip blacks for thirty-two years, these "head-bands," as he calls them, are spoken of, at page 72, as being much worn in his time, in the fabrication of which they took great pains.

hands. Mr. M. Cullough and Mr. White, the purser of H.M. Ship *Calcutta*, dind with me; in the eve they returnd on board.

Monday, 24. A.M.—At 7 the convicts were all musterd and put into different gangs for work. At 1 P.M. people employed cutting wood, &c., &c.

Tuesday, 25. A.M.—At 8 the British flag was hoisted at the camp for the first time in honour of His Majesty's accession to the throne. At 12 the Royal Marines fird 3 vollies in honour of the day. At 1 H.M. Ship *Calcutta* fird 21 guns on the same occasion. The day was exceeding hot. At 12 the thermomiter stood at 92. Confind to my bed the major pt. of the day. At ½-past 6 it was exceedingly cold; the sudden chance from heat to cold is very great here, much more than in England.

Wednesday, 26. A.M.—Being very ill, was confind to the marquee. Mr. Edward Brumley, surgeon of H.M. Ship *Calcutta*, came on shore to visit me, and Capt. Woodriff sent me a bottle of port. P.M.—At 5 the Capt. came to the camp and drank tea with me, likewise Mr. Brumley.

Thursday, 27. A.M.—Being very ill, confind to my bed all day. P.M. —The Governor came to see me, and requested me to go on board H.M. Ship *Calcutta* a few days for change of air.

Friday, 28. A.M.—The day being wet, I continued very ill at the camp. Visited by Capt. Woodriff and the Governor.

Saturday, 29. A.M.—At 9 Capt. Woodriff came to the camp, and at 11 I went on board with him, very unwell.

Sunday, 30. A.M.—Continued unwell on board H.M. Ship *Calcutta*.

Monday, 31. A.M.—Do. At 6 P.M. rain. At 8 much lightning. At 10 a very dreadful tempest, the lightning very severe. Mr. Tuckey, &c., surveying the harbour; the lightning so bad that the boat was obliged to return.

Tuesday, 1 *November*. A.M.—Continual rain, with a heavy thunderstorm; the thermomiter 93 at 12, and down to 50 in the eve. Receivd a letter from the Governor respecting my health.

Wednesday, 2. A.M.—Rain at intervals. Being much better was able to go to the camp; waited on the Governor. At 11 a complaint came before me as a majestrate that Robert Cannady, servant to Mr. Humphreys, had promised Buckly, the Governor's servant, a waistcoat for a pair of shoes, which he had taken and worn, and would not return the waistcoat; but after hearing them on both sides I had the waistcoat given to Buckley. A.M.—At 12 received stores, &c., from the Commissery. Lieut. Houston, Maculloh and White dind with me. In the eve returnd on board with Mr. Tuckey. At 9 Mr. Tuckey, Lieut. Patteshal, and self supd with Capt. Woodriff.

Thursday, 3. A.M.—Not so well. Mr. Tuckey went surveying. In the aft. Mr. Harris came on board with Mr. White.

Friday, 4. A.M.—Better. Mr. Harris continued on board, Mr. Houston on shore. Continual boats going to and from the ship with colonial stores. This day the Governor discharged the *Ocean* transport, Capt. Merthew, Mr. Harris on board [1] to Launceston.

---

[1] NOTE.—This word seems originally to have concluded the day's entry, the following words, " to Launceston," being in quite different ink, and most probably written at an after period.

Saturday, 5. A.M.—Employed in clearing H.M. ship *Calcutta* of stores, &c., for the colony. At 6 P.M., being very much better, I went on shore with Mr. Harris; and Lieut. Houston and MacCulloh supd with me. My friends on board the *Calcutta* would feign have kept me longer.

Sunday, 6. A.M.—At 9 I waited on the Governor; the day was so unfavourable, I could not do duty. At 10 I walkd with the G. to see his new garden, Capt. Woodriff and Lieut. Pattishal came and met us; at 1 P.M. Capt. W. had all the officers, but Lieut. Donovan, who was under an arrest, to dinner with him. I dind with the Governor of Pt. Phillip, and a very pleasant day we had; all the officers on board were very merry. Mr. Collins,[1] with 6 men in a large boat, saild with dispatches from the camp to Governor King at Port Jackson; he was to stop at the *Calcutta*, to take letters, &c., &c., to the Governor.

Monday, 7. A.M.—The *Calcutta*'s boats employed bringing stores on shore for the colony from the ship. I dind with the officers at the mess. At 4 P.M. we were informed that Mr. Collins could not get out of the harbours mouth. The married men employed building houses for themselves; 2 in a house.

Tuesday, 8. A.M.—At 10 Mr. Bowden and self went across the island to the opposite shore, to see whither we could observe Mr. Collins, but could not; on our return we were informed that he was not out of the harbour. There we see the most dreadful surge I ever beheld. At 4 P.M. we returnd. The soldiers wifes are permitted to build in the same manner.

Wednes, 9. A.M.—Three men of the convicts are missing from the camp. The men employed in mounting the guns, and making a battery.

Thursday, 10. A.M.—At 8 Mr. Bowden and self walkd to Arthers Bonnet, the S.W. point of the opposite shore from the encampment, and walkd to the enterance of the harbour, from thence to the *Calcutta*, where we dind and slept. I killd a duck. Mr. Collins this morn got out of the harbour in the boat.

Friday, 11. A.M.—At 9 I returned to the camp with Mr. Tuckey and Mr. Bowden, and we dind with Mr. Houston.

Saturday, 12. A.M.—A party of 6 men went out armd in search of 5 convicts that had excaped into the woods; 8 convicts in all absent. A.M.—At 11 all the officers military and civil attended with the Governor and Capt. Woodriff to the parade, and from thence all the convicts at divine service; the sermon preachd was to return Almighty God thanks for our safe arrival here. 2 P.M.—A party went and dind on board the *Ocean* with Capt. Marthew. I stayd there—

Sunday, 13—all night. Lieut. Pateshall kill a kangaroo.[2]

---

[1] NOTE.—Mr. William Collins was the Governor's cousin. He was afterwards Port Officer of Hobart Town and married the sister of Mr. James Hobbs. The names of the six men (convicts) who accompanied Mr. William Collins in this open boat expedition to Port Jackson were:—1. John Rawlinson; 2. Urias Alexander; 3. Christopher Forshas; 4. Wm. Thomas; 5. James Price; 6. David Wakefield. For this service they all received a conditional pardon.

[2] NOTE.—The Rev. Mr. Knopwood has entered the transactions of two days in one division of the page; the Saturday's business being in the margin. The entry is copied exactly as it is in the original.—[C.]

Monday, 14. A.M.—At 9 we came to the camp. What officers could be spared from H.M. ship *Calcutta* came and dind at the camp off the kangaroo, and very excellent it was, the dimensions as follows:—

	F.	I.
Length from the end of the tail to the nose	7	6
Of the hind leg	2	11
Fore leg	1	8
Head	0	7
Ear	0	6
Neck	0	10
Tail	3	6
Yard	0	6
Stone bag	0	3
Breadth of the skin at the haunches	2	6
Fore quarter	1	8

It weigh'd when skin'd, the head off, liver, heart, and entrails taken out, 68 lbs.; the skin of a dark brown color.

Tuesday, 15. A.M. At 2 p.m. I went on board the *Calcutta*, where I slep; at 5 p.m. the dimensions of a sea elephant killd on shore by the barge's crew of H.M. Ship *Calcutta*, at Port Phillip:—

	F.	I.
Length from the nose to the end of the tail	12	0
The round of the body	5	2

Weight more than 200 lbs.
The skin of a light-brown colour; the head like a bull-dog.

Wednesd, 16. A.M.—At 4 the *Ocean* transport, Capt. Merthew, drop'd down near the harbours mouth; at 8 brought too, the tide much against him; at 9 I arrived at the Camp; at ½-past, five of the convicts that had escaped were brought to the camp; at 11 burid the ship's cook of the *Calcutta* on shore. In the aft I went a shooting and kill a teal; Lieut. Dowers and a party came and supd with me.

Thursday, 17. A.M.—At 4 I went a shooting; no success; at 8 returned. At half-past ten Capt. Woodriff arrived at the camp with many of his officers that could be spared. 11 the garrison was under arms; ½-past all the convicts were clean dressd, and assembled on the left side of the Parade, and the Lieut. Governor's Commission was read by the Rev. R. Knopwood, Chaplain to the Colony; when that was done, the Military fird three vollies, and all gave three cheers to His Honor. The day would have passd off with the greatest joy, but His Excellency[1] was obliged to punish the 5 deserters that were brought to the camp to deterr others from deserting. P.M.—[2]   Captain Merthew got out of the Bay of Port Phillip. [*Note in margin.*]—*Ocean* arrid at Pt. Jackson on the 24 November.

Friday, 18. A.M.—At 8 we observd H.M. Ship *Calcutta* standing for Arthers Seat; and at 0 Lieut. Johnson, of the Royal Marines, Mr. Humphries, and self went in my boat for the first time to Yellows Point; we caught some fish, but I killd a couple of very handsome

---
[1] So written.——[2] Partially indistinct.

[specimens] of Banks Cockatwo; we returnd to dinner. See the *Calcutta* at anchor. At 5 hard rain and a dreadful tempest, which continued till late at night.

Saturday, 19. A.M.—At 11 see the *Calcutta* move her station toward Arthers Seat; at 8 three of the deserters returned to the camp. We receivd letters from the *Calcutta's* boat that the natives had obliged the woodmen to return on board. The *Calcutta's* boat went arm'd and relivd the men; the number of blacks were about 400. At 12 a party were sent to pitch a tent near the Governors garden, to give notice if the blacks were approaching the camp. This morn I sewd coucumbers, and onion seeds, and melons. At 4 p.m. heavy rain, with dreadful thunder and lightning.

Sunday, 20. A.M.—At 7 H.M. Ship *Calcutta* was under weigh, and standing for Fresh Water River. At 11 the military, &c., &c., all assembled; at $\frac{1}{2}$-past all attended the Governor at divine service. The day was very fine. At 8 a.m. rain.

Monday, 21. A.M.—Moderate breezes and clear. At 2 p.m. the thermomiter stood at 96 in the shade, and in the sun, by the side of the marquee, 118°. At 4 Mr. Harris and self, with Stewart, a convict, went in my boat a fishing; I caught three maiden rays. We returned to the camp by 8 in the eve; it very soon came on to blow and rain.

Tuesday, 22. A.M.—Strong breezes; at 11 rain; $\frac{1}{2}$-past, a heavy storm of thunder and lightning and hard rain with squalls. P.M.—At 1 more moderate. Receivd a pocket compass from the store.

Wed. 23. A.M.—In the morn Mr. Humphries, Lieut. Johnson, and self went in my boat to the Yellow Bluff to catch fish, but finding the wind too much we were obliged to return. In the afternoon I kill a teal. Continual rain with thunder and lightning.

Thursday, 24. A.M.—At 8 rain; 10, fine settled wr. 3 p.m. I walked to the opposite shore, across the island to the S.S.E. part of the shore; see a great many of the Banktian cockatoos.

Friday, 25. A.M.—At 10 Mr. Bowden and self walkd to the opposite shore to Arthers Bonnet, but found very few shells, the tide come in too rapidly. At $\frac{1}{2}$-past 7 [p.m.] Mr. M. Collough arrivd in the camp from H.M. Ship *Calcutta*; he walkd it from the Fresh River where ship layd watering [*The Yarra*], not less than 45 or 50 miles, a very great undertaking. He and a party sup'd with me. At 9 Sarjent Thorns wife was deliverd of a boy—the *first child born on the settlement of Port Phillip*.[1]

Saturday, 26. A.M.—Very unwell. Employed erecting a new signal staff near my marquee. Mr. M. Collough and self dind at the mess. In the eve I walked to the Governors gardens. At 11 p.m. rain with a fresh breeze.

Sunday, 27. A.M.—This morn at 10 the thermomiter stood at 96 in the shade. At 11 the military, &c., attended divine service. At $\frac{1}{2}$-past 12 continual thunder at a distance to the N.W. of the encampment. P.M.—At 4 the tempest increas'd, and at 9 it was very violent with rain.

Monday, 28. A.M.—At 9 Lieut. M. Culloch, Mr. Humphries, and self went in my boat to the Fresh Water River, on the E.S.E. side of

---

[1] William James Hobart Thorne still [1878] lives, and resides at Lewisham, Tasmania.

the Bay, where H.M. Ship *Calcutta* was watering; they were cutting wood. The distance across from the camp to the ship not less than 30 miles per water. At 7 we got on board; at ½-past it raind and blew very hard, with thunder and lightning. That eve Mr. Pattshall with the watering party left the shore, having waterd the ship.[1]

Tuesday, 29. A.M.—The wind blowing contrary, H.M. Ship *Calcutta* could not leave her station; all hands remaind on board.

Wednesd, 30. A.M.—This morn we weighd anchor and went to Arthers Seat; it blew strong breezes that we could not get on shore.

[The 3 following entries refer to the *Calcutta* taking in 55 tons of fresh water at the Yarra; information which was of course known to Mr. Knopwood, who obtained these entries from that ship's log.—*Ed.*]

Remarks on board H.M. ship *Calcutta* at Port Phillip and Hobson's Bay.

Friday, 18 [*Novr.*] Wind West. A.M.—Light breezes from the west. At 6 weighd and made sail from One-tree Point; launch attending to the N. side of the channel. At 10 receivd intelligence that the carpenters at Arthers Seat wanted ammunition and assistance, he being visited by the natives in great numbers. At 30 past 10 passd the camp at South, dist. 5 or 6 miles. At noon Lat. obsd. 38° 19 south. P.M.—Strong squalls with thunder and lightning and rain. At 2 anchored with the b. bower in 6 fms., fine sand; the camp bearing W. b S. ¼ S.; Arthers Seat E. ½ S. and the end of the island, shoal N.E. ½ N. Boats employd getting off the timber from under Arthers Seat.

Sunday, 20. Wind S.W. A.M.—Fresh breezes and cloudy wr. At 5, weighd and made sail for the river, boats sounding a head. At 15 past 5, past the buoy on the Island Shoal. Steerd N.N.E. for the river, having 10 and 11 fms., 3 miles off shore. At 30 past 9, shortend sail and preparing to anchor. At 10, came too with the best bower in 4¾ fms., fine sand. The enterance of the river at E.S.E., off shore 1½ mile.[2]

Wednesday, 30. Wind N.W. A.M.—Strong breezes and squally wr. At 5, cleard haws and unmoord ship and hove short on the small bower. At 9, sent a pety officer and 2 men to fetch the launch down the harbour. At 30 past 9, weighd and made sail, the launch following Strong breezes and squally; hauld ranges on the cables. Course steerd S.S.W. Soundings from 6 to 10 fms., fine sand and clay. At 11, shortend sail, not seeing the buoy on the Island Shoal. Supposd to have been washd away or sunk. At 30 past 11, shortend sail and came too with the small bower in 6 fms., clay bottom—

The entrance of the Harbour	...	West.
The Camp	...	W.S.W. ½ W.
Yellow Bluff	...	S.W. b. W.
Arthers Seat	...	E.S.E. ½ E., off shore 1½ mile.

[1] This day, it is stated by Labilliere, that Richard Garratt, prisoner, was married to Hannah Harvey, free.—The first marriage.—*Ed.*
[2] Off the present Alfred Graving Dock, Williamstown.

At 12, a very severe gale—a hurricane. The wind at that time shifted round the compass with dreadful lightning and thunder, and heavy swell from the N.W. P.M.—Rain, with squalls at intervals.[1]

[Journal resumed.]

Remarks at Sullivan Bay Camp, &c., December 1, 1803.

Thursday, 1. A.M.—Strong breezes and a very great surge. No boat able to go on shore or to the camp.

Friday, 2. A.M.—Strong breezes and rain, with thunder and lightning. No boats able to go [to] the camp, or on shore, the surf being so much.

Saturday, 3. A.M.—At 9, the weather being moderate Mr. Humphries and self landed, with Lieut. Houston, at the bottom of Athers Seat. We walkd to the camp, no boat being able to go up, the distance of the walk about 12 miles. That day I diud with the officers of the mess.

Sunday, 4. A.M.—Moderate breezes and fair. At $\frac{1}{2}$ past 10, the military parade. At 11, both civil and military went to divine service, and all the setlers and convicts. H.M. ship *Calcutta* advanced a little way to One Tree Point.

Monday, 5. A.M.—Moderate breezes and fair. H.M. ship *Calcutta* at 10 anchored at her old station off One Tree Point.

Tuesday, 6. Some of the officers of the *Calcutta* came on shore. Mr. Brumley [Bromley], surgeon, and self, with a party, dind with Mr. Houston off goose at his tent. At 6, Mr. Brumley, Humphries, and Harris and self, went to my summer house, where we smokd till near 1 A.M.

Wednesday, 7. Thermomter 96, at 10 A.M. A.M.—$\frac{1}{2}$ past 10, Mr. Brumley, Harris, Humphries, and self, went to the S. b. West part of the coast with our guns and fish spears. The tide coming in we returnd to the camp. In our way there I killd the most beautiful bird of the bittern species, havi—[indistinct]. P.M.—At 9, we observd a native fire near Arthers Seat. $\frac{1}{2}$ past, lightning at a distance.

Thursday, 8. A.M.—This morn I walked to the S.West part of the coast to see whether there was a sail coming from Pt. Jackson, being in great expectation of one every day. Mr. Tuckey, and a party of the *Calcutta* officers, on shore.

Friday, 9. A.M.—At 4, Lieut. Tuckey, R.N., McCulloch, R. Marines; Mr. White, Purser of H.M. ship *Calcutta*; Lieut. Johnson, R.M.; Mr. Bowden, Surgeon; Mr. Harris, Surveyor; with 3 soldiers armd, and their survants, set off for Western Port. Mr. Sladden and self engaged on some business. That Lee had been writing again Mr. Clark and Mr. Ingle.

Saturday, 10. A.M.—At 11, Mr. Sladden and self sat till 3 P.M. enquiring into an accusation that Lee should bring forward agst Manning for coining. After a minute investigation found it only a malicious transaction.

I set my white hen on 21 egg this morn.

---

[1] The log-book of the *Calcutta* was found by Labilliere who gives these entries in full.—[*Ed.*]

Sunday, 11. A.M.—At 10, the military, setlers, and convicts, asembled. At 11, performd divine service.

Monday, 12. A.M.—At 10, a signal was made from the post on the S.W. side of the island that a ship appeared in sight, which we immediately communicated to the *Calcutta*. At 11, I went on board to dinner. At 4, we obserd the ship to be the *Ocean* transpord, Capt. Merthew, taken into Government service by Governor King for 4 months. The ship brought Mr. Collins and the crew that went to Port Jackson, and dispatches to Lieut. G. Collins. By him we were informd that there was a settlement formd on Van Dandemens Land by a part of the convicts, male and female, under the command of Lieut. Bowen, River du Nord[1], the River Derwent, on the south shore of Van Diemens Land; and that the *Ocean* and *Lady Nelson*, which sailed on the 28 of November, and the *Ocean* on the 29 of November, have come to Pt. Phillip to remove us there, or where the Lieut. Governor should think proper. Early this morn Lee and another convict went to the Governors garden and procured a gun and ammunition from the gardner, by saying that he came from the Governor, and had orders to receive it.

Tuesday, 13. A.M.—At 10, Capt. Woodriff came on shore. The Lieut. Governor informd us that H.M. ship *Calcutta* was going to Port Jackson on Sunday 18 of this month. I went on board, and there I slept.

Wednesday, 14. A.M.—At 11, a signal was made that a strange sail was in sight. At 3 P.M. she came to an anchor. The *Francis*, schooner, from Port Jackson, sent round by order of Governor King, for to remove the settlement to Van Diemens Land. He brought dispatches from thence for that purpose. At 7, I returnd to the camp. The party of gentlemen returnd from Western Port. Lieut. Tuckey slept in my marquee, *Francis*, schooner.

Thursday, 15. A.M.—At 9 Mr. Brumley, surgeon of H.M. Ship *Calcutta*, came on the shore and took breakfast with me. We dind with the officers at the camp. This eve he and a party smokd their pipes with me.

Friday, 16. A.M.—At 9 the *Francis*, that came from Port Jackson, removed near the camp to be repaird. At 7 P.M. I went on board H.M. Ship *Calcutta*. Capt. Woodriff came on shore and took his leave of me in my marquee. Set the spotted hen.

Saturday, 17. A.M.—At 11 H.M. Ship *Calcutta* moved her station nearer the harbour's mouth, to Sandy Bay. At 3 P.M. she anchord. At 4 got under weigh again, and moved within 2 mile and ½ of the mouth of the harbour. At 10 P.M. Mr. Collins brought Government dispaches. Mr. Harris, Humphries, Collins, Capt. Merthew supd there. This eve Lieut. Pateshall and Lt. Dowers, Lt. M. Culloch went and caught some very fine crawfish. I took leave of Capt. Woodriff.

Sunday, 18. A.M.—At 6 I took leave of all the officers of H.M. Ship *Calcutta;* took my boat and went to the camp, where I arrivd at ½-past 8. At 9 I heard that H.M. Ship got out of the bay of Pt. Phillip,

---

[1] This was the name given by D'Entrecasteaux, subsequently by Hayes of the Bombay Marine called the Derwent, on the south shore of Van Diemen's Land. Bowen's settlement was established at Risdon, so named after the 2nd officer of the *Lady Nelson* which vessel conveyed the party.

and was standing with a fair breeze to Port Jackson. The Lt. Governor is under the necessity of directing that the people who are employed in the preparations which are carrying on for removing the settlement do continue to work to-day, by which order divine service will not be performd. At 4 P.M. I dind with the Lt. Governor.

Monday, 19. A.M.—Fresh breezes. The convicts employd erecting a warf for to load the ships. At 3 P.M. I walked to the S.W. side of the harbour to see whither we could observe any ships, but did not; returnd home at 7. Pritchard ran away from the camp.

Tuesday, 20. A.M.—Fresh breeze N.W. At ½-past 12 a strong N.W. wind, with very great heat. With the marquee all open in front the thermomiter was 92 in the shade. The people employd carrying on the warf to remove the settlement. At 5 P.M. the wind changed to S.W.; rain.

Wednesday, 21. A.M.—Moderate breezes and clear. At 2 P.M. took my boat and went a fishing; caught some very fine maiden reys near Arthers Seat. The wind at 5 came against us, and with very great difficulty we reachd the camp that night. At 10 rain.

Thursday, 22. A.M.—People employd at the getty. P.M.—Extreme cold, and hard gales from the S.W.

Friday, 23. A.M.—More moderate, but cold, and high sea from the S.W. side of the coast across the land.

Saturday, 24. A.M.—At ½-past 9 Mr. Collins, in a large boat, and the *Francis* saild to Port Dalrymple, Vandiemens Land. I went a fishing and caught 8 very fine crayfish, one mullet, and two dotterel I shot. I may with truth say I went out for birds and fish for my dinner, not having any to dress but a few peas. At 10 very fine weather. I sent the Governor crayfish, and the gentlemen of the mess and other friends.

Sunday, Xms. day, 25. A.M.—The weather very fine. At ½-past 10 the military assembled. At 11 civil military setlers and convicts, with the Governor, attended divine service; Xms. sermon. After service I publickly baptizd Sarjent Thorn's child. The Governor, Lieut. Johnson, Mrs. Powers, and Mrs. WhiteHead stood for the child, the first born in the colony; the Gov. namd it Hobert. The Governor invited me to dine, but was engaged prior. At 1 P.M., the thermomiter in the shade 82, I dind with the gentlemen of the mess at Port Phillip. Last night a most daring robbery was committed by some person or persons, in the Commissary's marque. While he was in bed they stole a gun which was hung up near the side of the bed, and took a pair of boots which were at the bed side. The sentry saw a man come from it, but thought he was his servant. The hospital tent was likewise robbd.

Monday, 26. A.M.—I walkd to the S. side of the island to see the surf, which was very great. I dind with the Lieut. Governor at 4. At 10 smokd a pipe with Mr. J anson.[1] ½-past ajornd to the Commissary's marquees. 11 the drum beat to arms by reason of some of the convicts had made their escape. The pigeons set.

Tuesday, 27. A.M.—At 9 Lieut. Lord, of the Royal Marines, and self walkd to the south side of the shore with our guns. At 3 P.M. we returnd. The eve a party came and smokd their pipes. At 9, 6

---

[1] Properly, J'Anson.

convicts endeavourd to make their escape; they were beset by a look-out party and one man shot, very much wounded. At 10 much lightning and rain.

Wed., 28. A.M.—At 1 Corporal Sutton returnd with the information of 1 man, by name Charles Shore, was shot and much hurt; a cart and men were sent to bring him to the camp. Mr. Bowden went for the man and one taken prisoner. At ½-past 11 I examind the prisoners, and carried the report to the Governor. At ½-past 8 Anchors was detaind by the order of the Governor and taken to the gard house.

Thursday, 29. A.M.—At 9 rain and the weather very cold. The people getting off stores to load the *Ocean*. At 4 I dind with the Lieut. Governor, who communicated to me the purport of a letter of the necessity that the civil establishment should form themselves into a patrol of a nigh in case of an insurrection. The thermomiter 63 at 3.

Friday, 30. A.M.—The morn much finer than for some days. The people employ'd in getting off the guns from the warf. At 7 P.M. a party returnd from searching all round by Arthers Seat and across to Shank Point after some prisoners that escap'd when the man was shot. Rain in the morn. One of the soldiers of the signal tent was shot at by the deserters from the camp, convicts.

Saturday, 31. A.M.—Moderate breezes and clear. At 6 P.M. the thermomiter 75. No information respecting the deserters from the camp. At 7 Capt. Merthew, of the *Ocean* transport, calld upon me. Great fires made at a distance from the camp; supposed set on fire by the party that escaped from the camp. At 10 we see a native fire across the bay, on the N.W. side of it, towards the lagoon; the natives were very distinctly observed by the fire. The people employd loading the *Ocean* transport. Two soldiers of the R. Marines taken up and carried to the guard house accus'd of mutany. Deserters from the camp, convicts—Mac Allennan, George Pye, Pritchard, M. Warner, Wm. Buckley; Charles Shaw, wounded and brought to the camp; Page, taken same time when Shaw *was shot*, G. Lee, and Wm. Gibson.

Sunday, *January* 1. A.M.—The Lieut. Governor, being desirous of expediting the removing the stores as fast as possible for loading the *Ocean* transport for our embarking to Van Diemens Land, is under the necessity of ordering the prisoners to work this day as on other. At 10 it was a very cold day, with rain. P.M.—At 4 Mr. Janson and self dind with the Governor, and had ducks and green peas, with fresh beans. In the eve observd fires of the natives.

Monday, 2. A.M.—The morn very cold. At 2 P.M. the civil officers met to consult upon the plan of the association; and at 9 P.M. Mr. Janson and self kept watch; 11, much rain. Officers of the night watch—Revd. R. K., Mr. Janson; C. Sign, London.

Tuesday, 3. A.M.—At ½ past 4 we went to bed. Report at 10 to the Governor all well in and near the camp. P.M.—At 3 great fires near the camp, made by convicts. Officers of the night watch—Mr. Fosbrooks, Mr. Hopley; C. Sign, Exeter.

Wednesday, 4. A.M.—Moderate and fair. Some of the civil officers being unwell, at 9 P.M. I go on the night watch; a very fine night. At 12 all well in and near the camp. Officers of the night watch—Revd. R. Kd., Mr. Bowden; C. Sign, Bath.

By His Honor David Collins, Esq., Lieutenant-Governor of a Settlement or Settlements to be formed in Bass's Straits, New South Wales.

A plan of an association of the civil officers of the settlement having been submitted by them to the Lieut.-Governor, he is pleased to approve thereof, and to authorise them, which he hereby does, to carry the same into effect.

The most probable means of this association rendering a service to the settlement is principally by forming a night watch, to patrole from the beating of the taptoo to that of the reveillie, during which time they will search such places as may be deemed necessary for the discovery of any felony, trespass, or misdemeanour; and for the apprehension and securing for examination any person or persons who may appear to them concerned therein, either by entrance into any hut or dwelling, or by such other means as circumstances may render expedient.

Cognizance is to be taken during the day, as well as by night, of such convicts as may sell or barter their clothing or provisions, as well as of such as gamble for either of the above articles or money; and, upon detection, instantly place them in confinement.

Upon receiving any information of a robbery having been committed during the night, they will use the most effectual means to trace out the offender or offenders, so that they may be brought to justice.

One of the members of the association will, at the morning parade, report the occurrences of the night to the Lieut.-Governor, to whom they may have access at all hours.

When challenged by a sentinel, the officer on duty will give the countersign, which shall be sent to the Revd. Mr. Knopwood for that purpose at sunset.

The persons who are joined with them in this duty will, when challenged, answer "Night watch," and advancing to the sentinel make themselves known as such. To prevent mistakes, their names will be left with the guard. As the military are to give every assistance they may require, so they will be cautious not to interfere with them in the discharge of their duty.

Two of the undermentioned gentlemen will meet each night, taking with them four of the persons named hereafter; and they will patrol at such hours as may be best calculated not to interfere with the military rounds or patroles.

A tent will be pitched for their accommodation in the rear of the guard tent; and the front of the tent is to be considered as their alarm post, where all the members of this association will assemble and wait for orders when the drum shall beat to arms.

The gentlemen will each be provided with a brace of pistols, and suitable ammunition. The other persons will each be furnished with a short staff.

This association is to take place on Monday the 2d of January 1804.

Officers of the association and principles of the night watch :—

Revd. Mr. Knopwood,	Mr. Harris,
Mr. Janson,	Mr. Fosbrook,
Mr. Bowden,	Mr. Hopley.
Mr. Humphrey,	

Subordinates of the night watch :—

Mr. John Ingle,

Wm. Thomas Stocker,	Matthew Power,
Andrew Whitehead,	James Groves,
John Boothman,	Francis Shipman.

1. John Sculler.	4. James Taylor.
2. Patrick M. Carty.	5. John Hindes.
3. John Crates.	6. Sanders Van Strutten.

Crombe.

Given under my hand, at Head Quarters, Sullivan Bay, Port Phillip, this 1 day of January 1804.

DAVID COLLINS, Lieut.-Governor.

The 6 soldiers mutiners from Giberalter.
Crombe died at Port Phillip.

Thursday, 5. A.M.—Men employd in loading the *Ocean* transport. P.M.—Moderate and fair wr. At 9 P.M. we musterd all the prisoners, fearing that any should be absent. I set up late looking out after some prisoners. Officer of the night watch—Mr. Hopley; C. Sign, Penzance.

Friday, 6. A.M.—At 5 Mr. Wm. Stocker and 2 men and self armd went to the harbours mouth. Did not find the trace of any convicts. At 3 P.M. returned. Killed a red bill, &c., at 9. Rain. Officer of the night watch—Mr. Harris; C. Sign, Exmouth.

Saturday, 7. A.M.—At ½ past 2 P.M. the drum beat to arms; the military and all the officers of the association, with the subordinates, attended. Each man received a brace of pistols and 4 rounds of cartridge and balls, and 1 lb. of bread, and 1 lb. of beef, ½ a pint of spirits. At ½ past 3, 9 soldiers armd with the same rounds of cartridge, sarjant-major (MacCauley), 1 drummer, and the gentlemen of the association and subordinates—in the whole, military, 11 ; association, 18—went in search of some convicts that had escaped from the camp. We all went first to the lagoon and to the harbour mouth to the west, from thence to the flagstaff to the south, beyond Needle Point ; then took a course S.E., and back to the camp, which we reached at 7 P.M. We found many places where they had been, and some of their things. It was computed that the distance we walked could not be less than 50 miles, some said more.

Sunday, 8. A.M.—Dark cloudy wr. People employd loading the *Ocean*, by which means we had not divine service performd. P.M.—At 8 rain ; 9, fine wr. The thermomiter at 64. My brown hen had 7 young chickings. Officers of the night watch—Bowden and Fosbrook ; C. Sign, Tinmouth.

Monday, 9. A.M.—All the morn engaged on justice business. P.M.—Clear wr. Receivd of Governor Collins three gallons of spirits. Officers of the night watch—Mr. Harris, Mr. Hopley; C. Sign, Torbay.

Tuesday, 10. A.M.—Moderate and clear ; people employed variously. At 2 P.M. Governor Collins, Lieut. Lord, Mrs. Powers, and self went in the Governor's boat on board the *Ocean*, and dind with Capt. Merthew ;

at 7 we returned to the camp. On duty—R. Kd., Mr. Janson ; C. Sign, Norwich.

Wednesd., 11. A.M.—Very hot day at ½ past 11. Punished 2 men, Taylor and Blackmore, for contempt of the military, with 100 lashes each. At 12 heard the report of a gun at a distance from the harbour; sent a man to the flagstaff ; 10 minutes past hear the report of cannon. At 2 P.M. Capt. Merthew came to the camp and informed the Governor that the report of cannon was the 1 mate seal'd one of the guns from the *Ocean*. My man returned from fishing, and caught 2 rock. In the eve at 9 we observd 2 large native fires on N.W. Therm. 92 & 94, with all the canvas down. On duty—Fosbrook and Bowden ; C. Sign, Hope.

Thursday, 12. A.M.—Moderate and hazy. At 2 P.M. observd a schooner coming into the Bay ; at 3 she came to anchor near the *Ocean* transport ; at 4 a boat landed from her ; she came from Pt. Jackson, ship namd the *Edwin*. In the eve Mr. Janson, Lieut. Johnson, R.M., came and smokd a pipe ; at ½ past 11 I went a round in the camp to see if all was quiet, when I unfortunately spraind my ancle, very bad. On duty—Mr. Harris and Hopley ; C. Sign, Ramsgate.

Friday, 13. A.M.—Extremely hot this day, and confid to my marquee. P.M.—People employd in loading the *Ocean* transport. At 7 the Lt. Gov. requested I would not attempt going on guard this night. On duty—Mr. Janson ; C. Sign, Broadstairs.

Saturday, 14. A.M.—Rather better ; at 11 the Lt. Governor called on me ; at 4 P.M. the thermomiter 92 ; at ½ past 6 the thermomiter 76. This day twelvemonth I received my appointment as chaplain to the settlement or settlemens of New S. Wales. On duty—Mr. Fosbrook, Bowden ; C. Sign, Settingbourne.

Sunday, 15. A.M.—At 7, rain. ½ past 10, it blew very hard, with rain, which continued till ½ pas 12 P.M. At 4 thunder and lightning. At 8 information was given from the *Ocean* that Capt. Merthew had 2 men drownd by the boat upsetting from Swan Island. At 9 the tempest very severe. On duty—Harris and Hopley.

Monday, 16. A.M.—The day very hot. At 1 P.M. MacAllnan [McAllenon] went to the Lieut. Governors garden and surrendered himself, with a gun that was Mr. Fosbrooks the Commissarys. At 2 he was brought into the camp. On duty—Mr. Janson ; C. Sign, Henley.

Tuesday, 17. A.M.—Engaged all the morn in taking the deposition of Dan Mac Allenan, the prisoner that escaped with Pritchard and the party when Charles Shaw was shot. Saild for Kings Island the *Edwin*. On duty—Mr. Fosbrook and Bowden ; C. Sign, Woodstock.

Wed.. 18. A.M.—The day very fine. At 11 the thermomiter stood at 82. At 1 P.M. ther. 92 in the shade, 110 in the sun. At 1 the military assembled on the parade in their new cloaths and fird 3 excellent vollies. At ¾ past 3 a hut belonging to Lieut. Johnsons, of the R. Marines, took fire and burnt down, with another of Lieut. Lords, and very near setting the marque's on fire. Observation of the thermomiter taken by Mr. Harris in his marque :—

Hours.	Shade.	Sun.
A.M.—7	68	...
12 noon	92	117

	Hours.	Shade.	Sun.
P.M.—	½ past 1	97	...
	2	...	127
	¼ past 2	101	130
	½ „ 2	102	132
	3	102	120
	10	83	...

This has been by far the hotest day since we came to the camp. On duty—Mr. Harris and Mr. Hopley ; C. Sign, Charlotte.

Thursday, 19. A.M.—At 9 a strong hot N.W. wind, and the country all on fire about Arther Seat, and to the N.E. of it. At 11 rain. P.M., at 4, rain. At 9 very hard rain, with lightning and thunder. On duty —Mr. Janson ; C. Sign, Crane.

Friday, 20. A.M.—Moderate wr. and cool. At 2 P.M. came to anchor the *Ann* from Pt. Jackson, with dispatches from Govr. King to Lieut. G. Collins. On duty—Mr. Fosbrook and Bowden ; C. Sign, Baker.

Saturday, 21. A.M.—Engaged all the morn on business, taking the deposition of Chs. Shaw. At 1 P.M. information was given that 2 vessells were in sight from the Flag-staff, standing towards this harbour. At 3 a brig came in sight. At 4 came to anchor the *Lady Nelson*, brig, from Pt. Jackson, and the *Edwin* from Kings Island. On duty— Harris and Hopley ; Adams.

Sunday, 22. A.M.—At 6 the *Lady Nelson*, brig, and *Ann*, cutter, anchord opposite to the camp very near the jetty end. At 9 very hot. ½ past 10 the military assembled. At 11 the Lt. Gov., civil and military officers, attended divine service, and all the convicts. At 1 we observd the country on fire all round Arthers Seat, and to the N.East. At 9 I went upon guard, my let (leg ?) being very much better. On duty—Rev. R. Knopwood, Mr. Janson ; C. Sign, Simondz.

Monday, 23. A.M.—At 11 observd a large fire near the camp, between the Yellow Bluff and the camp. Set upon business respecting Hartley at the mess room. Lieut. Sladden and Mr. Harris for the first time there. On duty—Mr. Fosbrook and Bowden ; C. Sign, Champion.

Tuesday, 24. At 11 A.M. the Court sat again and finishd the business. At 10, 1 Lieut. R. Marines went on board with 20 soldiers. At 2 P.M. 120 of the convicts went on board the *Ocean* transport with their baggage. At 3 one of the prisoners that had been absent a long time returnd in a very weak state ; his name Jones. On duty—Harris and Hopley ; C. Sign, Ellen.

Wed., 25. At 10 A.M. all the setlers that were to embark on board the *Lady Nelson* (Mr. Simonds, Commander) went on board. Employd packing up all day. At 4 P.M. I dind with Lieut. Johnson at the mess. Eve, smokd a pipe with Mr. J anson. All the convicts that were to embark on board the *Ocean* went on board. On duty—Knopwood and Janson ; C. Sign, Carr.

Thursday, 26. At 10 A.M. struck my marquee and sent every thing on board. I dind with Mr. J anson. At ½ past 5 p.m. the Lieut. Governor and self went in his boat, and at 6 got on board the *Ocean* transport to take our passage to the Derwent River. Officers on board —Lieut. Lord, R. Marines ; Mr. Harris, surveyor; Mr. Humphrys, mineralogist ; Mr. Bowden, assist. surgeon. We engaged to give Capt. Merthew 4 shillings per diem and to find us with every thing.

Remarks on board the *Ocean*, transport, Port Phillip Harbour,
January 1804.

Friday, 27. Wind N. East. A.M.—The wind moderate. At ½ past 1 p.m. a fresh breeze. At 2 weighd anchor and went to the Harbours mouth. At 3 anchord—all on board.

Saturday, 28. At 8 the wind at S.East, unable to sail. All remain [on] board the *Ocean*. We observd a very large fire near the camp.

Sunday, 29. A.M.—At 10 Capt. Merthew, Mr. Humphrys, and self, went on shore for a walk. Returnd at 4 p.m. to dinner. We heard from the camp that many of the natives were about it, and that one was in the camp.

Monday, 30. A.M.—At ½ past 4 weighd anchor, and made all sail out of the harbour of Port Phillip.[1] At 3 p.m. I dind with the Governor. At 6, the wind being still against us, we were in sight of land about Port Phillip. At 7 the *Lady Nelson*, brig, in company.

Tuesday, 31. A.M.—The wind contry.; made very little progress during the night. At 9 the *Lady Nelson*, brig, in company. At 7[2] the wind still unfavourable, S.E. b. E. Made little progress; but the wind a very fresh breeze.

Distance from Port Phillip to the River Derwent per sea 420 miles.

Ship *Ocean*, transport, from Port Phillip towards the River Derwent, Capt. Merthew. Owners, Mr. Hurriss, of Newcastle. Jan. 30, 1804.

February.

Monday, 30. Wind S. b. W., S.S.E. A.M.—At 3 hove short. At 4 weighd, with variable light airs. ½ past 5 came round when on the bar with the heavy swell and the ripplings, occasioned by the ebc tide running so fast out of the harbour. Tkd. ship to the westward. 8, Cape Shank bore S. 68° E. Harb. mouth N. 52. E. Noon, Cape

---

[1] "Nothing could offer a more imposing picture of reposing solitude than the wilds of Port Phillip on our first arrival. Here Contemplation, with her musing sister Melancholy, might find an undisturbed retreat. Often at the calm hour of evening I have wandered through the woods—

"'Where the rude axe with heaved stroke,
    Was never heard the nymphs to daunt,
    Or fright them from their hallowed haunts.'

"The last hymn of the feathered choristers to the setting sun, and the soft murmurs of the breeze, faintly broke the death-like silence that reigned around; while the lightly trodden path of the solitary savage, or the dead ashes of his fire, alone pointed out the existence of human beings. In the course of a very few weeks the scene was greatly altered; lanes were cut in the woods for the passage of the timber carriages; the huts of the woodmen were erected beneath the sheltering branches of the lofty trees; the "busy hum" of their voices, and the sound of their axes, reverberating through the woods, denoted the exertions of social industry, and the labours of civilization. At other times, sitting on the carriage of a gun, in front of the Camp, I have contemplated with succeeding emotions of pity, laughter, and astonishment, the scene before me. When I viewed so many of my fellow men sunk, some of them from a rank in life equal or superior to my own, and by their crimes degraded to a level with the basest of mankind; when I saw them *naked*, wading to their shoulders in water to unlade the boats, while a burning sun struck its meridian rays upon their uncovered heads, or yoked to and sweating under a timber carriage, the wheels of which were sunk up to the axle in sand, I only considered their hapless lot, and the remembrance of their vices was for a moment absorbed in the greatness of their punishment."—[*Tuckey*, p. 185.]

[2] Correctly copied.

Shank S. 83. E. Entrance Port Phillip N. 56° E. P.M.—Moderate breezes and clear wr. 4, Cape Albeny, Otway, S. 51 W., dist. 6 lgs., *Lady Nelson*, brig, in company.

Tuesday, 31. Wind East. A.M.—Moderate breezes and hazy. At noon fresh breezes. P.M.—Do. wr., the land of Pt. Phillip in sight. At 8 tkd. ship. 12, do. wr.

(NOTE.—Entries for the days above have been made before, only differently worded.—C.)

Wed., Feb. 1. Wind E. b. N., E. ½ N. A.M.—Moderate breezes and hazy. ½ past 6, tkd. ship At noon fresh breezes and hazy wr., *Lady Nelson*, brig, *not* in sight. P.M.—Do. wr. 10, tkd. ship to the southward.

Thursday, 2. Wind N.W. A.M.—At 3 light airs and hazy wr. Stood to the east. At noon see the land. Cape Liptrap N. 35 E., and Willsons Promentary S. 77° E., dist. off shore 3 lgs. P.M.—Light breezes and hazy. At 4, Willson Promtary., N. 80° E. Round Island, South. 76° E., dist. 3 lgs. At the end of Willsons Pro. is a very remarkable rock. with a deep cave, a great way in. The Promantary very high hills. Round Island very beautiful and exceedingly high. Sounded 35 fathoms.

Friday, 3. Wind N.N.W., E. ¼ N., east, E.b.N., E. ⅓ S., N.E.b.N. A.M.—At 2 wore ship. Light airs and variable, with rain, and severe lightning to the east. ½-past 3 wore ship. 6 Round Island N. 11° W. dist. 6 miles. ½-past 10 tkd. ship to the nthward. 11 Hogen's Grop. S. 11 E. dist. 5 miles; fresh breezes and squally, with rain. Hogan's Groop a cluster of islands. 1 P.M.—Barren Islands west, Hogain's Groop S.E., and Kent's Groop S. 71° W. ½-past 1 tkd. ship; in spanker. 3 tkd. ship; split main top gal. sail, unbent it and bent another. Spoke the schooner *John* from Sidney bound to Kings Island. At 4 Hogain's bore S. 25° E.; strong gales and squally. At 5 Hoggain's Group bore S.E. 3 miles; bore up to run into the straits again. At 7 close reeft the top sails. At 8 Round Island N. ¼ W. dist. 5 miles. At ½-past 11 saw some of the islands: wore ship; strong gales and squally, with rain; severe lightning from the S.E.

Saturday. 4. Wind East, E. ½ N., W.N.W., west, W.b.S. A.M.—Strong gales and hazy. At 5 *wore ship* back again for the R. Derwent; set the fore sail; more moderate. At 7 more moderate; made more sail. At 8 Willson's Promontary N. 40° E. At noon Willson's Promontary N. 75° E., and the islands off the Promontary N. 62 E., where the very remarkable cave is like a stage waggon. P.M.—Fresh breezes and cloudy, with a heavy head sea. At 4 saw the Broken Water bearing S.b.W. about 6 miles, Round Islands bearing N. 62 W. about 6 miles. At 6 Hoggan's Group S. 55 W. and rocks to the northward N. 59 W. dist. 5 miles. At 7 Hog. Group south 67° W. dist. 3 or 4 leagues. ½-past 8 Kent's Group bore south. At ½-past 8 saw the land to the S.E.; a very dark night; steard east. At ½-past 11 strong gales and squally wr.; in all sail for scudding. Latt. obsd. 39.29 south.

Sunday, 5. Wind S.W.b.W., W.S.W. A.M.—Strong gales and heavy squalls, with continual rain. At 5 the N.E. part of Ferneux Islands S. 28° W. dist. 6 leags. At 8 do. wr.; saw another of Ferneux

Islands S. 33 W. dist. 7 leags; set storm mizen stay sails. 11 strong gales and squally, with a heavy shower of sleet. At noon the Pattrots Rock bore S. 78 W. dist. 7 leags, and Cape Barren S. 26 W., and the [1] extremity N. 88 W. Latt. obsd. 40.04 south. P.M.—Strong gales; under close reef. main top sails, fore sail, and fore topmast stay sail. At 4 Cape Barren bore S. 70° W. At 6 strong gales. At 7 saw the land to the southward bearing S.S.W. At 9 more moderate. At 11 fresh breezes, with a heavy head sea.

Monday, 6. S.S.W., S.b.W., south. A.M.—Fresh breezes and clear wr.—At 4 do. wr. At 6 strong gales and squally; close reef the saills. At noon strong gales and hazy w.; no observation. P.M.—Do. wr. At 4 more moderate and clear; made more sail.

Tuesday, 7. N. east. A.M.—At 7 sprung up a breeze from the N.E. At noon light breezes and cloudy. P.M.—Fresh breezes and cloudy. At 6 fresh breezes and squally. At 12 strong winds and hazy, with some rain. Latt. obsd. 41° 29 south.

Wed., 8. North, N.b.W., S.S.W., W.b.S., S.W., S.W.b.W. A.M.—At 2 more moderate moderate and cloudy. At 5 the main top sail yard broke in two in the middle, unbent the sail and got the yard down. Saw the land a head, Van Diemens Land. At ½-past 6 bore up more to the southward. At 10 the island of Cape Pillar S. 46° W. dist. 6 lgs. At 11 strong wind and squally, with heavy showers of rain. At noon the outer point of Cape Pillar Island bore S. 85° W. Latt. obsd. 43° 16′ south. P.M.—Tkd. ship; squally, with showers of rain. At 4 strong gales and squally, with showers of rain. At 7 Cape Bassalter [2] N. 82 W., and the island, south point, N. 70° W. dist. 7 leagues. At 9 strong squalls and heavy rain, with severe lightning. At 12 heavy squalls.

		1804.				
Tuesday	Jan.	31	...	...	...	54 miles.
Wed.	Feb.	1	...	...	...	80 miles.
Thursday	—	2	...	...	...	80
Friday	—	3	...	...	...	38
Sat.	—	4	...	...	...	67
Sund.	—	5	...	...	...	140
Mond.	—	6	...	...	...	87
Tuesd.	—	7	...	...	...	48
Wed.	—	8	...	...	...	134
Thur.	—	9	...	...	...	72
Friday	—	10	...	...	...	57

Thursday, 9. S.b.W. S.W.b.S., S.S.W. ¼ W., S.W.b.S., S.S.W., S.S.W. A.M.—At 2 wore ship; strong winds and cloudy, with lightning from the eastward. At 6 strong winds and clear wr. At 8 Cape Bassalter N. 87 W. At 9 wore ship. At noon strong gales and squally, with rain. Latt. obsd. 43.28 south. P.M.—Strong gales and squally. At ½-past 3 wore ship. At 4 Cape Bassalter S.W., being then one with the south point of the island. At 7 Cape Bassalter bore west, and the

---

[1] Cannot make out whether this word is northern or southern.
[2] Cape Basaltes, better known as C. Raoul.—[C.]

island, south point, N. 85° west. Cape Bassalter is one of the capes that you pass on the starbord side as you enter the bay ; it is the most remarkable of any that you see. This morn at 9 o'clock we were coming up the mouth of the river with a very fine breeze, but was obliged to put back the wind was so much agst. us.

Friday, 10. S.b.W. A.M.—At 3 more moderate and cloudy ; 8, light variable airs, inclining to a calm. At noon Cape Bassalter bore S. 85 W. ; sprung up a northward favourable light breeze from the northward. Latt. obsd. 43° 19 south. P.M.—At 2 fresh breezes and cloudy wr. ; at 3 squally ; in studding sails. At 6 Cape Bassalters N.W. ; sounded in 43 fathoms, white sand with brown specks. At 7 light breezes ; Cape Bassalters bore south 88 east. At 8 fresh breezes and hazy with squalls ; at ½ past 8 wore ship ; at 10 sounded in 35 fthms. ; ½ past 11 wore ship ; at midnight sounded 37 fthms. This night we were in Storm Bay, tacking repeatedly from shore to shore.

Saturday, 11. N.N.W., W.b.S., West. A.M.—At 2 hazy with rain ; at 3 wore ship ; at 4 Cape Bassalters E.b.S. ; made sail. At 5 tackd ship and plyd to windward up Storm Bay. At 7 fresh breezes and light squalls ; at 11 strong gales and squally with rain. P.M.—At 2 strong gales, with very heavy gusts of wind ; wore ship. At 3 down top gallt. yards, and bore up for Frederic Henry Bay. At ½ past anchord in 8 fthms. ; Cape Deslace[1] S.S.E., and the north end of Frederick Henry Bay, Island N. 65° E. ; latter part more moderate and cloudy. At 4 Lieut. Lord Mr. Humphries landed with 4 convicts armd to walk to the Riv. Derwent, dist. 14 or 15 miles by the charts. The first English ship anchord in this bay.

Ship *Ocean*, at anchor, in Frederick Henry Bay, Van Diemens Land, Feb. 1804.

Sunday, 12. W.N.W. A.M.—Fresh breezes and cloudy, with squalls at times. At 10 Capt. Merthew, Mr. Bowden, Mr. Collins, and self went on shore ; we went armd. Capt. M. and self left them ; we landed on the shore W.b.N., lagoon of salt W.N.W., fresh lagoon N.W.b.W. At the back of the high hill we see a great number of wild fowl and one emew, quails, bronswin, pigeons, and parrotts. At 4 we returnd to the party we left, and got a great quantity of oysters. It appeard to me that the natives were much better supplied with fish and birds than those at Port Phillip. The trees are very large and good, and a great deal of underwood. Near the fresh lagoon, which was large—more than 12 or 14 miles round—was a great quantity of flax and very fine   ; besides ducks and teal were snipes, and I think a woodcock was flushd. At ½-past 6 we returnd in a very heavy gale of wind, with hard rain.

Monday, 13. W.N.W. A.M.—Strong breezes, with heavy squalls of wind and rain. At 10 a party were sent on shore to get oysters, but the tide did not suit the lagoon. 17 of the natives were seen by the party ; they reported the natives to be men well made, entirely naked, and some of them had war wepons ; they had a small boy with them

---

[1] Cape Deslaco of the charts, near Pipe Clay Lagoon.—[C.]

about 7 years old, and did not appear to flee from them. P.M.—At 3 Capt. Merthew and Mr. Collins went on shore to get oysters.

Tuesday, 14. W.N.W. A.M.—Fresh breezes and hazy wr. Unable to sail, the wind against us. 4 p.m. Capt. Merthew went on shore a short time.

Wed. 15. Calm, N.W. A.M.—First part light variable winds, inclining to a calm; at 4 sprung up a breeze from the N.W.; weighd and made all sail. At 10 calm, light airs; ½-past light airs from the S.E. The centre of Betseys Island S.W.b.S. At noon tkd ship to the eastward. P.M.—½-past 1 tkd. ship; at 3 round Betseys Island, and bore up for the enterance of the harbour. At ½-past 3 saw a boat a-head, which came alongside with Mr. Simonds, commander of H.M. Brig *Lady Nelson*, and went with us up the River Derwent. At ½-past 6 anchord in Risdon Cove,[1] in 4 fthms. Latter part light breezes and hazy.

Remarks, Risdon Cove, Van Diemens Land, Feb. 1804.

Thursday, 16. A.M.—The morn very fine. At 10 the Lieut. Governor, self, and Lieut. Lord, of the Royal Marines, went on shore to see the settlemen form'd by Lieut. Bowen, of the Royal Navy. As we left the ship, Cap. Mertho, of the *Ocean* Transport, saluted Lieut. Coll. Coll., the new Governor, with 11 guns. When landed we were received by Lieut. More, the commandant of the New South Wales Corps, Mr. Mongarrett, the surgeon, and Mr. Wilson, the storekeeper; the camp consisted of 16 privates, 1 sarjant, 1 drum and fife. After examining the camp, gardens, water, &c., it was the general opinion to be not calculated for a town. At 2 the Lieut. Gov. returnd on board. I dind with Mr. Mongarret at his house, on the N.-East side of the river. The watering place is by no means good. Capt. Bowen returnd to Port Jackson with an intention of going to England.

Friday, 17. A.M.—At 10 the Lieut. Governor, Mr. Collins, and self went to examine a plain[2] on the S.W. side of the river; the plain extensive, and a continuel run of water, which is very excellent; it comes

---

[1] Risdon Cove, improperly called "Restdown," was named by Lieut. Bowen after the 2nd officer of the *Lady Nelson*, which vessel carried Bowen and his party from Sydney to form the settlement in June 1803.—*Ed.*

[2] It is difficult to determine in what sense Mr. Knopwood uses the word *plain* here and elsewhere, all the surface about Hobart Town being undulatory, and, at the time he writes of, much wooded. The following is the description of the place as it was in 1804, written by the chief officer of the *Lady Nelson* [*Jorgen Jorgensen*] (and published in Hobart Town, 1835), who assisted to establish both Risdon and Hobart Town :—"During our absence," that is at Port Phillip, to remove the second draft of Collins' people to the Derwent—"the station at Risdon was found ineligible, and the present site of Hobart Town was ultimately determined on. We landed at Sullivan's Cove, and having pitched our tents, spades, hoes, saws, and axes were put into the hands of prisoners, and we commenced clearing away as fast as we could. As I walk up and down the streets of this now crowded and large town, I cannot always divest myself of the remembrance of what it was at that time—32 years ago. The spot where the Bank of Van Diemen's Land, the Hope and Anchor, and the late Mrs. Kearney's habitation now are was then an impervious grove of the thickest brushwood, surmounted with some of the largest gum trees that this island can produce, and all along the rivulet, as far up as where the Old or Upper mill now is, was impassable from the denseness of the shrubs and underwood, and the huge collection of prostrate trees and dead timber which had been washed down by the stream, and were strewed all around. These had in parts blocked up the channel, and many places which are now dry and built upon, or cultivated in fruitful gardens, were covered with rushes and water." Jorgenson says the *Lady Nelson* was a small brig, of

from the lofty montain, much resembling the Table Montain at the Cape of Good Hope. The land is good, and the trees very excellent. The plain is well calculated in every degree for a settlement. At 5 we returnd and dind with the Gov., much delighted with the excursion. The new settlement is 6 miles lower down the river than the present one, which is a great advantage, besides the landing of the stores so much better.

Saturday, 18. A.M.—At 11 the Gov., Mr. Harris, Capt. Mertho, and self went and examined a part of the river to see a plain for the settlers, but the Gov. did not approve of it. The ground appeared to be much injured by the torrents of rain. The trees are very large and good. At 5 p.m. the Gov. went on shore to the settlement on the N.E. side of the river, and ordered the tents to be struck and sent on board the *Lady Nelson*. At 6 a little rain; they have not had a good shower of rain for 4 months.

Sunday, 19. A.M.—Strong breezes and small rain. At 6 weighd anchor and dropd down the river towards Sullivan Bay, but the wind coming on to blow hard, came to anchor at 12. At 3 weighd and anchord in Sullivan Bay, near the small island[1]; Capt. Mertho, Mr. Collins, and self went on shore, see some very fine trees.

Remarks, Sullivan Cove,[2] River Derwent, Van Diemens Land, Feb. 1804.

Monday, 20. A.M.—Part (of?) the military this morn went on shore, and a part of the convicts, to pitch their tents. P.M.—At 4 the Governor and some of the civil officers went on shore. He orderd my marquee to be pitchd very near his, as it was at Pt. Phillip. In the eve returnd on board. At 6 the military landed and as many convicts as could be sent on shore.

Tuesday, 21. A.M.—At 10 I went on shore to see my marque pitched; returnd to dinner on board the *Ocean*. At 6 p.m. the Lt. Governor went on shore, having landed all his baggage, &c. At 7 I went and slept at my marque for the first time, and the Lieut. Governor honoured my name for parol, the first given on the new settlement, and Lieut. Lord's name for the C. Sign. My marque is pitched near the Gov., on the left of him. I slept at the camp for the first time, and so did the Lt. Gov. Parole, Knopwood; C.S., Lord.

Wed., 22. A.M.—Clear wr. and fine. At 8 went on board the *Ocean*, Capt. Mertho, to breakfast, having few things unpackd. At 9 returnd to the camp. 11 Mr. More, Commandant of Risdon, waited upon Lieut. Gov. Collins, having some men deserted from his settlement. Employd getting my things in order. P.M.—I dind on board the *Ocean*, and at 7 p.m. left the ship and came to the camp. Mr. Wilson, the Commissary of Ridson Cove, calld upon me. C.S., Brown.

Thursday, 23. A.M.—Very fine weather. At 10 Mr. Harris and self walked to see the country. Mr. Mountgarret, the surgeon of Risdon

---

65 tons; and of the *Ocean*, that "she sailed so badly that we were obliged to assist her coming up the river." Knopwood says nothing about her entry into the harbour in this undignified manner.—[C.]

[1] Hunter's Island, now swallowed up in the "Old Wharf."
[2] Sullivan Bay, Port Phillip, and Sullivan Cove, Tasmania, were named by Collins after Mr. John Sullivan, permanent Under-Secty. for the Colonies.—[*Ed.*]

Cove, calld on me. P.M.—The convicts employd in preparing a warf at the landing place on the island. Preparing a ser. for Sunday. C.S., Mountgarret.

Friday, 24. A.M.—Do. wr. Many fires of the natives around, but none came near to the camp. I dind with Mr. Lord and Mr. Humphries. See two kangaroos in the eve, but did not shoot any. Preparing for the same. C.S., Averne.

Saturday, 25. A.M.—Do. wr. Preparing a ser. for Sund. Early this morn a bandycoote killd two of my fowls, of my white hens. Capt. Mertho calld on me. C.S., Innis.

Sunday, 26. A.M.—At 10 the military paraded; ½-past all the convicts, settlers assembled, and the Lieut. Gov., with the officers of the new colony, heard divine service. The sermon, by request of the Lt. Gov., was upon the prosperity of the new settlement, and to pray to God for a blessing upon the increase of it. Mr. More, the Commandant, and Mr. Wilson, the storekeeper from Risdon Cove, attended divine service. At 1 p.m. Lieut. Lord, Mr. Humphrys, Mr. Collins, Mr. Simmons, of H.M. Brig *Lady Nelson*, and self went in the Gov. black cutter to Risdon Cove, where I did duty to all the convicts, &c., &c. I dind with Mr. Mont-garret, and returnd in the eve. C.S., Winter.

Monday, 27. A.M.—This morn we had rain. Mr. Montgarret, from Risdon Cove, visited the camp, and he informd us that they had not had rain for 4 months. P.M.—Do. wr. The convicts employd in making some store houses on the island. C.S., Anderson.

Tuesday, 28. A.M.—We had rain all night. Caught a spotted cat which had killd my fowls, and the Governor's gamekeeper brought me a large kangaroo, the first killd in this colony. C.S., Varlo.

Wednesday, 29. A.M.—Moderate and clear. The Commandant of Risdon Cove came to the camp, Lt. More, of the New South Wales Corps. P.M.—At 3 I walked some distance; see many of the native huts, but none of them. C.S., Latham. Letters for England by the *Lady Nelson*, brig: Mr. Tylor, Mrs. Pettit, Col. Mitchel, Adjut. Pettit, Revd. Mr. More, John Kirby, Esq., Wm. Tustins, Esq., Earl Spencer,[1] Earl Clermont, Ld. Vis. Sudley, Hon. Capt. Gard,[2] the Dowager Lady Spencer.

Thursday, March 1. A.M.—Very fine weather. H.M. Brig *Lady Nelson* was to have saild this day with dispatches to Port Jackson, but they were not finishd. C.S., Flight.

Friday, 2. A.M.—This morn went a shooting early, and killd a quail. Dind on board the *Ocean* with Capt. Merthow. In the eve Mr. More and Mountgarret calld upon Capt. Merthow; stayd late. C.S., Campbell.

Saturday, 3. A.M.—Employd in writing letters. At 4 Mr. Simonds, H.M. Brig *Lady Nelson*, dind with me. At 6 we took a walk; I killd 4 quails, two of which I gave to Mr. Mountgarret and two to the Governor. In the eve fresh breezes.

---

[1] Mr. Knopwood was formerly private chaplain in this family.
[2] Probably the Hon. Allen Hyde Gardner, R.N., Captain of H.M. Ship *Resolution*, of which Knopwood was chaplain; a very intimate friend.

Sunday, 4. A.M.—At 11 the Governor and all the officers, &c., &c., attended divine service. At ½-past 12 sent all my letters on board the *Lady Nelson* brig. Dind with Capt. Merthow on board the *Ocean* transport. C.S., Despatch.

Monday, 5. A.M.—At 9 I went on board the *Ocean* with Mr. Humphrys. 10 Capt. Merthow, Mr. Brown (the botanist), and we went to Risdon Cove, where we dind with Mr. Mountgarret. At 4 we all went up the Derwent River, where we slept on the west side of it, about 17 miles from the camp; I killd two black swans. C.S., Herdsmans Cove; Parole, Excursion.

Tuesday, 6. A.M.—At 5 we all got in our boats and went 5 miles up the river and breakfasted; on the east side of the river got some more swans. At 10 we got into the boats again and went 10 miles further up, where we dind, and pitchd our boat sails for a tent. At 4 Mr. Mountgarret and Mr. Humphrys left us for Risdon Creek. Capt. Merthow and self went a shooting; killd a pigeon. At 6 a.m. H.M. Brig *Lady Nelson* saild for Pt. Jackson with a fair wind. C.S., Pillar.

Wednesday, 7. A.M.—At 6 we breakfasted. ½-past 7 Capt. Merthow and self went a shooting 15 miles up the river. Mr. Brown went up the mountains a botanizing. The river took these directions, where the falls of water were:—1, fall reach, E. to W.; 2d., from S.E. to N.W.; 3rd reach, S.-W.; 4th, W.S.W.; 5th reach, N.b.W. We walkd on the west side of the river; the hills, &c., very high. When one side of the river was hilly the other a vally, and it continued so for more than 40 miles from the camp, where there was an extensive plain of very few trees. We see kangaroos, emews, pigeons, and parrotts. At ½-past 4 we return to the hut we left in the morn. During our walk we a great many native hutts and the fires they made; no doubt they see us. In the eve the natives made a fire near where we slep, on the west side of the river. C. Sign, Hogan.

Thursday, 8. A.M.—At 5 rain, with hard squalls. We struck our canvass and saild for Herdsman's Cove, where we reachd about 10 and breakfasted; the land appeard not very good. At 12 as we were coming from thence a native appeard, but the distance was too great to discover much of him. Strong breezes and squally. At 5 we arrivd at the *Ocean*, where we dind, and went to the camp at ½-past 6. C.S., Palmer.

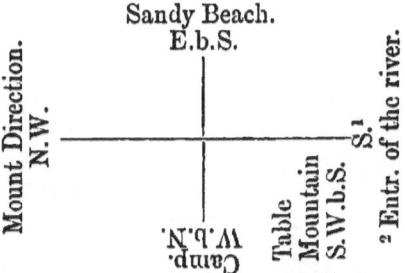

The first party that went on excursion up the river.

---

[1] South in copy.   [2] An illegible word here.

Friday, 9. A.M.—At 8 many of the natives were about the camp, but not prevaild upon to enter; Cap. Merthow and Mr. Brown had an interview with them on the shore near the *Ocean*. The people employd about the Lt. Governor's house. P.M.—In the eve Mr. Bowden and self took a walk. The Governor slept in his house for the first time. C.S., Townson.

Saturday, 10. A.M.—Moderate and fair. Went out a shooting and killd some quails. P.M.—At 4 [1] a schooner appeard in sight. Name the *Pilgrim*, Capt. Dillano, who has the *Perseverance*. At 6 a boat came on shore with the Governor of Risdon Creek. Lt. Bowen, of the Royal Navy, received letters from Pt. Jackson from Mr. Brumley and Lt. Houston, who is now appointed Governor of Norfolk Island. C.S., Native.

Sunday, 11. A.M.—At 11 performed divine service. At 2 p.m. Mr. Humphry and self went on board the *Ocean* and dind with Capt. Mertho. In the eve Lt. Bowen, Lt. Moore, Mr. Mountgarret came on board the *Ocean*, and stayd late; likewise the Capt. of the schooner dind there, Mr. Delano. C.S., Bowen.

Monday, 12. A.M.—Employd variously. Capt. Dunnow,[2] of the schooner *Pilgrim*, calld upon me. P.M.—In the eve walked with my gun. C.S., Integrity.

Tuesday, 13. A.M.—At 3 it blew a perfect gale of wind, which continued some time. At 11 Mr. Moore, Mr. Mountgarret, calld upon me. P.M.—At 4 I walkd out with my gun, and kill a very fine kangaroo. At 6 returnd to the camp. The first kangaroo that had been killd by any of the gentlemen in the camp. C.S., Hunters River.

Wed., 14. A.M.—Mr. Moore and Mr. Wilson calld upon me. P.M.—Mr. Wilson and Lt. Lord dind with me. C.S., Buckingham.

Thursday, 15. A.M.—Gov. Collins sent for me on business. P.M.—At 3 I went out a shooting; no success. C.S., Farren.

Friday, 16. A.M.—At 5 I went out with my gun and returnd at 10; no success. At 12 I put up three quails near Mr. Bowdens marque, and killd them. A 4 p.m. Lieut. Lord, Mr. Humphry, Mr. Brown dined with me. Mr. Mountgarret, Mr. Collens, Capt. Mertho, Mr. Moore were to have dind with me, but could not get down time enough. They came to me at 5 p.m., and took wine with me. C.S., Pitt.

Saturday, 17. A.M.—Very fine weather. 4 p.m., Captain Bowen, the Governor of Risdon Creek, and Mr. Mountgarret, Lt. Lord, dind with me. C.S., St. Patrick.

Sunday, 18. A.M.—At ½ past 10 I married Mrs. Ann Skelthon to Corp. Gangel, in the Royal Marines, at Lt. Governor Collins house. The weather unfavourable that we could not have divine service performd. Mr. Wm. Todd Wright came on shore; he dind with me.

---

[1] An American Bostown.

[2] It will be noticed throughout this copy of Knopwood's journal, which I have followed with very great exactness, that, with all the advantages of a high-class education, he spells very carelessly, especially proper names, which he writes very variously. The names of Lieut. Moore, Mr. Humphries, Captain Mertho, Mr. Mountgarrett, Dr. Bromley, should all be written as I give them, but he usually writes them in some other way. Dunnow, as he writes it here, is Dillano and Delano elsewhere, &c., &c.—[C.]

At 3 Lt. Lord and self went on board the *Pilgrim*, an American schooner, Capt. Delano, and stayd till 6 p.m. C.S., Peru.

Monday, 19. A.M.—At ½ past 8 Lt. Lord, Wm. Wright Todd, breakfasted with me. At 10 Mr. Moore calld upon me. C.S., Straits.

Tuesday, 20. Employed all the day with Capt. Delano and his mate Mr. Mile. Mr. Wilson sup'd with me and Mr. Harris. C.S., George.

Wed., 21. Mr. Wilson and Mr. Harris breakfasted with me, and Mr. Wilson and Mr. Wright Todd dind with me and stay'd the day. A young man on board Capt. Mertho ship. His father was Capt. of H.M. ship *Queen Charlotte* that was blown up. C.S., Nile.

Thursday, 22. A.M.—Mr. Wilson breakfasted with me. Confind to my marque with a spraind ankle.

Friday, 23. A.M.—Mr. Wilson breakfasted with me. At 1 p.m. I dind with Mr. Lord, and met Capt. Bowen and Mr. Mountgarret, Mr. Wilson from Risdon Cove, and Mr. Humphry. After tea they all came to see me and stayd late. C. S., Virginia.

Saturday, 24. Mr. Lord and self went on board the *Pilgrim* schooner, and Capt. Delano came on shore with us. I dind with Mr. Lord. Saild the *Ocean*, transport, to Pt. Phillip for the civil, military officers, &c., &c., &c. Parole, Fair Winds ; C.S., Ocean.

Sunday, 25. A.M.—Mr. Lord and self breakfasted with Mr. Humphry on board the American schooner. At ½ past 10 performd divine service. Captain Delano and self dind with Lt. Lord. In the eve they came to me. C.S., Georgia.

Monday, 26. A.M.—At 6 saild the American schooner, Capt. Amasa Delano, for Kents Bay. At 11 Mr. Humphry and self went in a boat to Risdon Cove, on a visit to Governor Bowen, and dind with him. Met Mr. Bowden with their dogs. They caught 6 young emews, about the size of a turkey, and shot the old mother. C.S., Kentuchy.

Tuesday, 27. A.M.—At 9 Mr. Mountgarret, Mr. Humphrey, and Mr. Brown and servants, with 10 days provisions, to go to the head of the river. Mr. Wilson and Lt. Moore came and stayd the eve with us. C.S., Otway.

Wed., 28. A.M.—Gov. Bowen and self walkd about the wood with our guns. At 4 p.m. Mr. Wilson and Mr. Moore came and took wine with us. C.S., Serle.

Thursday, 29. A.M.—This morn Gov. Bowens young friend was confind to her bed. At 10 Lieut. Moore and self came to camp, and Mr. M. dind with me. C.S., Towry.

Friday, 30, *Good.* A.M.—This day was strictly observd throughout the Camp. At ½ past ten all the officers in the camp, military and convicts, attended divine service. At 10 p.m. it blew very hard, which continued all night. C.S., Orde.

Saturday, 31. A.M.—At 9 dark weather, blowing hard. P.M.—Do. wr. I went out a shooting in the eve ; no success. The weather continue to blow very much. C.S., Mann.

April, Sunday, 1, *Easter Day.* A.M.—At ½ past 10 all the officers, &c., &c., attended divine service. After that Lieut. Lord, Royal Marines, and Mr. Harris, pertook of some Norfolk ham with me, the best we ever eat. At 4 p.m., Mr. Bowden and self dind with Lieut. Lord, and was very merry. C.S., Nelson.

Monday, 2. A.M.—Strong breezes and squally wr. from the S.West. At 11 Mr. Bowden and Mr. Lord and self went out with his dogs and killd a kangaroo, and we dind with him. C.S., Raven.

Tuesday, 3. A.M.—At 11 Mr. Bowden and self went to Risdon and dind with Mr. Bowen the Governor. At 6 we returnd to the Camp. C.S., St. Helens.

Wed., 4. A.M.—At 9 Governor Bowen sent a boat for me to stay the week with him. Lt. Moore and Mr. Wilson came in the eve. C.S., Witworth.

Thursday, 5. A.M.—Governor Bowen and self after breakfast went up of Mount Direction on the N.East side and came down the S.West, and had a very long walk. The view was grand. At 2 p.m. the boat returnd from the first fall of the river with Mr. Mountgarret: Mr. Brown, the botanist; and Mr. Humphry, the mineralogist. They went in search of the head of the river but could not find it. C.S., Elgin.

Friday, 6. A.M.—The weather being so bad we could not venture this morn. P.M.—At 4, Governor Bowen, Mr. Humphry, and self, went into the boat, with an intention to go to Sullivan Camp. Mr. H. went, and Capt. Bowen and self returnd to his house. We see a very great whirlwind in the river. At 9 much lightning in the eve. C.S., Geneva.

Saturday, 7. A.M.—At 11 Mr. Mountgarret, Mr. Brown, and self, got into the boat, and Mr. Moore and[1] came to Sullivan Camp. They and Mr. Bowden dind with me. The wind very much from the S.W. C.S., Jasper.

Sunday, 8. A.M.—The weather so very bad that no duty could be performed. At 4 p.m. Lt. Lord, Mr. Humphry, Mr. Harris, Mr. Bowden, dind with me off kangaroo. Continual rain and wind all day and night. C.S., Patience.

Monday, 9. A.M.—At ½ past 9 the gentlemen that dind with me yesterday breakfasted with me. At 11, Lt. Lord, Mr. Harris, and Humphry and self, went to the settlers farms, but had no success with our guns. At 4 p.m. I dind with Mr. Lord and Humphry. C.S., Grinfield.

Tuesday, 10. A.M.—At 9 Mr. Lord and Humphry breakfasted with me. At 2 p.m. I went out with my gun and kill'd a couple of pigeons. C.S., Hood.

Wednesda, 11. A.M.—Mr. Humphry breakfasted with me, and we walkd to the Table Mountain, where I killd a *white hork*, the first that has been seen in this country; a very great curiosity. We returnd home at 5 p.m. Mr. Wilson smokd a pipe with me. Mr. Milne went to Risdon to have his examination taken before Mr. Bowen and Mr. Mountgarret. C.S., Wallace.

Thursday, 12. A.M.—Mr. Lord, Humphry, and Mr. Wilson from Risdon Cove, breakfasted with me and dind with me; in the eve he went home. C.S., Jamaica.

Friday, 13. A.M.—Mr. Humphry, Lord, and Mr. Mountgarret, breakfasted with me, and Mr. Harris went with me a shooting. No success. I dind with Mr. Lord. C.S., Martinique.

---

[1] Some omission here.

Saturday, 14. A.M.—Nothing perticular. I dind with Mr. Lord and Mr. Humphrys. C.S., Malta.

Sunday, 15. A.M.—At ½ past 10 the soldiers, &c., attended for divine service, but the wr. was so very cold that the Lt. Governor deferrd it by reason of the wr. At 3 p.m. Governor Bowen, from Risdon, calld upon me. At 4, Lt. Lord, Mr. Humphry, and Mrs. Sarjent, dind and drank tea with me. C.S., Minorca.

Monday, 16. A.M.—I took a long walk with my gun, but had no success. At 4 p.m. I dind with Mr. Lord and Mr. Humphry. C.S., Derwent.

Tuesday, 17. A.M.—Mr. Lord and Humphry breakfasted with me. At 10 receivd letters from Governor Bowen and Mr. Mountgarret. At 11 a strange sail appeard. 1 p.m. she anchord in the Bay. The *Pilgrim*, schooner, Capt. Dillano. At 2 he calld upon me with a friend of his, Capt. Smith. In the eve they took a pipe with Lt. Lord. C.S., Good order.

Wed., 18. A.M.—At ½ past 6 Capt. Bowen, and Mr. Wilson from Risdon Cove, calld on me, and took me with them to Ralphs Bay, where we breakfasted on shore, and walkd to Frederick Henry Bay. Many of the natives were there. At ½ past 8 we went on board the *Integrity*, cutter, from Kents Bay, commanded by Mr. Rushworth. C.S., Integrity.

Thursday, 19. A.M.—Employd about looking out for a situation for a garden. At 2 p.m. Lt. Lord, Mr. Harris, and self, went on board the *Pilgrim*, schooner, and dind with Captain Dillano. At 4 came on shore. Mr. Mountgarret calld on me. C.S., Chesterfield.

Friday, 20. A.M.—Mr. Brown returnd to the Camp, and calld upon me. He had been with an intention to get to the River Ewen, but could not. He found another river, which ran due south from the Camp.¹ I dind with Mr. Lord. C.S., Buccleugh.

Saturday, 21. A.M—Engaged at home all the morn upon justice business. Mr. Mountgarrett and Mr. Harris dind with me. C.S., Norfolk.

Sunday, 22. A.M.—At 10 the weather being bad could not perform duty at the camp; at 11 Capt. Bowen came to the camp to Lit. Gov. Collins, and I returnd home with him. C.S., Montrose.

Monday, 23. A.M.—At 10 Capt. Bowen, commandant at Risdon Cove, assembled all the military and convicts, and punishd 3 mutiners, who was going to raise a disturbance in the camp; at 2 he and self came to Sullivan Cove, and stayd with me. Siled this morn the *Pilgrim*, schooner, Capt. Dillans, to the South Cape, a sealing. C.S., St. George.

Tuesday, 24. A.M.—This morn employd writing to Sidney; at 4 P.M. I took out my gun, with Nettle, and killd a native hen, which first took the sea, and Nettle brought it out. This day twelvemonth we weighd anchor, and anchord at St. Helens in company with the *Ocean* transport. C.S., South Cape.

---

¹ There must be some mistake in this description. North-West Bay River is probably intended, but which in no part of its course is nearer "the Camp," that is, Hobart Town, than a dozen miles.—[C.]

Wednesday, 25. A.M.—At 8 Mr. Mount Garret and Mr. Brown calld on me; we breakfasted at Lords. At 11 Mr. Mount Garret and self walkd opposite Risdon Cove, where I left him, and returnd to camp. Mr. Harris spent the eve with me. Sailed: the *Industry*, cutter, for Sidney, Mr. Rushworth, commander. C.S., Port Jackson.

Thursday, 26. A.M.—At 11 Capt. Bowen calld upon me; in the eve took a walk with my gun, no success. C.S., Watson.

Friday, 27. A.M.—At 11 the Lt.-Governor and self went and markd out a burial ground at a distance from the camp. Receivd a letter from Capt. Bowen to visit Risdon Cove, but could not; in the eve took a walk. C.S., Byng.

Saturday, 28. A.M.—At 10 Mr. Mount Garret came to the camp; at ½ past 2 P.M. I buried Mr. Edwardes child. The Lt.-Governor and all the officers attended at 3. I went to Risdon Cove with Mr. Mountgarret, Mr. Bowden, Mr. Harris, and dind there. This day twelvemonth we took our departure from England. Capt. Bowen and Mr. Wilson went with the mutiners prisoners to land them on an island 8 of them, and all Irishmen. C.S., Hampstead.

Sunday, 29. A.M.—At 11 I performed Divine Service at Risdon by order of Lt. Governor Collins, and dind with Mr. Mountgarret. C.S., Barnet.

Tuesday, May 1. A.M.—At 6 I got up to see a dog run a kangaroo, but could not find. Returnd to Mr. Mountgarrets to breakfast. Continual rain all the morn. At ½ past 10 came to Sullivan Cove Camp. Mr. Brown dind with me. C.S., Winter.

Wednesday, 2. A.M.—Remaind at home. At 4 P.M. dind with Mr. Harris; met Mr. Bowden and Mr. Collins. C.S., Stratford.

Thursday, 3. A.M.—Took a long walk in the morn; at 2 P.M. we heard the report of cannon once from Risdon. The Lt. Governor sent a message to know the cause. At ½ past 7 Lt. Moore arrived at the camp to Lt. Governor Collens, and I receivd the following note from Risdon:—

Dear Sir,

I beg to referr you to Mr. Moore for the particulars of an attack the natives made on the camp to-day; and I have every reason to think it was premeditated, as their number farr exceeded any that we we ever heard of. As you express a wish to be acquainted with some of the natives, if you will dine with me to-morrow, you will oblige me by christining a fine native boy who I have. Unfortunately, poor boy, his father and mother were both killd; he is about two years old. I have likewise the body of a man that was killed. If Mr. Bowden wishes to see him desected, I will be happy to see him with you to-morrow. I would have wrote to him, but Mr. Moore waits.

Your friend,
J. MOUNTGARRET, Hobert, six o'clock.

The number of natives I think was not less than 5 or 6 hundred.—J. M.

At 8 Lt. Moore came to my marquee and stayd some time; he informed me of the natives being very numerous, and that they had wounded one of the settlers, Burke, and was going to burn his house down and ill treat his wife, &c., &c. C.S., Coventry.

Friday 4. A.M.—Neither myself or Mr. Bowden were able to get a boat to go to Risdon. Mr. Harris and Mr. Lord dind with me. C.S., Litchfield.

Saturday, 5. A.M.—At 6 I went out with Mr. Lords doggs, and kill a couple of kangooros; at 20 minutes past 7 returnd home to breakfast with Mr. Lord; I dind with Mr. Lord. C.S., Newcastle.

Sunday, 6. A.M.—At 10 the weather so wet that divine service could not be performd; at ½ past 11 a strange sail appeard coming up the river; at 1 P.M. anchord in the bay the *Nancy*, cutter, from Pt. Jackson with despatches for Lt. Gov. Collens; at ½ past 2 we obserd the Risdon whale boat returning home; she had been out eight days with Gov. Bowen and Mr. Wilson. C.S., Nancy.

Monday, 7. A.M.—At 11 waited on the Lt. Governor respecting my garden by the house; at 3 P.M. Mr. Shipman measured the ground. C.S., Knutsford.

Tuesday, 8. A.M.—A very sharp frost; at 11 Capt. Bowen, Mr. Wilson, and Lt. Moore came to the camp; the two first gentlemen dind with me, and in the eve Mr. Moore came and stayd till quite late. C.S., Liverpool.

Wednesday, 9. A.M.—At 10 Mr. Mountgarret came to the camp and called upon me. P.M.—I took a walk with my gun. C.S., Stone House.

Thursday, 10. A.M.—I stayd at home all the morn; at 11 Capt. Bowen, Mr. Mountgarret and Mr. Wilson came to the camp. Mr. M. and W. and self dind with Mr. Lord. Capt. Bowen slept at my marque. C.S., Mount Edgecombe.

Friday, 11. At 11 A.M. Lt. Lord and self went to Risdon with Capt. Bowen. Mr. Lord returnd in the eve, and I stayd there. I xtiand a young native boy whose name was Robert Hobert May. C.S., Cawsand.

Saturday, 12. A.M.—In the morn we took a walk to see where the natives attacked the camp and settlers. C.S., Sattram.

Sunday, 13. A.M.—At 9 Capt. Bowen and self returnd to the camp; and at 11 performd divine service; at 3 p.m. Capt. Bowen and self dind with the Lt. Governor; in the eve Capt. Bowen and Mr. Harris went to Risdon. C.S., Fowey.

Monday, 14. A.M.—I took a long walk. Mr. Lord breakfasted and dind with me. Mr. Harris and Mr. Moore returned to the camp in the eve. C.S., Ashburton.

Tuesday, 15. A.M.—Engaged all the morn upon justice business. Mr. Moore returnd to Risdon in the eve. C.S., Chudleigh.

Wednesday, 16. A.M.—At daylight Lt. Lord and self went out with the dogs after kangaroo, but had no success; at 3 P.M. Mr. Wilson, Capt. Bowen, Mr. Mountgarret came to the camp; they brought down the native boy for Lt. Governor Collins to see; at 4 Mr. Brown and Mr. Humphry came to the camp, they had been out 16 days, and got to the River Huon by land; ½ past 4 we all dind with Mr. Lord, except Mr. Mountgarret; in the eve they called upon me, and Captain Bowen slept at my marquee. C.S., Dartmoor.

Thursday, 17. A.M.—Capt. Bowen, Mr. Wilson, Mr. Lord, and Humphry breakfasted with me; at 11 Capt. Bowen and Mr. Wilson returnd to Risdon; at 5 P.M. Mr. Mountgarret and Mr. Brown came to the camp. C.S., Tavistock.

Friday, 18. A.M.—Sailed at 7 the *Nancy* for Kings Island a sealing; 4 P.M., rainy weather, which continued all night. C.S., Blandford.

Saturday, 19. A.M.—Continuel rain and cloudy wr.: at 6 P.M. the *Nancy* in sight working out of the river; at 7 Mr. Harris came and smokd a pipe with me; at 8 Mr. Mountgarret calld upon me from Risdon. C.S., Dorchester.

Sunday, 20. A.M.—At ½ past 10 performed divine service, attended by His Honor the Lt.-Gov., &c., &c.; at 4 P.M. I dind with Mr. Lord and Humphry. Thermomiter 62 at ½ pas. 12 A.M. C.S., Salisbury.

Monday, 21. A.M.—I took a long walk in the morn; at 2 P.M. Mr. Brown calld upon me from Risdon. C.S., Norfolk.

Tuesday, 22. A.M.—At 10 Mr. Harris and self walkd to the bay opposite Risdon, when Capt. Bowen sent a boat for us. We dind with Lieut. Moore of the New South Wales Regt. Capt. Bowen and Mr. Wilson dind with us there. I slept at Capt. Bowns. C.S., Menrirs.

Wednesday, 23. A.M.—I stayd at Risdon all day at Capt. John Bowns. Mr. Mountgarret and Mr. Brown went to Hobert Town Camp. C.S., Return.

Remarks Hobert Camp, River Derwent, Van Diemen's Land, 1804.

Tuesday, 24. At 6 A.M. Mr. Mountgarret and self went out with his doggs to kill kangaroo; in a very short time we killd a large one. At 11 Capt. Bown and self came to the camp, and dind and slept at my marquee; at 10 we heard the report of a gun from Hunters Island (the store houses); at ½ past the sarjant who had been sent there to protect the island was brough prisoner, having robbd the store houses of spirits and leather, &c., &c. C.S., Receive.

Friday, 25. A.M.—At 8 Capt. Bown went to Risdon, and I went and chose a place for my garden. Set the white hen on 11 eggs. C.S., Cows.

Saturday, 26. A.M.—At 11 I took a walk to the government farm, and dind with Mr. Lord.

Sunday, 27. A.M.—At ½ past 10 the Governor and all the officers, &c., attended divine service; at ½ past 5 Mr. Bowden, Harris, and self dind with Mr. Lord and Humphrys. C.S., Forum.

Monday, 28. A.M.—At 10 Mr. Humphrys and self went up the mountain on the S.E. to look for the *Ocean* [the ship], but could not see it. C.S., Liphook.

Tuesday, 29. A.M.—At 10 Mr. Wilson and Lieut. Moore from Risdon calld upon me. Mr. Moore and self dind with Lt. Lord and Mr. Humphry. C.S., Knitesbridge.

Wednesday, 30. A.M.—At 10 Lieut. Lord, Lieut. Moore, Mr. Humphreys breakfasted with me, and in the eve Lt. Moore, Mr. Harris smokd a pipe with me. C.S., Brenttford.

Thursday, 31. A.M.—At 10 Lieut. Moore breakfasted with me, and at 11 I went to Risdon Cove with him; dind and slept at his house. Calld on Capt. Bowen. C.S., Surry.

Friday, 1 *June*. A.M.—At 11 Capt. Bowen and self came to the Cam, and he returnd back to dinner, and Mr. Humphry with him. C.S., Kew.

Saturday, 2. A.M.—At 10 Capt. Bowen sent me a large quarter of kangaroo. Mr. Wilson and Mr. Humphrys came to the Camp. At ½-past 5 p.m. those two gents, Lieut. Lord, Harris, and Bowden dind with me, being my birthday. C.S., Walton.

Sunday, 3. A.M.—At 11 the weather was so bad that divine service could not be performd. At 12 all the officers, civil and military, and settlers met at my marque to consult on the price of labour, &c., &c., and deliverd the report to the Lit. Governor. In the eve. Mr. Harris smokd a pipe with me. C.S., Retreat.

Monday, 4. A.M.—This day, being H.M. Birthday, was not observd as a holiday by reason of the *Ocean* transport not being arrivd from Pt. Phillip with the remainer of the civil and military officers, marines, and convicts, but will be kept on her arrival at this colony. Mr. Harris, Mr. Bowden, and self dind with Mr. Lord and Humphrys. Parole, Long live the King.

Tuesday, 5. At 7 a.m. His Honour the Lt. Governor, with Mr. Harris, the Surveyor-General, and Mr. Collins, the Harbour Master, went in the Lt.-Gov. cutter to Betsey's Island to survey it; and they returnd to camp at ½-past 10 p.m. The aft. and night blew very hard from the S.W., that they were obliged to land at Sandy Bay,[1] 5 or 6 miles from the Camp, and walk in. C.S., Cumberland.

Wednesday, 6. A.M.—At 11 Mr. Wilson and Lieut. Moore, from Risdon Cove, came to the Camp. In the eve I took my pipe with Mr. Harris. A very fine day after [indistinct] an eve. Mr. Harris and self had our new gardens measured out. C.S., Lee.

Thursday, 7. A.M.—Breakfasted at Lt. Lords, and walkd with Mr. Wilson near Risdon. Went to see the Government farm, &c.; returnd and dind with Mr. Harris. C.S., Look out.

Friday, 8. A.M.—At 10 Mr. Wilson came to the Camp; at 11 I went to the Island to look out for the *Ocean*. At 2 p.m. I took a walk; and in the [eve] drank tea with Mr. Lord. At 4 a.m. Mr. Collons, the harbour master, went in the white cutter to Betsey's Island to land 2 convicts there, to keep a look out for ships, and to make a signal at the appearance of any—by fire. C.S., St. Vincent.

Saturday, 9. A.M.—At 9 Mr. Wilson breakfasted with me, and we both went to Prince of Wales Bay, opposite Risdon Cove, where I left him, and did not get back till 5 p.m. to dinner. Capt. Bowen, from Risdon, came on purpose to see me, but I was from home. C.S., Fear.

Sunday, 10. A.M.—The weather so bad that divine service could not be performed, the wind so much. At 8 p.m. the white cutter returned with Mr. Collens, the harbour master, from Betsey's Island. C.S., Douglass.

Monday, 11. A.M.—At home all the day; the people employd at the magazene and other buildings. P.M.—Took a long walk; home to dinner in the eve. C.S., Bodmin.

---

[1] Sandy Bay is not nearly so far from Hobart Town, but it should be remembered that it was all bush, with its obstructions, in 1804, and it would appear double its real distance.—C.

Tuesday, 12. A.M.—Very strong breezes. At 12 Capt. Bowen, in the whale boat, and Mr. Brown with him, Mr. Mountgarret, in his boat, went to Adventure Bay; they passd the Camp at ½-past 12. I walked to the farm. At 4 heavy squalls, which continued all night. C.S., Goldsmith.

Wed. 13. A.M.—Very heavy gusts of wind and bla [indistinct], with hard rain at intervals. At 12 Mr. Wilson came from Risdon, and was very nearly lost in the bush. The winds strong; many trees round the Camp torn up by the wind. P.M.—The wr. continue, with very hard gales. At 8 do. wr., and much lightning. Mr. Wilson dind and stayd the day with me. C.S., Adventure Bay.

Thursday, 14. A.M.—At ½-past 2 continuel bad wr. A gun was fird from Hunters Island as signal that a fire was seen upon Betsys Island. The day very bad. Do. wr. at 3. P.M.—More moderate. Mr. Collins, the harbour master, went into Ralphs Bay, where he was to continue all night. C.S., Cornwell.

Friday, 15. A.M.—Moderate wr. At 11 I walked with Mr. Wilson to the settlers, and he went on to Risdon. P.M.—Do. wr. C.S., Signal.

Sat. 16. A.M.—At 4 stormy wr. and rain; at 8 more moderate P.M. C.S., Penzance.

Sunday, 17. A:M.—At ½-past 10 I walked to the settlers, and the Lt.-Gov. and Mrs. Powers came there and heard Divine Service; we returnd to the Camp. At 3 I dind with the Governor, and took tea with him. Thos. Salmon, my man, killd a very large kangaroo—a forester. C.S., York.

Monday, 18. A.M.—I breakfasted at Mr. Lords. Mr. Harris, with shipman and 2 men, went to the head of the river that supplied the Camp and settlers farms with water; Mr. Humphrys went with him. I walkd with them 3 or 4 miles from the Camp; returnd to dinner. *See* a remark given me by Mr. Harris and Mr. Humphry when they surveyed the river at the beginning of the book. C.S., Sandwich.

Tuesday, 19. A.M.—Mr. Lord breakfasted with me; and at 11 I walked to look for the *Ocean*, but could not see her. I dind with Mr. Lord at his new house. Mr. Humphry returnd in the eve from the mountain [Mt. Wellington]. C.S., Deal.

Wednesday, 20. A.M.—Lieut. Lord and Humphrys breakfasted with me. At 6 p.m. Mr. Harris returnd from the mountain. At 3 p.m. Capt. Bowen and Mr. Mountgarret return to Risdon from their excursion. C.S., Law.

Thursday, 21. A.M.—I breakfasted with Mr. Lord and Humphrys. At 5 p.m. Mr. Collins returnd in the white cutter from Betsys Island, &c. He went to the River Houin, and report it to be by far the most eligible situation for a settlement; the great supply of fresh water, good land, and trees, and the anchorage safe and good. He see many of the natives, and was conducted to the town[1] by some of them, where there were about 20 families; he stayd all night with them. They were all very friendly; he see 3 of their cattemerans, or small boats made of bark, that will hold about 6 of them. At 8 we heard the

---

[1] This must mean their own assemblage of wigwams.

report of a gun, and likewise in the nigh; supposed a ship in Frederick Henry Bay. C.S., Somers.

Friday, 22. A.M.—At 7 Mr. Collens in the white cutter and black boat went into Ralphs Bay, with an intention to go to Frederick Henry. Continual rain all this morn. At 4 p.m. we observd a ship coming up the river. At 9 Lieut. Johnston landed from the *Ocean*, which had brought the party we had left at Pt. Phillip, after a passage of thirty-three days, during which she had a gale; 21 days laying under her bare poles, expecting for some days that the ship would have went down, the sea so high, and the wr. so bad. C.S., Coke.

Saturday, 23. A.M.—Moderate. The *Ocean* under sail. At 11 Mr. Mountgarret and Mr. Brown came from Risdon. At 4 p.m. I went there with them, and slept at Mr. Mountgarrets. C.S., Ocean.

Sunday, 24. A.M.—At 11 performd divine service. At 5 p.m. came home and waited upon the Lt. Governor. *Ocean* not come up. C.S., Mansfield.

Monday, 25. A.M.—The *Ocean* under sail. At 4 p.m. she came to an anchor in Sullivan Cove. At 5 I dind with Lt. Lord and Lt. Johnstone. In the eve Capt. Mertho and Lt. Sladden and Mr. Janson came there. The camp equipage landed. C.S., Mertho.

Tuesday, 26. A.M.—At ½-past 10 the Marines landed from the *Ocean*, and the prisoners landing their things. At 1 p.m. my man Salmon killd a kangarro; length from the end of the tail to the nose seven feet two inches, length of its tail 3 f. 4 i. and a half, the weight of one hind qr. 25 lb., circum-fr. of the tail 1 foot 4 inch.; the whole weight of the kannarro was 150 lbs.

Wednesday, 27. A.M.—At 10 Mr. Wilson, from Risdon, came to the camp. At 3 p.m. all the prisoners landed and encampd at Hobart Town. Lt. Johnstone and Mr. Wilson dind and stayd all night at my marque. C.S., Hall.

Thursday, 28. A.M.—Lt. Johnstone and Mr. Wilson breakfasted with me, and I walked to the farms with Mr. W.; he took a boat to Risdon. Lt. Johnstone dind with me. This eve we heard a great many whales in the river very near us. C.S. Raymonds.

Friday, 29. A.M.—Mr. Harris and Lt. Johnston breakfasted with me. In the eve we dind with Mr. Harris. C.S., Jacobs.

Saturday, 30. A.M.—At 10 Groves and self walked to the farm'; and in the eve Mr. Fosbroke, Mr. Harris, and Lt. Johnston dind with me. I killd 3 kangaroo rabbits. C.S., Farm.

Sunday, July, 1. A.M.—At 9 I married Mr. Ingle to Miss Rebecca Hobbs. At ½-past 10 Lt. Johnston and self went to Risdon, by order of Lt.-Governor Collins, and performd divine service there. We passed so many whales that it was dangerous for the boat to go up the river, unless you kept very near the shore. At 4 p.m. we dind with Capt. Bowen, and Lt. Sladden came there in the eve. We were going from his house I spraind my ankle very bad, and was obliged to sleep at Lt. Moore's. In the eve continual rain. C.S., Carlton.

Monday, 2. A.M.—All this morn continual rain. At 11 Mr. Wilson and self came from Risdon to Hobart Town. P.M.—Do. wr.

Tuesday, 3. A.M.—Moderate and clear wr. At 10 Mr. Mountgarret and Mr. Bowen calld upon me from Risdon. 8 p.m. Mr. Wilson came and slept at my marque.

Wednesday, 4. A.M.—Mr. Wilson breakfasted with me; afterwards he went to Risdon. At 2 p.m. I dind with Captain Mertho on board the *Ocean*. C.S., Bristol.

Thursday, 5. A.M.—Being much better this morn took a walk with Mr. Harris after sitting as magistrate upon some business respecting Robt. Stewart, who we orderd 50 lashes and to be sent into a gang. C.S., Pye.

Friday, 6. A.M.—Moderate wr. At 5 p.m. Captain Bowen and Lt. Johnston dind with me, and Capt. Mertho, Mr. Mountgarret came. In the eve Capt. Bowen returnd. C.S., Dunchurch.

Saturday, 7. A.M.—Engaged at home on business all day. In the eve Lt. Johnston dind with me. Lt. Moore came down from Risdon. In the eve much rain. C.S., Dunstable.

Sunday, 8. A.M.—The weather so cold and wind blowing that divine service could not be performd. At 11 Capt. Bowen and Mr. Wilson calld upon me. In the eve I dind with Lt. Johnston. C.S., Landaff.

Monday, 9. A.M.—At ½-past 12 Capt. Mertho and Mr. Mountgarret calld upon me, but was engagd upon business with Mr. Harrises servt. At 5 p.m. Lt. Johnson called upon me. C.S., Nash.

Tuesday, 10. A.M.—At 8 the Lt.-Gov. sent for me, and both of us attended punishment of John Rogers, who receivd 50 lashes, and Thoms Green 100 lashes. Afterwards I breakfasted with the Governor. At 10 Groves and self took a walk. In the eve I dind with Lt. Johnson and Capt. Mertho. C.S., Bull.

Wed., 11. A.M.—Mr. Harris breakfasted with me; afterwards engaged upon business till 11; then Mr. Wilson came to the camp and dind with me. In the eve he went to the point opposite Risdon, but could not get a boat, therefore came back and slept at my marque.

Thursday, 12. A.M.—At 9 Mr. Wilson and self walkd oppsite Risdon, where we see Lt. Moore, and he set us over the water; it blew very hard all day. I dind and slept at Capt. Bowen's. Very bad wet weather.

Friday, 13. A.M.—Do. weather till 3 p.m., when I came to the camp and supd with Lt. Johnsonn.

Saturday, 14. A.M.—Mr. Harris and self engaged all the morn in trying some men who had robbd the stores, and found them guilty. I went to the *Ocean* as magistrate, and took some things that were there. In the eve Lt. Johnson dind with me and G. Collins, the Lt.-Gov. son. C.S., Gill.

Sunday, 15. A.M.—The wr. so cold that divine service could not be performd. Lt. Moore and Mr. Mountgarret calld upon me. C.S., Boidel.

Monday, 16. A.M.—Detained at home with G. P. Harris on justice business. Lt. Johnson dind with me.

Tuesday, 17. A.M.—Lt. Johnson and self walkd to the farm, where I left him to go to Risdon to see Capt. Bowen. I returnd home to dinner. C.S., Curtis.

Wednesday, 18. At 1 p.m. Mr. Harris and self dind with Capt. Mertho on board the *Ocean*. After tea we all came on shore. C.S., Glynn.

Thursday, 19. A.M.—At 5 it began to rain. 8 fine wr., but the mountain covd. with snow. Mr. H. and self engaged upon business. At 10 rain, which increasd, and at 1 p.m. it blew a hard gale, the wind from the S. east; all the hills covd. with snow around; a very bad night of wet. C.S.,

Friday, 20. A.M.—Continuel hard rain. At 12 more moderate. P.M.— At 7 Lt. Johnson return from Risdon, where he had been on a visit, and slept at my marque. C.S., Harrington.

Sat., 21. A.M.—Moderate, but rain at intervels. At 10 my man Salmon and self went out with our guns, and killd a couple of kangarros by 12 o'clock. Lt. Johnson and Mr. Wilson breakfasted with me.

Sunday, 22. A.M.—The wr. exceedingly cold; all the mountains around coverd with snow, perticulary the table mountain. At 3 p.m. Capt. Bowen, Mr. Wilson, and self dind with Lieut. Johnson. In the eve Capt. Metho came. Capt. Bowen slept at Lt. Johnson's. We had an eclipse of the moon visible. C.S., Eclipse.

Monday, 23. A.M.—At 9 I breakfasted with Lt. Johnson and Capt. Bowen; returnd to Risdon as soon as breakfast was over. Mr. Harris and self engaged on justice business. At ½-past 10 married Samuel Gunn, a prisoner, to Miss Paterson, a free woman. At ½-past 2 I took a walk, and returnd home to dinner at 5; the hills coverd with snow. C.S., Return.

Tuesday, 24. A.M.—After breakfast I went out with my gun in hopes of getting a kangarro. I see 2, but could get any; killd a kangarro rabbit. C.S., Amendment.

Wed., 25. A.M.—Sent my man Thos. Salmon out with my gun, but he had no success. At 1 p.m. Capt. Bowen from Risdon calld upon me. At 3 I took a walk in hopes of killing something for dinner, but could not. C.S., Sidney.

Thursday, 26. A.M.—At 11 I walkd opposite Risdon, when Mr. Wilson took me over in a boat, and I dind with Capt. Bowen. Slept at Mr. Wilson's. C.S., Penshurt.

Friday, 27. A.M.—In the morn I took a walk to the saw pitts, and breakfasted with Capt. Bowen; his man brought home a very large emew. At 3 p.m. we dind; and ½-past 4 Capt. Bowen, Mr. Wilson, and self got into a boat and landed at the setlers. We see a great many porpuses and a very large whale near us. C.S., Hyde.

Saturday, 28. A.M.—At 12 Mr. Mountgarret calld upon me, and we both went on board the *Ocean*. At 2 p.m. the Lt. Governor and Mrs. Powers came; they stayd till 5 p.m., when I went on shore with them. Mr. and Mrs. Groves and little boy drank tea with me this eve; much lightning with rain.

Sunday, 29. A.M.—The wr. so bad, blowing hard, that divine service could not be performd. At 1 p.m. it blew a perfect gale of wind from . At 4 p.m. Lt. Johnson and Mr. Wilson dind with me. In the eve Mr. W. came and slept at my marque.

Monday, 30. A.M.—At 7 Mr. Wilson went to Risdon. At 8 Lt. Johnson went up with orders for every one to embark on board the *Ocean*. At 4 p.m. Mr. George Collins, son of the Lt. Governor's, and Mr. Wright Todd dind with me. ½-past 8 p.m. Lt. Johnson calld on me; he informd that every one was embark on board but Capt. Bowen, who slept at the farm, at the house which he built for Martha Hays. The wind blowing very fresh, and a great quantity of snow upon the mountains. C.S., Pearson.

Tuesday, 31. A.M.—Engaged in writing letters for England. At 10 p.m. a boat arrived in the cove from the *Alexander* whaler, Capt. Rodes, belonging to the house of Mr. Hurry, Capt. Mertho's house. She had been in the South Seas, and had very great success. I got my certificate[1] signd.

Wed., August 1. A.M.—Mr. Rodes, the Master of the *Alexander*, whaler, breakfasted with the Governor, and afterwards call'd upon me. He informed me that he had some things from Port Jackson for me. In the eve Capt. Bowen and Mr. Wilson calld upon me.

Thursday, 2. A.M.—At 8, Lt. Lord, Mr. Harris, and self, went and breakfasted with Capt. Mertho. Mr. Rodes went early in the morn to his ship at Adventure Bay. At ½ past 10 Henery Hakin went in the white cutter for the Lt. Governors dispatches. C.S., Antrim.

Friday, 3. A.M.—At 10, engaged all this morn upon business with Mr. Harris. At 3 I dind with Capt. Bowen at his house at the farm. Mr. Wilson there. I returnd home to tea.

Sat., 4. A.M.—Engaged in writing letters all the morn. 5 p.m. Lt. Johnson dind with me. Henry Hakin, the Lt. Governors coxwain and pilot, returnd from the ship *Alexander* in Adventure Bay. He brought me a dog from Lt. Houston, and informd us that he see a ship at a distance out of the river.

Sunday, 5. A.M.—The *Ocean*, transport, was to sail this day, but was prevented. The Governors despatches were not ready. At 5 p.m. a boat arrived from the *Lady Barlo*, a ship from Pt. Jackson with cattle, &c., &c. Sent all my letters on board the *Ocean*, Capt. Mertho. The Lt. Governors coxwain went down to the *Lady B.* to pilot her up. Mrs. Pettit, Adjt. Pettit, Ld. Spencer, Ld. Sudley, Wm. Tustin, Esqr., — Donovan, Lt. Houston. C. S., Ocean.

Monday, 6. A.M.—At daylight I went out with my man Salmon in search of kangarro, but could not find any. Returnd home at 11. 2 p.m. Mr. Harris and self went on board the *Ocean*, transport, Capt. Mertho, to dinner, where we met Mr. Mountgarret, Lt. Moore, and Mr. Brown [? Bowen], who were going to Pt. Jackson. At 7 we came on shore.

Tuesday, 7. A.M.—At 11 we observed the East India [Extra] Company ship *Lady Barlow* beating up the river. Lt. Johnson dind with me. At 8 she anchord in Sullivan Bay. C. S., McAskill.

Wednesday, 8. A.M.—At 9 the Lt. Governor sent me some letters, which were from England, Mr. Pettit, &c., and likewise from Mr. Marsden. At 3 p.m. I dind with the Lt. Governor, and met Capt.

---

[1] These are to certify the Right Honble. the Lords Commissioners of His Majesty's Treasury that the Revd. Robert Knopwood hath been in the execution of his office as Assistant Chaplain of the settlements in New South Wales from the date of his appointment to the day of the date hereof.

Given under my hand at Government House, Hobart Town, Derwent River, Van Diemen's Land, this twenty-ninth day of Feb. 1804.

D. C., Lt. Governor.

McAskill, belonging to the *Lady Barlow*, one of the Companys East India ships. 7, went on board the *Ocean*, transport, to take leave of Capt. John Bowen, who was going to Pt. Jackson, and likewise Capt. Merthow, who was going to leave this settlement. C.S., Menzies.

Thursday, 9. A.M.—At 8 this morn saild our friend Capt. Mertho, who commanded the *Ocean*, transport, which came from England in company with H.M. ship *Calcutta*, Capt. Dan. Woodriffe. The *Ocean* brought out settlers, stores, &c., &c., for the colony at Port Phillip, under the command of Lt. Gov. Collins of the Royal Marines. The settlement at Pt. Phillip did not succeed, and the *Ocean* removed it to the River Derwent, Van Diemens Land. C.S., Success.

Friday, 10. A.M.—At 4 p.m. the *Alexander*, whaler, anchord in Sandy Bay, near the east side of the river, to take whales. At 5, Capt. McAskill and self dind with Lt. Johnson. At 8 he went away. ½ past, Capt. Rhodes, of the *Alexander*, whaler, came and calld upon me there. He slept at my marque. C. S., Success.

Saturday, 11. A.M.—Captain Rhodes went away, and after breakfast I walkd to the farm. Calld on Martha Hays, &c. Returnd home to dinner. C.S., Nelson.

Sunday, 12. A.M.—The *Alexander*, whaler, Capt. Rodes, caught 2 whales opposite the Camp. At 3 p.m. the following gentlemen dind on board the *Lady Barlow* with Capt. McAskill :—Lt. Governor Collins and Mrs. Powers, Capt. Sladden, Lt. Johnson, Lt. Lord of the Royal Marines, Wm. J anson, Mathew Bowden, Leonard Fosbrook, G. P. Harris, and self. We were all very merry. C.S., Long live.

Monday, 13. A.M.—At ½ past nine I went in the launch to Risdon for some plank, &c., that I left there. The *Alexander*, whaler, caught a very fine whale. At 5 Mr. Bowden, Fosbrook, Johnson, and self, dind with Mr. Harris. This eve we sent a letter to His Honor the Lt. Governor, and in the eve he calld upon me, and requested to speak to me upon business. Capt. Rhodes slept at my marque. C.S., Ganges.

Tuesday, 14. A.M.—Capt. Rhodes, Mr. Harris, and Lt. Johnson, breakfasted with me. At home all the morn. At 5 Lt. Johnson dind with me. The people emptied the *Lady Barlow* of stores. C. S., Britannia.

Wed., 15. A.M.—At 8 the Lt. Governer sent two men to begin my house, and this morn Gun and Foreshaw began mending my boat, and Eodem literd, which was sent to the Lt. Gov. was withdrawn after a meeting of all the officers. Capt. Rhodes, of the *Alexander*, whaler, came on shore and took an early dinner. At 5 p.m. I went on the Parade, where the Gov. and Lt. Johnson was walking. The Gov. was very pleasant, and on our coming away to my markwequee said that all was amicably settled. C.S., Escort.

Thursday, 16. A.M.—This morn a party of us was to have dind on board the *Alexander*, whaler, Capt. Rhodes, but the rain was so much that we were prevented.

Friday, 17. A.M.—Lt. Johnson breakfasted with me, and afterwards walkd to the farm, and I dind with Lt. Johnson. The *Lady Barlow* landing her stores for Mr. Collins. C.S., Montague.

Saturday, 18. A.M.—At home all the morn. At 4 p.m. I dind with Mr. Harris. C.S., Pelham.

Sunday, 19. A.M.—Mr. Harris breakfasted with me. At 12, Captain Sladden, Lt. Johnson, Mr. Harris, and self, went on board the *Lady Barlow* to settle our bills, &c., with Capt. MacAskill. At 6 p.m. I dind with Lt. Johnson, and Capt. Rhodes calld upon me there. They all went on board the *Lady Barlow*, and stayd very late. C.S., George.

Monday, 20. A.M.—At 9 the masons began to lay the foundation of my house, and the carpenters at work; the *Lady Barlow* making preparations for sailing.

Tuesday, 21. A.M.—At 10 a boat came from the *Alexander*, whaler, Captain Robt. Rhodes. 11, Lieut. Johnson and self went on board and dind. At 7 Capt. MacAskill and Mr. Collins came on board and stayd some time. In the eve it blew very fresh, and they went on board.

Wednesday, 22. A.M.—At 9 Capt. Rhodes and self went out in search of kangarrois, but could not see any. We returnd to dinner.

Thursday, 23. A.M.—At 10 Capt Rhodes and self came to the camp, and in the eve dind with Lt. Johnson. Mr. Bowden and Mr. Fosbrook came and spent the eve there. Hamond.

Friday, 24. A.M.—Capt. Rhodes slept at my marque and breakfasted with me. C. S., Oldman.

Saturday, 25. A.M.—At 11 took a walk with my gun and dogs. Killd a small brush kangarro. Continuel rain and very hard squalls of wind. Lt. Johnson dind with me. Very hard gales of wind during the eve. C.S., Defiance.

Sunday, 26. A.M.—Severe gales of wind with hard rain. At 8 more moderate. 10, saw Capt. Rhode of the *Alexander*, whaler, kill 2 whales. Lt. Johnson dind with me. C. S., Victor.

Monday, 27. A.M.—More moderate but hot winds from the N. West. In the afternoon walk to the farm with Lt. Johnson and returnd home to dinner. Groves came and sat with me in the eve. Very hard gales of wind.

Tuesday, 28. A.M.—Very hard gales during the night and morning. At 8 more moderate and rain. Took a long walk; and at 5 dind with Lt. Lord and Humphry, Capt. and Mrs. Sladden there. C.S.,

Wednesday, 29. A.M.—At 11 Lt.-Governor and self went to the farm, and when he returnd he gave me the counter sign, which is to be delivered every day to me. C.S., Venus.

Thursday, 30. A.M.—At 11 Lt. Governor Collins swore the following gentlemen in as magistrates, as appointed by His Excellency Gov. King:—Revd. R. Knopwood, Wm. Sladden, G. P. Harris, Esq. At 5 p.m. Mr. Harris, Lt. Johnson, and Mr. Fosbrook dind with me. C.S., Juno.

Friday, 31. A.M.—At 11 Capt. Sladden, Mr. Harris, and self sat as majtrates, concerning Mr. Blinkworth, a settler. In the eve much rain. C.S., Mars.

Saturday, 1 *September*. A.M.—At 10 took a walk; saw no kangarro. At 3 p.m. rain. At 5 I dind with Lt. Johnson, and as we were sitting down to dinner a large kangarro came very near his marque, and through the camp. ½-past 9, the centinel fird at a man near the magazeene, and he escaped. C.S., Culloden.

Sunday, 2. A.M.—Moderate and clear weather. Capt. Rhodes calld upon me. P.M.—At 4 rain. At 5 Lt. Johnson and Captain Rhodes dind with me, and he stayd all night. C.S., Elliott.

Monday, 3. A.M.—A very fine morning. At ½-past 11 Lt. Gov. Collins and self walkd to the farm, and there took his boat and went to Risdon Cove; the Gov. ordered all the houses that were there to be pulld down.[1] At 4 p.m. we arrived in the camp, and I dind with him. C.S., Goliath.

Tuesday, 4. A.M.—At 12 Lt. Johnson and self walkd to the farm; and in the eve dind with him. Met there Lt. Lord, Mr. Fosbrook, and J anson. My boat was finished. C.S., Illustrious.

Wed. 5. A.M.—At 11 I walkd to the farm, where I took my boat and went to Risdon Cove with my dogs. At 4 p.m. went and killd a large kangarro. I slept at Mr. Mountgarret house that was. Rain and snow. C.S., Genner.

Thursday, 6. A.M.—At 5 sent my man out with the dogs. At 6 I went out after ducks; saw very few. At 10 returnd. He killd a kan. At 1 p.m. left Risdon and came to Hobert Town, and dind with Mr. Harris. C.S., Musgrave.

Friday, 7. A.M.—At 10 saild a whaling the *Alexander* ship, Capt. Rhodes, to Adventure Bay. Lt. Johnson and Mr. Harris dind with me.

Saturday, 8. A.M.—This morn the weather remarkably fine. At 11 I went out a fishing; no success. Mr. Harris and self dind with Mr. Fosbrook. C.S., Brenton.

Sunday, 9. A.M.—Very fine wr. In the eve much lightning. At 11 fresh breezes. C.S., Garrow.

Monday, 10. A.M.—Strong wind, with rain. At 2 p.m. I walkd to the farm, and dind with Lt. —[illegible]. Mr. Groves came to me in the eve. C.S., Clarence.

Tuesday, 11. A.M.—Moderate wr., and fine. C.S., Hobart.

Wed., 12. A.M.—At 11 Lieut. Johnson and self took a long walk to Millers, the settler; In the eve I dind with him; Capt. Sladden and Mr. Humphry calld and took wine. The day very hot, but the Table Mountain coverd with snow. C.S., Colossus.

Thursday, 13. A.M.—Lt. Johnson and self [w]alk to the garden, and home by the Government [blank]. C.S., Nisus.

Friday, 14. A.M.—At 11 Lt. Johnson and the Lt. Governor went to the farm; the Gov. returnd, and Mr. Johnson and self went to Risdon. In the eve I dind with him. My man Salmon brought home 2 kangarros. C.S., Longford.

Saturday, 15. A.M.—This day all the civil and military dind with Mr. Fosbrook, the commissary, except Mr. Hopley, who was not invited. C.S., Manners.

Sunday, 16. A.M.—Divine service was to have been performed at the farm, but the wr. was so very wet I could not go there. At 4 p.m. thunder was heard very loud, and the Table Mountain was coverd with snow. Mr. Fosbrook and self dined with Lt. Johnson. C.S., Grampus.

Monday, 17. A.M.—The majestrates sat. In the eve continuel rain. The people employd at building houses for the civil officers. C.S., Liverpool.

---

[1] The proprietor of the land on which the Risdon settlement stood was the late Thomas George Gregson, Esquire, who died four or five years since. I called, with an intimate friend of his, upon him during his last illness, when the latter shewed me the remains of these houses—mere broken walls. I suppose these ruins still exist —C., 1878.

Tuesday, 18. A.M.—Fresh breezes and clear. At 2 p.m. thunder. At 6 I dind with Lt. Johnson; and had a very severe gale, with hard rain. ½-past 10, the drum. C.S., Leeth.

Wednesday, 19. A.M.—At 3 very bad wr.; and at 6 the wind and rain very much. At 8 the mountain was coverd with snow. 11, I walkd to the farm, and killd a kangarro. Sent my man forward to Mr. Millers, the settlers, where he slept. Lt. Johnson dind with me. C.S., Alert.

Thursday, 20. A.M.—At 9 I went to the farm in my boat to meet my man, who was out at Mr. Millers, the settler, to kill a kangarro; at 11 he came there; had bad luck, killd only one. I met Lt. Johnson at the farm, and we went and called upon Martha Hays. Lieut. Johnson rode to Hobert Town, Capt. Bowens mare.[1] At 4 p.m. dind with Mr. Bowden, and met there Lt. Johnson and Mr. Fosbrook. C.S., Bognor.

Friday, 21. A.M.—The day very hot from the N.W. winds. At 1 p.m. Lt. Gov. Collins and Mrs. Powers went in my boat to the farm; they took their provision with them to dine. Sent my man Salmon to Risdon to kill kangarro. Lt. Lord returnd from the opposite side of the river, and kill 5 kangarros. Hackin, the Lt. Gov. keeper, came from the settlers farm and brought in 4 with him. C.S., Broadstairs.

Sat. 22. A.M.—The day very hot. At 3 p.m. rain, and heard thunder. This day I began to dig a well at my new garden. At 1 p.m., it being H.M. Coronation day, the colors were hoisted. C.S., Happy reign.

Sunday, 23. A.M.—Rain at 10. 1 p.m. I went to the farm and performd divine service; returned to Hobert Town, and Lt. Johnson dind with me. My man Salmon returnd from Risdon, and brought three large kangarros, which my young dogs killd—Spot and Alexander. C.S., Parsons.

Monday, 24. A.M.—The wr. very hot, and the large flies begin to be very troublesome. I stayd at home all the morn upon justice business and Mr. Harris. Returnd 56 lbs. of kangarro into H.M. store, for the use of the sick, at 6d. per lb. C.S., Melbourne.

Tuesday, 25. A.M.—At 11 Mr. Harris and self markd out a place of 2 acres for a garden. Martha Hays and mother came to the camp and calld on me. C.S., Gloucester.

Wednesday, 26. At 11 I went in my boat with my dogs part of the way to Risdon. Killd a wild duck. At 4 p.m. Lieut. Johnson met me, and we went across the water to Risdon. We went out to look for kangaroos; no success; returnd and slept at Mr. Mountgarrets house. When Salmon met us on the 22nd inst. he caught a young kangarro, and left it with the 2 men that were there as watch over the convicts; the creature is so tame that it followed one of the men down to where the boat lai'd, a mile from the house. In the eve it ran about the room, and playd with the dogs; not one of them offerd to kill it.

Thursday, 27. At 4 a.m. we got up. At 6 we went out and had a very long walk up the mountains. At 9 we returnd home to breakfast; we saw only one kangarro, which we killd. At 1 p.m. Lt. Johnson and self came to my boat from Risdon to Hobert Town, and we dind with Mr. Fosbrook. C.S., Adolphus.

---

[1] First mention of any horse in the colony.

Friday, 28. At 9 R[a]in, Lt. Lords servants, returnd with 5 kangarros from the opposite side of the river. At 5 p.m. Salmon returnd from Risdon with a large forest kangarro. At 11, while in bed, I heard the report of a gun. C.S., York.

Saturday, 29. A.M.—At 8, Mr. Fosbrook, the commissary, informd me that his marquee was attempted to be robbd, but was prevented by his firing at them; they had cut part of the marque, near a box of clothes, &c., &c. At 5 p.m. dind with Lit. Johnson. C.S., Wertemberg.

Sunday, 30. A.M.—The morning so very windy that divine service could not be performd. This morn two men began to cut down and burn off 2 acres of ground for me at my new garden. At 7 the wr. began to be very windy; and at 10 a heavy gale came on, which increasd till near 12. C.S., Saxton.

Monday, 1 Oct. A.M.—At 1 it blew a perfect hurricane; many trees and the store tent upon Hunters Island was blown down. At 4 I expected every moment that my marquee would have been blown down. This day the brickmakers began to make some. At 10 the wr. began to moderate. At the parade of the Royal Marines this morn the Articles of War were read by Capt. Lieut. Sladden, acting as adjutant. After the parade a court martial was held, by order of Lieut. Coll. Col., of the Loyal Marines, upon a Private Woolley. At 5 p.m. the military assembled at the parade, and marched off to the place of punishment. Wooley was sentenced to receive 200 lashes for drinking with a convict named Plunket, each of which men received one 100 each. N.B.—The Lieut. Gov. and Lt. Col., of the Royal Marines, the same morn breakfasted with a convict and his wife, by the name of Mathew Powers; she always lives at the Col. table. C.S., Fenshaw.

Tuesday, 2. A.M.—At 5 I went up with my boat near Risdon to Mr. Millers farm to kill ducks, &c.; had bad luck. At 5 p.m. returnd; killd only one duck. Dind with Lt. Johnson. C.S., Hope.

Wednesday, 3. A.M.—The day remarkably fine. At 4 p.m. all the civil and military officers dind with me, Captain Sladden, Lieuts. Johnson and Lord, Messrs. Harris, J anson, Bowden, Fosbrook, Humphrey. The dinner as follows:—Fish, kangaroo soup, roast kid—saddle, roast kangarro—saddle, 2 fowls pellewed with rice and bacon, rost pig.[1] C.S., Colnet.

Thursday, 4. A.M.—At 10 Groves and self went in my boat down the river a fishing, but had very bad success. At 1 while we were there the Lt. Governor ordered the guns to be scaled on Hunter's Island. In the eve returnd, and Lt. Johnson dind with me.

Friday, 5. A.M.—At 12 all the civil and military officers met at Mr. Bowden's to consult about a plan of building a subscription room, when we all wrote to the Lt. Governor to prove the plan to him. At 1 the Lt. Gov. and Mrs. Powers went to the farm in his boat. C.S., Loring.

---

[1] NOTE.—The remainder of the leaf (which it may be presumed contained originally the enumeration of the wines drank, &c.), has been cut away, thus destroying very nearly an entire entry on the other side of the 6th; and the whole of the next leaf has also been removed, which must have contained the entries of the 7th, 8th, and 9th, all of which are wanting. [C.]

Saturday, 6. A.M.—At 7 Groves came to me and we—[the remainder of the entry gone.] C.S., Cesar.

[The entries of the 7th, 8th, and 9th all cut out.]

Wednesday, 10. A.M.—This morn Salmon killd a kangarro; the day very hot. At 5 p.m. Lt. Johnson, Mr. Harris, Bowden, and Fosbrook dind with me off of emew, and very excellent it was. C.S., Straits.

Thursday, 11. A.M.—At 10 very squally, with rain. 4 p.m. all the officers, civil and military, dind with Mr. Bowden at his new house; Mrs. Sladden was at the dinner. C.S., Procter.

Friday, 12. A.M.—A very fine morn. At 1 p.m. the sea breeze came, and I went in my boat to Millers, the settlers. At $\frac{1}{2}$-past 4 I went out with my dogs; saw one kangarro, but no success. I slept at Millers. C.S., Darnley.

Saturday, 13. A.M.—At 3 I got up and breakfasted; and at 4 Mr. Miller and self with my man went in my boat up the river nearly as far as Herdsman's Cove. We walked about till nearly eleven, when we returnd to Millers. Afterwards I came to Hobert Town and dind with Mr. Harris. In the eve I drank tea with Mrs. Groves. C.S., Falmouth.

Sunday, 14. A.M.—The day very warm. At $\frac{1}{2}$-past 2 performd divine service at the hospital to all the sick. $\frac{1}{2}$-past 3 I dind with His Honor the Governor. C.S., Fox.

Monday, 15. A.M.—This morn Salmon took my dogs and went with Henry Hacking, the Lt. Governor's keeper, up the river. At 5 p.m. I dind with Lt. Johnson. At 6 very hard rain, which continued all night. C.S., Chesterfield.

Tuesday, 16. A.M.—Early this morn the Governor's boat went for his keeper and Hacking up beyond Risdon; they had no success, and the boat took them to Risdon. Lt. Johnson and Mr. Harris dind with me. This day twelve months we landed from His Majesty's Ship *Calcutta* at Port Phillip, New South Wales, and all the military and convicts were encampd there. C.S., Landing.

Wednesday, 17. A.M.—At 8 I sent my boat for Salmon, and he returnd with the Gov. keeper. He informd me that on the first day my dogs killd a very large *emew*, but could not find it; last eve they killd 3 kangarros. Mr. Harris went up the river with some men with him.

Thursday, A.M.—At 7 I went in my boat to Risdon. The wind come so much against me that with very great difficulty I got to the farm, where I left my boat and walkd to Hobert Town. In the eve Lt. Johnson dind with me. C.S., Massey.

Friday, 19. A.M.—This morn my man returnd with the boat. I sent the Governor a dish of green peas, the first that had been seen; they were taken from Mr. Moor's garden at Risdon. At 5 p.m. I dind with Lt. Johnson, and met Mr. Humphry there. No success this day after kangarros. C.S., Penn.

Saturday, 20. A.M.—The morn very hot. At 4 p.m. rain, which continued some time. At 9 observed a very fine night rain bow from the S.S. west, which continued some time; then we heard[1] the rain very much from the mountain. C.S., Walter.

---

[1] Probably *had*.

Sunday, 21. A.M.—At 10 rain, accompanied with thunder and lightning. At 12 the wr. very fine. P.M.—Very cold, and excessive hard gales of wind, which continued all night. Mrs. Sarjant came into the camp to live with her husband. My little white hen haching her yaind;[1] the 2d brood since Feb. last. C.S., Mexico.

Monday, 22. A.M.—10 do. wr., with rain. Salmon killd a kangarro. We had very violent squalls of wind and hard rain. At 5 p.m. Lt. Johnson dind with me. C.S., Hague.

Tuesday, 23. A.M.—My little white hen came off with 7 young chickings. A.M.—At 10 the Lt. Governor and self in his boat went across the river to see what ship was coming in. At 12 we returnd and concluded to be the *Alexander* whaler, Capt. Rhodes. At 8 p.m. a boat came on shore with the Captain. Capt. Rh. I dind with Lt. Johnson. C.S., Vivian.

Wednesday, 24. A.M.—At 6 I sent my boat to Mr. Millers the settlers, with Groves in it. At 11 the Governor, Mrs. Powers, and self went in his boat up the river with an intention to dine at Millers (the Governor took every thing with him). At 12 o'clock the weather came on very bad that we were obliged to run into the farm cove, and went on shore and dind at Mr. Hobbs house, the day was so wet. At 5 p.m. I walkd to Millers, where I slept, and Mr. Groves likewise.

Thursday, 25. A.M.—At 5 we got up and breakfasted; sent Salmon out with the dogs to meet us at Mr. Harris hut. At 8 we got there, 14 miles from Miller's. Salmon came with a kangarro; we breakfasted there. At ½-past 9 we got in the boat and went up the river 2 miles, where we met Mr. Harris and party returning; we went back and gave them the provisions that I brought out with me. At 11 we pitched the tent and stayd there all night. Mr. Groves and self went to see Herdsmans Cove and the land there.

Friday, 26. A.M.—At 7 we breakfasted, and at 9 Mr. Harris went on measuring the course of the river. 12 I got into my boat (Salmon this morn killd 2 kangarros), and we went for Risdon. I killd 3 black swans. At 2 we arrived at Risdon, where we dind, and slept at Mr. Mountgarrets house.

Saturday, 27. A.M.—Early this morn Salmon went out with the dogs, but had no success. We breakfasted there, and at 10 came away and arrived at the camp. I killd 2 black swans. Mr. Harris returnd to the camp and dind with me. C.S.

Sunday, 28. A.M.—Cold rainy wr. At 1 p.m. all the convicts were musterd at one of the huts to see respecting their clothing. At ½ past 2 performd divine service to the sick at the hospital. 4 Capt. Rhodes, of the *Alexander* whaler, dind with me and Mr. Harris and Lt. Johnson. C.S., Bligh.

Monday, 29. A.M.—Strong winds. At 12 I went on board the *Alexander* with Mr. Bowden to take sanwidges. At 5 p.m. Cap. Rhodes, Mr. Humphrys, Mr. Janson, and self dind with Mr. Harris. Capt. Rhodes stayd all night at my marque. C.S., Thompson.

Tuesday, 30. A.M.—Cap. Rhodes breakfasted with me. At 12 Mr. Fosbrook, Harris, Janson, Bowden, and self went on board the

---

[1] This word is correctly copied. [C.]

Alexander to take tiffin. At ½-past 1 Mr. Harris, J anson, and self came away; the other two gentlemen were going up to Risdon with Capt. Rhodes in his boats. C.S., Hope.

Wednesday, 31. A.M.—I sent my man Salmon with my dogs to kill kangarro for the Governor, his dog Paddy being staked. C.S.

Thursday, November, 1. A.M.—At 12 I walkd to the farm. At 5 Mr. J anson and Lt. Johnson took a stake with me. My man returnd from kangarro hunting with the Governor's keeper; they went out the morning before and brought home 4 large forest kangarros. C.S., Steele.

Friday, 2. A.M.—At 8 I went across the river with my boat and Mr. Groves with me. At 3 p.m. the Governor's boat returnd from Betseys Island and brought with them a native man. The man was much coverd with charcoal, and had a bag made of kangarro skins about his neck which containd teeth of one of the tribe. The same aft. he was dressd in trousers and a shirt and jacket given him by the Governor. C.S., Dryden.

Saturday, 3. A.M.—This morn I heard that the native man deserted from Hobert Town. At 10 Mr. Fosbrook and Mr. Bowden with Capt. Rhodes returnd from their excursion; they had very good luck, killd and took 17 black swanns. At 5 p.m. the weather began to blow from the N.W. At 8 it blew very hard gales from the same quarter. C.S., Gay.

Sunday, 4. A.M.—At 11 performd divine service, and His Honor the Lt. Governor, &c., &c., &c., attended. At 2 p.m. I performd divine service at the hospital. At 4 Mr. Harris and self dind with the Governor, and in the eve we had very severe gales of wind; expected every moment the marque to be blown over. Wind N.W. C.S., Churchell.

Monday, 5. A.M.—At 1 it raind very hard. 9 do. wr. 1 p.m. continuel rain. At 3 I dind on board the *Alexander*, Capt. Rhodes; came on shore at 8. The weather very bad with rain and wind. C.S., Plot.

Tuesday, 6. A.M.—The weather very windy. At 3 His Honor the Lt. Governor went on board the *Alexander* to dinner. Mr. Harris and self met him there. On his getting on board the crew gave him three cheers. We came away with him at ½-past 7. Spent the day very pleasantly. C.S., Young.

Wednesday, 7. A.M.—Capt. Rhodes and self went to the farm. At 5 p.m. the civil and military dind with Mr. J anson. C.S., Parnell.

Thursday, 8. A.M.—At 10 I went out a fishing with Groves, and caught some very fine flat heads. ½-past 12 we went on board the whaler. At 4 p.m. Mr. Harris, Capt. Rhodes, and self dind with His Honor the Lt. Governor. At 12 we had severe lightning. The people employd building huts, &c., &c. C.S., Mason.

Friday, 9. AM.—At 1 a very dreadful tempest of thunder and lightning. 2 it raind very hard, which continued some time. At 4 a hot wind came on from the N.W. At 3 p.m. Mr.Harris, Fosbrook, Bowden, and self dind on board the *Alexander*, Capt. Rhodes. C.S., Perrin.

Saturday, 10. A.M.—At 10 Capt. Rhodes and self went in his boat to Millers farm, where we were to have met His Honor the Lt. Governor. At 11 the wind blew very hard, which continued some time. Soon after we arrivd at Millers the Gov. sent a man to inform us that he could not come forward, but that he should dine at the farm and should be glad to see us at dinner there. We dind with him at his marque, and walkd home in the evening. The convicts who were marred had some houses building in their extra time. C.S., Return.

Sunday, 11. A.M.—At 11 performd divine service ; the Lt. Governor and all attended. Capt. Rhodes and Mr. Johnson dind with me. C.S., Gay.

Monday, 12. A.M.—Mr. Harris and self dind on board the *Alexander*, Capt. Rhodes, and Mr. Fosbrook and Mr. Bowden. C.S., Hobart.

Tuesday, 13. A.M.—Preparing my letters to England for the *Alexander* whaler. Settled with Capt. Rhodes. The Governor supplied Mr. Harris and self with 14 days' provisions and a boat. Letter for[1] Esq., Mr. and Mrs. P., Miss Kd., Wm. Tustin, Esq. C.S., Wilson.

Wednesday, 14. A.M.—Fresh breezes from the S.W. All hands employd as needful. Middle part more moderate ; at daylight clear. At 5 a.m. took the breeze from the N.W. ; took the anchor and bore for Storm Bay passage. At 6 a.m. went on board: Revd. R. Kd., G. P. Harris, and James Groves, with a Government boat mannd with the following men :—Henry Hakin, the Gov. coxwain, Powell, Garrett, Richardson, Davis, Atkinson, Scholar, Wm. Russell, Henry Miller, and Salmon. At 12 brought up in Storm Bay passage in 26 fathoms water with the peak of the table Mountain, which we gave the name of Mount Collins in honor of the Lt. Governor ; the mount bearing N.W., Point Louis N. by east 4 miles, the east point of Ile Bruny S.W. by S. dist. 4 miles. At 3 p.m. sent 3 boats for black swans, and Mr. Harris, Capt. Rhodes, Groves, and self on shore. It was the North Cove where the ship layd ; the soil very bad, all stones, and the tree not good. At sun set we returnd and the 3 whale boats ; they took 79 swans. This aft. when we layd at anchor we see 2 of the natives on Isle de Bruny.

Thursday, 15. A.M.—Fresh gales. At 2 the anchor came home squally, brought up in 12 fathms in a hard muddy bottom. At 12 sent a boat to Hobart Town with letters, and forsome sheet lead. Mt. Collins bore N.N.W., and Point Luis N.N.E., dist. 3 miles. The Isle Bruny, N.E. b. E., dist. 1 mile, the point from the westermost shore, that from the N.W. branch, W. by North, dist. 2 miles.

Friday, 16. A.M.—This morn we went to the opposite shore, where, after tracing the coast 6 miles, we arrived at a fine cove, which abounds with oysters. On the north side, a little above low water mark we found a large conger eel, which the Revd. R. Knopwood shot. It weighed 20 lb. We gave the name of the cove Conger Cove. In this cove we markd a tree—R. Knopd., R. Rhodes, Nov. 17, 1804. From the ship the tree is 4 miles, S.W. b. S. It stands from the rocks on the side of the hill. The boat up at Hobert Town.

---

[1] Name omitted.

On board the *Alexander*, whaler, Cap. Rhodes, Storm Bay Passage, November 1804.

Saturday, 17. A.M.—This morn we went on shore on Isle Bruny, and see many grass trees. The day was very wet. We killd a kangarro. The men took some black swans.

Sunday, 18. A.M.—At 8 observd a boat come round Point Louis. At 10 she came on board. Struck top gallant yards at meridian hard gales and squally. We continued on board with the boat belonging to Government. At 6 p.m. let go the other bower anchor. Hard gales. The wr. was so bad that we could not stir out.

Monday, 19. A.M.—At daylight more moderate. Hove in the small bower and secured it. At 8 sent 2 boats after black swans. At 10 they returnd with 21. This morn Capt. Rhodes, Mr. Groves, and self, went on Isle Bruny and killd a kangarro. After travelling in the country several miles we returnd to a point where we orderd the boats to. Here we markd 3 trees laying in the N.E. and S.W. direction. At the back of them Revd. R. K. put several sorts of seeds in the ground. The trees were markd as follow :—The Revd. Robt. Knopwood, Nov. 19, 1804; on the back D. G., for Daniel Groves, son of Mr. Groves ; and to the S.W. six paces R. Rhodes, Commander of the *Alexander*, whaler ; to the tree 24 paces S.W., G. P. Harris, Surveyor, Hobert Town ; and on the back J. Groves. This point I gave the name of Alexander Point, in honor of our friend Capt. Rhodes. The peaks of the Table Mountain bore N.N.W., and Conger Cove W. $\frac{1}{4}$ S., dist. 3 miles.

Tuesday, 20. A.M.—At 8 took up the anchor and got under weigh. At $\frac{1}{4}$ past 1 brought up in 8 fthms., about a mile distant from Green Island. At 3 we went on shore on Green Island, and got a dozen black swans eggs and some young birds.

Wed., 21. A.M.—At 4 took the anchor up and ran down the passage as far as the mouth of the River Huon. At 9 brought up in 8 fthms. At 10, 4 boats left the ship. At 3 we returnd, having been up the River Huon, where I see a beautiful island, which I give the name of Gardners,[1] in honor of my friend the Honble. A. H. Gardner, Capt. of H.M. ship *Hero*. We caught some crayfish and got some shells. At 4 the three boats returnd with 78 fine black swans. The *Alexander* layd at anchor near a small rock, much like Noahs Ark Rock at Simons Bay, Cape of Good Hope.

Thursday, 22. A.M.—At 8 the Government boat left the ship. $\frac{1}{2}$ past, Mr. Harris and Groves, in one boat, Capt. Rhodes and self in another boat, went up the River Huon. Opposite the Huon Island is a sunken rock, in the mouth of the river, which runs $\frac{1}{2}$ a mile long from east to west. We went up the river as far as the flats, where we pitch'd our tents ; made ready for dinner some black swans, which we caught in abundance.

In the River Huon, 1804. In the Storm Bay Streights, 1804.

Friday, 23. A.M.—At day light we got up and breakfasted. Sent the whale boat after swanns, and we went in the Government cutter

---

[1] Probably Garden Island, as it is now called.

up the Huon to the 1 fall. The river is by no means so fine as the Derwent, and as for the land there is none not even fit for a garden. At the first fall there is a small island in the middle of the stream. At ½ past 1 we returnd, and arrived at the Camp Point, where we left in the morn, where we dind and slept.

Saturday, 24. A.M.—At day light we got up, and at 3[1] a.m. made sail. At 8, or ½ after, we all got on board the *Alexander*, where she was laying near the Isle of Huon, in the Straights.

Sunday, 25. A.M.—At 10 a breeze sprung up. Mr. Harris, Groves, and self, went in the Government boat, and on our leaving the ship we gave them three cheers. Capt. Rhodes hoisted his pendant, and we were cheerd by all the crew. We went into a bay calld La Petit Anse, on the N.E. It being Sunday, and having come some way, I gave orders for the tents to be pitch'd, roasted some black swans, and there we slept. We observd many of the native fires. At 11 a.m. Capt. Rhodes saild back into the Straights.

In Storm Bay Streights, 1804.

Monday, 26. A.M.—Very early this morn we breakfasted, and at 6, with a party of our men, with Mr. Harris and Groves, went up a mountain, steering a N.E. b. E. course, and with very great difficulty we got up to the top of the mountain. We were three hour and a half going about 1 mile and a half. Upon the top we see a very fine cedar and sassafras. At 12 we returnd; got every thing ready for sailing. At ½ past 1 saild, and went into a bay near [the rest left blank]. We slept on the west side of Storm Bay Passage.

Tuesday, 27. A.M.—At 6 we breakfasted, and prepared to sail to Hobert Town. 13 minutes past 7 made sail, wind south, Green Island E.N.E. At 12 we observd the *Alexander*, Capt. Rhodes, under sail, beating out of the Streights.[2] At ½ past 1 we got on board. The wind came quite calm. At 6 we observd a schooner coming up the river. I sent the pilot, Henry Hakin, on board to take care of her. The wind [3]—— We all slept on board.

Wed., 28. A.M.—At 7, Mr. Harris and Groves went in the Government boat to Hobert Town after breakfast. Capt. Rhodes and self went in his boat. At ½ past 10 we arrived. I waited on the Governor. At 11, the *George*, schooner, Capt. Stewart, anchord in the Bay. I dind with the Governor. Capt. Rhodes slept in my marque. We were all much delighted with the excursion, and indebted to Capt. Rhodes for his kind attention to us. I brought the Houen pine home with me; the first seen.

Friday, 29. A.M.—Capt. Rhodes breakfasted and dind with me and Mr. Johnson. Found that the ground at my garden would not do. The well was very bad; salt water. C.S., Buffalo.

---

[1] Correctly copied. It should probably be 5.
[2] Correctly copied.
[3] Something left out here. [C.]

Remarks Hobert Town, River Derwent, Van Diemens Land, 1804.

Friday, 30. A.M.—Capt. Rhodes stayd with me. We walkd to the farm together. Calld upon Martha Hays. Little G. Collins dind with me. C.S., Kent.

Saturday, December 1. A.M.—At 10 Capt. Rhodes went in his boat to his ship ; the wind was more moderate. It was mentioned that Mr. Powers and Shipman had got their free pardon. C.S., Kents Bay.

Sunday, 2. A.M.—At ½ past 10 performd divine service. I read at church the General Order received from His Excellency the Commander in Chief of the division of the 2 counties, and the settlement at Hobert Town, under the command of Lt. Gov. Collins, should be calld Buckinghamshire, and the one under Lt. Col. Patterson[1] should be calld Cornwall. At 4, Mr. Harris, Capt. Steward, and self, dind with the Governor. Cornwall.

Monday, 3. The first fine day we have had for some time. Engaged all the morn upon justice business. The Governor gave me leave to exchange the ground for a garden. C. S., Buckinghamshire.

Tuesday, 4. A.M.—The day very hot. At 11 I went on board the *George*, schooner. At ¼ past 1 the Governor went to his farm to dinner, and Mrs. Powers. C.S., Northumberland.

Wed., 5. A.M.—At 9 I went in my boat down the river, and returnd at 3 p.m. At 5 all the civil an military dind with Mr. Johnson in his own house, it being his turn to give a monthly dinner. C.S., Cumberland.

Thursday, 6. A.M.—Engaged in planting pot8o [potatoes]. At 4, Mr. Harris, Fosbrook and Capt. Stewart, of the *George*, schooner, dind with me off mutton.

Friday, 7. A.M.—My man returnd with a very large emew. In the eve I took a walk. C.S., Derwent.

Saturday, 8. A.M.—Stayd at home writing letters to send to Port Jackson. In the aft. Groves and self walkd to the farm. C.S., Dispatch.

Sunday, 9. A.M.—The Governors despatches not being ready, and the wind blowing, we had no duty performd. At 4 p.m. Mr. Fosbrook, Bowden, Mr. Steward, of the *George*, schooner, and self, dind with Mr. Harris. Elephant Bay.

Monday, 10. A.M.—At 8 a very hot wind came on from the N. East, which continued till 1 p.m. We then heard thunder at a distance. At 2 it began to rain very delightful showers. At 4 I dind with Lt. Johnson. At 5 thunderd very much. C.S., Tuckey.

Tuesday, 11. A.M.—At 6, the *George*, schooner, Capt. Steward, got under weigh, and went down the river to Kings Island for seal skins. In the eve I took a pipe with Mr. Groves, the(n) drank tea with the Lt. Governor. C.S., Armstrong.

Wed., 12. A.M.—The coroners inquest sat upon the body of Bradley, on suspicion that he had receivd blows from fighting with Cole, a convict, but after a very minute investigation they brought in their verdict accidental death, from his falling upon some stump of trees and tools, &c., &c. George Collins dind with me. C.S., Harcourt.

---

[1] Properly Paterson.

Thursday, 13. A.M.—I went to my new garden, and had it markd out. C.S. [word omitted].

Friday, 14. A.M.—At 8 the Gov., son, and self, went up to Risdon in my boat. At 3 p.m. we came from thence, and dind with the Gov. at the farm. ½ past 9 Mr. Fosbrooks servt. arrivd at the camp, and informd me that his master, Mr. J anson, and Mr. Hopley, were lost in the woods. C. S., Bensley.

Saturday, 15. A.M.—I sent my man Salmon with Mr. Fosbrooks, supplied with ammunition and provision, in search of the three gentlemen that were lost. At 8 I went down with one of Government boats into Ralphs Bay in search of them. At 11 I observd 2 people walking upon the beech at a distance (by the help of my glass), upon which I fird a gun. Soon after I see a boat standing in for the land, and I made signals for her to come up. At 11 I got on shore, and to my comfort see Mr. Fosbrook and Mr. J anson, both of whom were then lost. They informd me that they had been lost since Thursday morn at 3 a.m., and had nothing to eat since that time but a few mussels and 4 oysters. Their chief support was the sprouts from the she oak. Mr. Hopley had left them that morn early, and on the arrival of the boat he informd us that he was pickd up by my man Salmon, and that it was impossible for him to have reachd the tent had it not been for Salmon. Mr. Fosbrook and J anson were going into the woods again had they not heard the guns from my boat. They informd me they were so exhausted they could not have survived another night. I first gave them some bread and weak spirits and water. At 1 we got into the boat and went to the tent, where I had some kangarro stakes dressd. At ½ past 3 we got into the boat and came to Hobert Town. C.S., Hanover.

Sunday, 16. A.M—At 10 the wr. was so bad that we could not have divine service performd ; at ½ past 1 I performed divine service at the farm. At ½ past 3 I dind with the governor. In the eve I smokd a pipe with Mr. Groves. In the eve some rain. Memorandum of Sunday, 16. Chris Forsha agreed to take care of my boat for one guinea a quarter. C.S., Portland.

Monday, 17. A.M.—The day very hot. I continued at home all the morn reading. In the eve I called upon Mr. Johnson. C.S., Bedford.

Tuesday, 18. A.M.—Detained at home all the morn. At 4 p.m. Mr. Harris dind with me. C.S., Russell.

Wednesday, 19. A.M.—The morn very hot. I prepared to go to Risdon, but was so unwell that I could not stir out. At 4 Mr. Harris and self dind with Mr. Fosbrooke. Sent my 2 men to Risdon after kangarros. C.S., Finsbury.

Thursday, 20. A.M.—The day exceedingly hot. Remaind at home all the day. C.S., Fitzroy.

Friday, 21. A.M.—At 9 the Governor and self went to the place where I fixed upon for a house. He gave orders that the groun[d] work should be began on Monday at ½ past 11. My two men returnd from Risdon and brought home with them 4 kangarros. Mr. Harris dind with me. The day so hot I could not dine in my marque; I dind at Mr. Harris house. Mr. J anson came in the eve. C.S., St. Thomas.

Saturday, 22. A.M.—The morn very damp, but not much rain. I took a walk with my gun. At 4 p.m. Mr. Harris Mr. J anson dind with me. The aft. was so wet that we went to Mr. Harris's house. C.S., Barkley.

Sunday, 23. A.M.—The morn damp. Divine service could not be performd. At 5 p.m. a strong breeze came on. C.S., White Hall.

Monday, 24. A.M.—The morn very wet. This eve being Xmas I went and took a pipe with Mr. Groves. C.S., Buckingham.

Tuesday, 25. A.M.—This day being Xmas day, at ½ past 11 all the civil military and free people, with His Honor the Lt. Governor, attended divine service. I was to have dind with the Gov., but was a long time before engaged to dine with a party at Mr. Bowdens. At 5 Mr. Harris, Fosbrook, J anson and self dind at Mr. Bowdens. C.S., Henley.

Wednesday, 26. A.M.—The wr. very cold at intervals. At 12 the same party met at Mr. Bowdens and took a second breakfast, and the same party dind with Mr. Bowden. C.S., Borough.

Thursday, 27. A.M.—Remained at home all this morn upon business. At 4 p.m. Mr. Harris and Mr. Fosbrook dind with me. C.S., King's Bench.

Friday, 28.—A.M.—Upon business all this morn with Mr. Harris. At 4 p.m. the Govns. son dind with me, and in the eve I went and took a pipe with Mr. Fosbrook. C.S., Market.

Saturday, 29. A.M.—At 11 my man returned home with 2 very large emews. At 4 p.m. thunder with rain. C.S., Clare.

Kangaroo killed by my dogs since August 24, 1804, which day I received 1 dog from Lt. Houston and on the 29 Capt. gave me another dog :—

August 25	...	Kangarro	1
Sept. 5	...	Do.	1
6	...	Do.	1
14	...	Do.	2
19	...	Do.	1
21	...	Do.	1
23	...	Do.	3
27	...	Do.	1
28	...	Do.	1
Oct. 9	...	An emew 60 lb. weight	1
10	...	Kangarro	1
13	...	Do.	3
22	...	Do.	1
25	...	Do.	1
26	...	Do.	2
Nov. 1	...	Do.	4
5	...	Do.	1
19	...	Do.	1
21	...	Do.	1
29	...	Do.	1

Dec.	1	...	Kangarro	...	1
	4	...	Do.	...	2
	6	...	A very large emew	...	1
	12	...	Kangarro	...	1
	13	...	Do.	...	1
	14	...	Do.	...	1
	18	...	Do.	...	1
	21	...	Do.	...	4
	26	...	Do.	...	2
	29	...	Emews	...	2

Sunday, 30. At 10 a.m. Mr. Harris, the Governor's son and self walked to the farm, where I performed divine service; all the convicts and settlers attended. At 4 p.m. thunder with some rain. ½ past 1 dined with Lt. Johnson. At 1 p.m., a very heavy hail storm. C.S., Newport.

Monday, 31. A.M.—At 10 continuel rain. In the eve I went and called upon Mr. and Mrs. Groves, where I stayed the eve. C.S., Hungerford.

BY AUTHORITY:
JOHN FERRES, GOVERNMENT PRINTER, MELBOURNE.

www.ingramcontent.com/pod-product-compliance
Lightning Source LLC
Chambersburg PA
CBHW030344170426
43202CB00010B/1240